EARLY MODERN CULTURAL STUDIES

Jean Howard and Ivo Kamps, Series Editors

PUBLISHED BY PALGRAVE MACMILLAN

Idols of the Marketplace: Idolatry and Commodity Fetishism in English Literature, 1580–1680
by David Hawkes

Shakespeare among the Animals: Nature and Society in the Drama of Early Modern England
by Bruce Boehrer

Maps and Memory in Early Modern England: A Sense of Place
by Rhonda Lemke Sanford

Debating Gender in Early Modern England, 1500–1700
edited by Cristina Malcolmson and Mihoko Suzuki

Manhood and the Duel: Masculinity in Early Modern Drama and Culture
by Jennifer A. Low

Burning Women: Widows, Witches, and Early Modern European Travelers in India
by Pompa Banerjee

Shakespeare and the Question of Culture: Early Modern Literature and the Cultural Turn
by Douglas Bruster

England's Internal Colonies: Class, Capital, and the Literature of Early Modern English Colonialism
by Mark Netzloff

Turning Turk: English Theater and the Multicultural Mediterranean
by Daniel Vitkus

Money and the Age of Shakespeare: Essays in New Economic Criticism
edited by Linda Woodbridge

Prose Fiction and Early Modern Sexualities in England, 1570–1640
edited by Constance C. Relihan and Goran V. Stanivukovic

Arts of Calculation: Numerical Thought in Early Modern Europe
edited by David Glimp and Michelle Warren

The Culture of the Horse: Status, Discipline, and Identity in the Early Modern World
edited by Karen Raber and Treva J. Tucker

The Figure of the Crowd in Early Modern London: The City and Its Double
by Ian Munro

Citizen Shakespeare: Freemen and Aliens in the Language of the Plays
by John Michael Archer

Constructions of Female Homoeroticism in Early Modern Drama
by Denise Walen

Localizing Caroline Drama: Politics and Economics of the Early Modern English Stage, 1625–1642
Edited by Adam Zucker and Alan B. Farmer

Re-Mapping the Mediterranean World in Early Modern English Writings
edited by Goran V. Stanivukovic

Islam and Early Modern English Literature: The Politics of Romance from Spenser to Milton
by Benedict S. Robinson

Women Writers and Public Debate in 17th Century Britain
by Catharine Gray

Global Traffic: Discourse and Practices of Trade in English Literature and Culture from 1550 to 1700
edited by Barbara Sebek and Stephen Deng

Remembering the Early Modern Voyage: English Narratives in the Age of European Expansion
by Mary C. Fuller

Memory, Print, and Gender in England, 1653–1759
by Harold Weber

Violence, Politics, and Gender in Early Modern England
edited by Joseph P. Ward

Early Modern Ecostudies: From the Florentine Codex to Shakespeare
edited by Ivo Kamps, Karen L. Raber, and Thomas Hallock

Women's Work in Early Modern English Literature and Culture
by Michelle M. Dowd

Race and Rhetoric in the Renaissance: Barbarian Errors
by Ian Smith

Masculinity and the Metropolis of Vice, 1550–1650
edited by Amanda Bailey and Roze Hentschell

Masculinity and the Metropolis of Vice, 1550–1650

Edited by

Amanda Bailey
and
Roze Hentschell

palgrave
macmillan

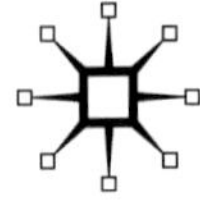

MASCULINITY AND THE METROPOLIS OF VICE, 1550–1650

First published in 2010 by
PALGRAVE MACMILLAN®
in the United States—a division of St. Martin's Press LLC,
175 Fifth Avenue, New York, NY 10010.

Where this book is distributed in the UK, Europe and the rest of the world, this is by Palgrave Macmillan, a division of Macmillan Publishers Limited, registered in England, company number 785998, of Houndmills, Basingstoke, Hampshire RG21 6XS.

Palgrave Macmillan is the global academic imprint of the above companies and has companies and representatives throughout the world.

Palgrave® and Macmillan® are registered trademarks in the United States, the United Kingdom, Europe and other countries.

ISBN: 978–0–230–62366–8

Library of Congress Cataloging-in-Publication Data

Masculinity and the metropolis of vice, 1550–1650 / edited by Amanda Bailey and Roze Hentschell.
p. cm. — (Early modern cultural studies, 1500–1700)
ISBN 978–0–230–62366–8 (alk. paper)
1. English literature—Early modern, 1500–1700—History and criticism. 2. Masculinity in literature. 3. Vice in literature. 4. London (England)—Moral conditions—History. I. Bailey, Amanda, 1966– II. Hentschell, Roze.

PR428.M37M38 2010
820.9'352109031—dc22 2009027526

A catalogue record of the book is available from the British Library.

Design by Newgen Imaging Systems (P) Ltd., Chennai, India.

First edition: March 2010

10 9 8 7 6 5 4 3 2 1

Printed in the United States of America.

Contents

Part III Remapping Misconduct: Sewers, Shops, and Streets

Figures

Series Editors' Foreword

In the twenty-first century, literary criticism, literary theory, historiography, and cultural studies have become intimately interwoven, and the formerly distinct fields of literature, society, history, and culture no longer seem so discrete. The Palgrave Early Modern Cultural Studies Series encourages scholarship that crosses boundaries between disciplines, time periods, nations, and theoretical orientations. The series assumes that the early modern period was marked by incipient processes of transculturation brought about through exploration, trade, colonization, and the migration of texts and people. These phenomena set in motion the processes of globalization that remain in force today. The purpose of this series is to publish innovative scholarship that is attentive to the complexity of this early modern world and bold in the methods it employs for studying it.

As series editors, we welcome, for example, books that explore early modern texts and artifacts that bear the traces of transculturation and globalization and that explore Europe's relationship to the cultures of the Americas, of Europe, and of the Islamic world and native representations of those encounters. We are equally interested in books that provide new ways to understand the complex urban culture that produced the early modern public theater or that illuminate the material world of early modern Europe and the regimes of gender, religion, and politics that informed it. Elite culture or the practices of everyday life, the politics of state or of the domestic realm, the material book or the history of the emotions—all are of interest if pursued with an eye to novel ways of making sense of the strangeness and complexity of the early modern world.

Jean Howard and Ivo Kamps
Series Editors

ACKNOWLEDGMENTS

Masculinity and the Metropolis of Vice, 1550–1650 began as a panel, entitled "City of Vice: Passion and Civility in Early Modern London," at the 2006 Renaissance Society of America meeting in San Francisco. We would like to thank Laurie Ellinghausen for taking part in that panel and for continuing the journey with us. Lawrence Manley generously agreed to be the respondent, and his insightful comments inspired us to pursue the collection. We owe much to Larry, whose seminal work on London has influenced so much of the work in this volume. This book would exist, however, only as a bright idea without the contributions of our authors whose superb scholarship, good cheer, and patience made editing this book a pleasure. For her support of all our endeavors, we are grateful to Barbara Sebek. At Palgrave, thanks are due to Ivo Kamps, Jean Howard, Brigitte Shull, Lee Norton, and the anonymous reader whose comments have helped to make this a better book. We are extremely grateful to Aaryn Richard for his excellent work on the index. Amanda Bailey would like to thank the University of Connecticut's Humanities Institute for the year-long Faculty Fellowship that allowed her to complete this project and Roze Hentschell for being an ideal coeditor. She is, as ever, grateful for Ross Lewin and Spencer Bailey-Lewin. Roze Hentschell would like to thank Colorado State University for sabbatical release time, during which this project was completed. She would also like to thank her colleagues in the English Department at Colorado State University, as well as Amanda Bailey, Patricia Fumerton, Catherine DiCesare, and Thomas and Eleanor Cram.

Introduction: Gendered Geographies of Vice

Amanda Bailey and Roze Hentschell

A place sheweth the man.

—Francis Bacon

The Subjects of Space

Scholars have detailed the vast and sprawling nature of late sixteenth-century London, which as the third largest city in all of Europe daily absorbed a steady influx of strangers from England and the Continent.[1] In 100 years, between 1550 and 1650, the city's population expanded from 80,000 to 400,000. By 1700, over half a million people lived in London.[2] One historian describes early modern London as "a city packed with people."[3] Although observations about London's rapid population growth typically frame discussions of the period's sweeping economic and social changes, only recently have we begun to relate general trends in urban growth to city-dwellers' specific, everyday lived experiences. Ian Munro in his book on the crowd, for instance, considers "the phenomenological implications of population growth in the city" and asks us to attend to "the visible and tangible presence of more and more *bodies*."[4] In her comparative analysis of early modern London and Paris, Karen Newman explores a new politics of proximity that heralded an awareness of urban space as constituted by and constitutive of social relations:

> The new space of the metropolis, the relentless saturation of what had been only recently empty and open spaces, the promiscuous encounters of the urban pedestrian, and the need to reduce spatial barriers and provide access to newly developing market spaces breached status boundaries and not only generated profound anxiety about order and place but also fueled the production of "the *subject* as an *individual*" that will eventually become Jameson's enlightenment subject and Ferguson's romantic consciousness.[5]

In seeking to historicize further how urban subjects experienced the relation between the social and the spatial, *Masculinity and the Metropolis of Vice, 1550–1650* asks what the space of the city meant for the doing of gender?[6]

The central premise of this volume is that "geography matters to the construction of gender."[7] Our understanding of gender as a social relation based in material practice recognizes gender as a function of space. Concomitantly, such an understanding acknowledges that spatial orders are comprehended through the gendered body. Early modern men and women experienced the city as a series of local sites that were gendered in imaginary and concrete ways. As Laura Gowing stresses, "in the early modern city, gendered space was defined not merely through particular configurations of space and time, but also through a sense of the city itself. The city was consistently imagined through gendered personifications, which had their own impact on gendered spatial practices. The early modern image of the city invoked tensions around space, place and gender."[8] On a symbolic level, urban spaces communicated gendered messages—whether by means of overt exclusion or tacit inclusion. On a material level, urban places created the conditions for certain uses and misuses, alliances and identifications, as well as new forms of mobility and constraints that had far-reaching consequences for the articulation and comprehension of gender.

Thus *Masculinity and the Metropolis of Vice* engages the insights of cultural geographers and social historians to complement a growing body of work on urbanization as a gendered process. This volume also, though, aims to fill a gap in the existing scholarship. While our contributors investigate the gendered spatial practices of early modern Londoners, they do not view masculinity as the static norm against which femininity is constructed.[9] In early modern London, access to patriarchal privilege was as varied for men as for women and, as the chapters that follow demonstrate, competing forms of manhood interfaced with a patriarchal ideology that was itself "muddled, contradictory, and selectively invoked."[10] Our guiding assumption is that patriarchy was flexible and heterogeneous and not a rigidly defined monolithic institution, exemplified by men's systematic domination of women. In this respect, the chapters in this volume seek to complicate earlier studies that construe London as a feminine entity. While neither ignoring contemporaneous representations of the city as a heroic matron or deceptive harlot nor overlooking popular depictions of predatory city women, our authors invoke a wealth of evidence to suggest that the city was not necessarily regarded as a feminized space only or as an environment of possibilities and perils solely for women.[11] The early modern city offered myriad opportunities for men to gain from, reject, or even revise patriarchal dictates.[12]

In exploring the relationship between urban culture and masculinity, this volume demonstrates that the provisional nature of manhood was most readily discerned in those contexts associated with vice. Literary scholarship has historically understood "vice" as tied to the stock character from medieval morality plays. "The Vice" or "Iniquity" was a servant of the Seven Deadly Sins who assisted them in their efforts to corrupt the souls of men. Hallmarks of The Vice included villainy and roguery and, by the late medieval period, clownish buffoonery.[13] The character was necessarily aligned with immoral practices, and thus vicious behavior was regarded as that which went against Christian ideals of human conduct. By the late sixteenth-century, however, "vice" had obtained more secular associations and a narrow Christian understanding of vice, where bad behavior was understood as a transgression against godly principles, had become more loosely defined. From the Latin *vitium* indicating a "fault, defect, failing," vice came to comprise "habits or conduct" that were "evil, immoral, or wicked" and represented an "indulgence in degrading pleasures or practices."[14] While immorality and wickedness still operated in the register of Christian judgment, vicious conduct involved a range of behaviors that troubled civic authorities and disrupted general understandings of civility.

The chapters in this volume are concerned with the ways that manhood was negotiated, made visible, and even engendered through the performance of misconduct. Attending to the linguistic connection between *virtus* and *vir*, as Bruce Smith suggests, can assist us in establishing the "fundamental connection between masculinity and conformity to ethical ideals. The link between the two consists in the root sense of *virtue* as inherent power or efficacy."[15] Male misconduct thus not only calls into question masculine virtue, but also serves to define it; it is only by recognizing vice that ideal male behavior can be understood, since "moderate masculinity requires forms of alterity for its definition."[16] As Todd W. Reeser has recently argued, ideal masculinity in the early modern period was commonly understood as consisting of moderation:

> The etymological association made between the Latin *virtus*...and *vir* (the Latin word designating "man" as a gendered being, in contrast to *homo*, or "mankind") was widely known, and since moderation was routinely considered one of the cardinal virtues of the period, it too was considered inherently male, a "fact" proven by the often assumed link of the linguistic sign and its etymological origin.[17]

The yoking of moderation and proper masculinity meant that vicious behavior, associated with various forms of excess, was by definition a challenge to and potentially a departure from manhood.

While vice in the early modern period continued to fall under the purview of canon and civic authorities (perceived as sin or crime), by focusing on its spatial implications these chapters offer a new framework for analyses of attitudes and activities increasingly targeted as disruptive. A fresh perspective on vice allows our authors to obtain purchase on the ambivalent representations of London evident in the period's sermons, advice manuals, guidebooks, pamphlets, and stage plays.[18] We argue neither that early moderns were pro-urban nor that those obsessed with the sins of a corrupt city reveal the truth of urban life. *Masculinity and the Metropolis of Vice* considers instead how the spaces of misconduct mapped the contradictory social logic of a city ambivalently poised as "a golden imperial city and ghost of its former grand self; Europe's trading hub and an employment wasteland for citizens and a thieves' paradise."[19] Vice in this period not only served as a metaphor for various sorts of cultural classifications but also provided a means for effecting real social divisions. As Tim Cresswell explains:

> By studying the margins of what is allowed we come to understand more about the center—the core—of what is considered right and proper. Transgression is also important in itself as an example of possible tactics for resistance to established norms. No hegemonic structure is ever complete, and it is always important to study the ways in which hegemonies are contested in everyday life...transgression (literally, "crossing a boundary") is often defined in geographical terms. Geography, then, can tell us a lot about transgression, and

> transgression, conversely, provides valuable insights into the way places affect behavior and ideology.[20]

If it was through the identification, regulation, and containment of vice that authorities delineated the licit and illicit and mobilized the exclusion or evacuation of the other, the occurrence of vice signaled the intrusion of the counterhegemonic. Not simply an object of inquiry, vice proves to be a key category of analysis for historical investigations of cities, raising a series of questions such as: how do particular places obtain a symbolic status that challenges their purported civic function? Or, how do certain urban spaces designated for particular persons and activities come to be known as places for alternative users? Of equal concern is how certain groups come to be associated with particular sites, which in turn confer attitudinal and even behavioral aspects onto their users. The chapters that follow mine the significance of the labeling of places as sites of vice and consider how people mobilize the symbolism of a given locale as a means by which to distinguish themselves. These chapters also explore how sites topographically situated on the city's periphery come to be seen as culturally marginal, as well as how perceptions of marginal places become linked to objects, practices, and modes of behaviors that represent not only the culture of marginal places but also the culture of the marginalized. In investigating how city centers attempt to define themselves in opposition to perceived margins, our authors illuminate the ways in which the legitimate depended on the illegitimate, such that even as vice was reviled in official discourse it remained "instrumentally constitutive of the shared imaginary repertoires of the dominant culture."[21] Finally, our contributors show that an examination of contested definitions and perceptions of vice offers a window onto the heretofore-overlooked liminal zones, composite spaces where the orthodox and heterodox mingled.

The Places of Men

The "metropolis of vice" was thus both a real place charted by the coordinates of particular locales—specific streets, churches, taverns, gaming houses, and playhouses—that made up early modern London's built environment and a space of the mind mapped in accordance with denizens' "emotional geographies" and "imaginary geograph[ies]."[22] The urban sites visited in this volume were never simply physical locations but continuously invented and reinvented by their myriad users. Even as streets and buildings remained anchored in the city's topography, they were always figuratively constructed and reconstructed through ever-shifting cultural contexts and the myths and meanings they generated. By presenting the city as a palimpsest of neighborhoods, streets, and edifices that officially and unofficially encouraged certain forms of gendered behaviors, our authors reveal the coterminous existence of many Londons: a capital, a port city, a neighborhood of alien workers, and an amorphous confederation of outcasts. The early modern Londoner Donald Lupton aptly notes "there are so many little worlds in her [London]" and, along similar lines, contemporary scholar John Twyning reminds us that "no city-dweller can inhabit the whole city even though the impact of that whole may be felt by her or him. In a sense, to live in a city is to occupy a locale (social, topographical, imaginary) which is distinct from, yet integrated with, all the other locales which make it up."[23] As an examination of *social spatialization*, or the social construction of the spatial formed by discursive and nondiscursive practices alike, this volume is interested in how vice came to be experienced and represented as gendered and collective.[24]

Much of this volume focuses on the behavior of men in public places and in doing so necessarily acknowledges late sixteenth-century London as a city of young men.[25] The centralization of England's political life in London, an unprecedented surge in population, and economic crises in the provinces led to the mass migration of so-called superfluous young men, second and third sons, who, because they were not heirs apparent, flooded into the city seeking places at Court, in elite households, within guilds, and at the universities and Inns of Court.[26] It was in this period that the ubiquitous "younger brother" became a London fixture, depicted within city-comedies, satiric tracts, advice literature, and serio-comic prose pamphlets as the "*Infans perdus* (or the Forlorne hope)," cast upon "the mercy of the World" having been bequeathed only "his wit" as "his best revenue."[27] The particular example of the second son was encompassed within the larger phenomenon of a growing presence of bands of male youths. Historians have recently turned their attention to the overwhelming numbers of men visibly struggling to survive in a competitive, anonymous environment, the majority of whom came to be classified as vagrants, beggars, tricksters, idlers, rogues, and rioters. The perceived problems associated with groups of men took on disproportionate attention, as evidenced by diverse materials ranging from official complaints of a rise in youth-related social problems, to moral invectives against idleness in young men and advice manuals warning sternly against rowdy behavior on the streets and at commercial venues.[28] Running through depictions of and responses to burgeoning urban male youth subcultures was the persistent belief that men in general and young men in particular made up a disruptive contingent.

Young men were perceived as unable to curb their appetites because they were emboldened by "the season of [their] Lust, and the houre wherein [they] ought to bee bad."[29] The young man was a "Shippe without [a] Pilot."[30] Because male youth were seen as in danger of becoming engulfed by a surfeit of vitality that inclined them to practice overindulgence in alcohol consumption, gambling, tobacco-smoking, and sexual activity, those in charge were imputed to scrutinize the deportment of male youth who were in "the 'dark' and 'dangerous' age."[31] Advice literature for householders is dominated by accounts of young men's communal "rioting" at various urban locales, such as the tavern, St. Paul's Cathedral, the Royal Exchange, or the Globe Playhouse, where youths "acquaint themselves too much with the licentious customes of the Cittie: as with quarreling, dycing, dauncing, deceiving, lustinge, braving, and indetting."[32] The public male subcommunities that formed on the city streets and at specific London sites confirm historian Paul Griffiths's accounts of groups of young men who met regularly at public venues to "talk, play, drink, eat, gamble, and whore away their time, engaging in some of the bold posturing and subversive impudence, which magistrates attributed to ill-advised and ill-nurtured youth."[33]

For John Wharton, Dean of the Cathedral of St. Paul's, "the vices [of youth] are most frequented . . . in London."[34] Perceived as excessive in appetite and impudent attitude, young male Londoners embodied an uncontrollable city. This sector of the population became associated with what Derek Keene describes as "a growing sense of the physical disorder of the metropolis and the social degeneration of its fabric."[35] If London's rapid growth led to crime, dilapidation, and disease, amoral and depraved young men, as constructed within the literature of the day, were seen as entering into a symbiotic relationship with a city that offered an array of temptations. While the city may have corrupted young men, their indulgences animated the dynamism of the urban environments in which they maneuvered. Patriarchal ideals of the day, exemplified by education at the Inns of Court, service to the church, or obedience to one's guild master, were expressed topographically. Gray's Inn, St. Paul's Cathedral, and Guildhall presumably stood as edifices of proper conduct. But activities that resisted or revised patriarchal ideals—like binge drinking at taverns, dicing at gaming houses, flaunting apparel in the middle aisle of St. Paul's, and trafficking in false wares at the city limits—also became incorporated into the cityscape. Although alternative forms of manhood were improvised and displayed at particular urban sites, these modes masculinity, in turn, revised the imaginative and cultural geographies of early modern London.

Chapter Overview

Masculinity and the Metropolis of Vice is organized into three sections, each one focusing on a group of specific urban sites, transgressive practices, and their implications for the meanings of manhood. In each instance, our authors are sensitive to the myriad forms of evolving urban imaginaries—how they disrupted traditional modes of representation or necessitated new aesthetic strategies. Stage plays, serio-comic prose pamphlets, sermons, advice manuals, satiric portraits, topographies, and official documents appealed to the competing interests of diverse groups as they constructed and deconstructed the city as "a polemical space."[36] Insofar as the city was textually produced, so too was vice. The celebratory treatment of urban vice in city comedy must be juxtaposed to the anxious response to transgressive behavior in advice literature and sermons. Urban satire focuses on the material aspects of vice, tying together social morality with the problems of property and possession. Complaint literature is driven by the subversive energies of figures such as the wily city-gallant, the prostitute, the prodigal, and the usurer who are produced and reproduced alternately as comic and menacing. While our authors analyze a range of literary and cultural forms, each demonstrates an understanding of vice as generated and sustained by gendered uses of urban space.

All three authors in part I, "Redefining Urban Masculinity: Taverns, Universities, and Gaming Houses," question the assumption that behaviors such as binge drinking or gambling compromised manhood. They engage the complexities of these ostensibly vicious conducts and the discourses surrounding them to argue for more nuanced understandings of urbane masculinity. Gina Bloom's "Manly Drunkenness: Binge Drinking as Disciplined Play" challenges the notion that excessive consumption of alcohol was necessarily associated with effeminacy, and she shows that drinking games created a "disciplined" activity that generated an alternative framework for early modern manhood. The culture of binge drinking in early modern London also produced a "recreational discourse" that overturned moralists' collocation of drink and unruliness.

By analyzing accounts of early modern drinking games such as those outlined in Richard Brathwaite's *The Law of Drinking*, as well as the material artifact of the wagering cups themselves, Bloom underscores how ritualized drinking had clear associations with the social graces and civilized behavior that characterized patriarchal masculinity in the period.

If Bloom's chapter shows us that ritualized alcohol consumption could recast vice as virtue, Laurie Ellinghausen's "University of Vice: Drink, Gentility, and Masculinity in Oxford, Cambridge, and London" demonstrates the productive role of drink in the lives of university students. By stressing the importance of the relationship between Oxford and Cambridge and the capital city, especially since so many graduates would go on to pursue careers in the metropolis, Ellinghausen's discussion of university drinking culture complicates contemporaneous views of drinking as vice that distinguished town from gown. Interpreting young men's drinking practices as part of a complex network of loss tied to "the failed promise of university education," she turns to the *Parnassus* plays, a set of three anonymous comedies performed at Cambridge, and the work of Thomas Nashe. Here she demonstrates that these authors recognized drink as a compensatory indulgence that could potentially ease the despair of socially disenfranchised students.

In "The Social Stakes of Gambling in Early Modern London," Adam Zucker provides an overview of the social relations underwriting early modern gaming. Exploring an array of primary texts in his examination of the spaces of betting and representations of the figure of the gamester, Zucker argues that the dynamics of wagering were of particular interest to those who performed at and attended the early modern theater. London's playhouses, he shows, were closely linked both materially and ideologically to London's culture of gaming, and his analyses of plays that stage wagering shed new light on gambling as "an overdetermined object of scorn and pleasure." While the period's response to gambling may appear as a blanket condemnation of risk, Zucker contends that many were attuned to the ways that gambling produced the conditions for a stylized mode of urbane masculinity, exemplified by the witty, tasteful gallant. Like Bloom and Ellinghausen, Zucker sees the practice of vice as creating a new space for an alternative form of manhood.

The chapters in part II, "Sexualizing the City: Cathedrals, Brothels, and Barbershops," highlight the unstable mixing of the proper and the profane. In "Carnal Geographies: Mocking and Mapping the Religious Body," Mary Bly investigates St. Paul's Cathedral as a popular staging ground for demonstrations of male sartorial and erotic appetite. Rather than regarding the church as merely a backdrop for illicit activities, such as the flaunting of sumptuous apparel, Bly stresses that the space of Paul's *as a cathedral* was crucial to understanding its male users' behaviors as transgressive. Both the church and its attached boys' theater offer a platform for displays of carnality, which echo Christianity's own emphasis on the sensual body of the young Jesus Christ. The tensions between erotic place and religious space are explored in *The Puritan*, the last play performed by Paul's Boys, which Bly argues is energized by its dense interweaving of religious vocabulary and sexually suggestive puns. By exploiting the symbolic coding of the cathedral both thematically and dramaturgically, *The Puritan* presents, Bly shows, a complex cartography of a "morally degenerative" London.

In " 'To what bawdy house doth your Maister belong?': Barbers, Bawds, and Vice in the Early Modern London Barbershop," Mark Albert Johnston explores the sexualization of a more quotidian site—the London barbershop and details its numerous activities and uses, as well as its indispensability to the stylish urban man. Providing the male population with both medical and cosmetic services, the barbershop also encouraged homosocial fraternization, intimacy, and entertainment. Some barbershops, however, also operated as brothels and were often sites where venereal disease was not only treated but also transmitted. Johnston engages a variety of texts that attest to the importance of barbers' services for the comportment of the urbane Londoner, but which also acknowledge that such services—aesthetic, medicinal, and musical, to name but a few—called into question the reputation of the patron, potentially placing him in "considerable mortal, moral, and social peril."

The chapters in part III, "Remapping Misconduct: Sewers, Shops, and Streets" focus on the perceived hazards of urban landscape, as the authors examine how those playwrights who represent civic crises map misconduct onto particular material spaces of the metropolis. The lens of cultural geography lead these authors to unexpected insights about the role played by new forms of capital in the construction of masculine virtue and vice. In "*Coriolanus* and the 'rank-scented meinie': Smelling Rank in Early Modern London," Holly Dugan investigates early modern London's nascent sewer system that traversed the city's boundaries and bifurcated its center. Reeking sinks, kennels, and ditches, Dugan shows, defined the metropolis on a visceral level and connected its dwellers through a shared olfactory landscape. Stench also served a more specific function, however, as a social marker that designated members of the lower ranks. Turning to Shakespeare's *Coriolanus*, Dugan explores how this play stages class warfare as the struggle over the elimination of unpleasant odors. The title character's animosity toward the "rank-scented" masses, Dugan argues, necessitates a new understanding of other "pungent struggles" in and around London, most importantly the nearby enclosure riots. By exposing the connections between offensive odors and "the metaphoric threats of city life," where civic disorder comes to represent the threat of invasion, Dugan demonstrates that Coriolanus' masculine *virtus* is challenged by the reeking, rioting multitudes.

Natasha Korda, in "Vicious Objects: Staging False Wares," looks to the market to present a more nuanced understanding of vice, as she considers not vicious subjects but material objects corrupted by defect. Although so-called virtuous wares were associated with "masculine vigor" and the male fellowship of the craft guilds, the unregulated production of goods manufactured and sold by foreigners, noncitizens, and women were regarded as morally and economically suspect, and often associated with iniquity and adulteration. The ritualized punishment for the production and sale of false wares was akin to that of sexual infractions and, like the shaming rituals to punish scolds, adulteresses, and prostitutes, were publicly *staged*. In addition to tracing the historical construction of corrupt commodities, Korda also considers the representation of false wares at the playhouse. Like the laborers whose participation in unofficial economies challenged civic patriarchal masculinity, players—by assuming a professional legitimacy that did not belong to them and by trafficking in stage properties that were themselves false wares—were also targets of charges of vice and effeminacy. By staging the contestation over the manufacture and sale of false wares, playwrights like Jonson and Middleton attempt to forge a new definition of civic masculinity to which professional players might lay claim.

The idea of the city as the theatrical place is not new, but Ian Munro moves beyond an analysis of London as an arena for social display to show that urban life constituted a mode of performance that radically revised the relationship between narrative and spectacle. In "City of Angels: Theatrical Vice and *The Devil is an Ass*," Munro explores demonic possession as a denial of masculinity, one that is intimately wrapped up in the pleasures of London. As the play's main character, Fitzdottrel, embraces unbridled consumption, he rejects the conventional roles of husband and landowner. London's sumptuous allure provides Jonson's character with a "permanent floating stage"; at the same time, the city appropriates the theater for itself and urban vice is seen as merely theatrical. The "urban epistemology" of the play, which posits London as an "irrational city," challenges the efficacy of its redemptive conclusion. By situating *The Devil is an Ass* in the context of the genre of *film noir*, Munro calls our attention to Jonson's representation of an urban culture that ultimately offers a world of simulation unmoored from any ascertainable moral foundations. For Munro, Jonson's *noir* London renders the theatrical representation of vice obsolete. The seductive city—awful and beautiful—consumes the theater into its own abyss of nonmeaning.

Conclusion

Masculinity and the Metropolis of Vice does not attempt to offer a comprehensive account of the vices practiced in early modern London. Nor do the chapters in this volume address all aspects of masculine misconduct. None of our contributors, for instance, examines the rising incidence of the regulation of vice instigated by the late seventeenth-century Reformation of Manners campaigns. Instead, this collection stages a productive encounter between Cultural Geography and Masculinity Studies in its investigation of the ways early moderns experienced and altered their urban environs through vicious behavior. Historians have observed that developing global economic systems were taking hold in capital cities at the very moment that a recognizably modern gender order also began to take shape.[37] The chapters in this collection ground this observation in sustained analyses of concrete practices and in doing so, elucidate the connections between gender formation and the opportunities and demands of emerging metropolitan capitalism. Although the masculine self may appear coherent across time and space, these chapters show that perceptions and experiences of masculinities in early modern England were predicated on one's access to and mobility across particular spaces. In seeking to investigate how gendered subjects were produced by what Habermas would come to call "the public sphere," this volume explores the myriad ways men distinguished themselves from women, boys, as well as from one another through the differential use of sites of production, consumption, display, and recreation. Much work remains to be done on the evolving social, cultural, economic, and moral conditions of manhood. Our hope is that *Masculinity and the Metropolis of Vice* will provide a fruitful jumping off point for further inquiries into the complex relations among space, place, and gender.

NOTES

1. On historical investigations of London see: A. L. Beier and R. Finlay, *London 1500–1700: The Making of the Metropolis* (London and New York: Longman, 1986); Steve Rappaport, *Worlds within Worlds: Structures of Life in Sixteenth-Century London* (Cambridge: Cambridge University Press, 1989); Ian Archer, *The Pursuit of Stability: Social Relations in Elizabethan London* (Cambridge: Cambridge University Press, 1991); Roy Porter, *London: A Social History* (London: Harmondsworth, 1994); Joseph Ward, *Metropolitan Communities: Trade Guilds, Identity, and Change in Early Modern London* (Stanford: Stanford University Press, 1997); Jeremy Boulton, *Neighborhood and Society: A London Suburb in the Seventeenth Century* (Cambridge: Cambridge University Press, 2005); Paul Griffiths, *Lost Londons: Change, Crime and Control in the Capital City, 1550–1660* (Cambridge: Cambridge University Press, 2008); and Vanessa Harding, *Short History of Early Modern London, 1500–1700* (Cambridge: Cambridge University Press, 2009). For recent studies on representations of London in culture and literature: Lawrence Manley, *Literature and Culture in Early Modern London* (Cambridge: Cambridge University Press, 1995); *Material London, ca. 1600*, ed. Lena Cowen Orlin (Philadelphia: University of Pennsylvania Press, 2000); Janette Dillon, *Theatre, Court and City, 1596–1610: Drama and the Social Space in London* (Cambridge: Cambridge University Press, 2000); *Londinopolis: Essays in the Cultural and Social History of Early Modern London*, ed. Paul Griffiths and Mark S. R. Jenner (Manchester: Manchester University Press, 2000); *Imagining Early Modern London: Perceptions and Portrayals of the City from Stow to Strype 1598–1720*, ed. Julia Merritt (Cambridge: Cambridge University Press, 2001); *Plotting Early Modern London*, ed. Dieter Mehl, Angela Stock, and Anne-Julia Zwierlein (Aldershot: Ashgate, 2004); Karen Newman, *Cultural Capitals: Early Modern London and Paris* (Princeton, NJ: Princeton University Press, 2007); Jean E. Howard, *Theater of a City: The Places of London Comedy, 1598–1642* (Philadelphia: University of Pennsylvania Press, 2007); and Darryll Grantley, *London in Early Modern English Drama: Representing the Built Environment* (New York: Palgrave Macmillan, 2008).
2. See Vanessa Harding, "The Population of London, 1550–1700: A Review of the Published Evidence," *London Journal* 15 (1990): 111–28; N. G. Brett-James, *The Growth of Stuart London* (London: George Allen & Unwin, 1935); Roger Finlay, *Population and Metropolis: The Demography of London, 1580–1650* (Cambridge: Cambridge University Press, 1981); and Jeremy Boulton, "London, 1540–1700," in *The Cambridge Urban History of Britain*, vol. 2, ed. Peter Clark (Cambridge: Cambridge University Press, 2000).

3. Griffiths, *Lost Londons*, xiii.
4. Ian Munro, *The Figure of the Crowd in Early Modern London* (New York: Palgrave Macmillan, 2005), 4.
5. Newman, *Cultural Capitals*, 69–70.
6. For the concept of "doing gender," see Judith Butler, *Gender Trouble: Feminism and the Subversion of Identity* (New York: Routledge, 1990), 41. For a discussion of space as social, see proponents of the new cultural geography who understand space as produced and reproduced by its users and hence as an arena of social, political, and economic struggle rather than as a passive and static entity. Analyses of the lived practices and symbolic meanings of space and place begin with the seminal work of Yi-Fu Tuan, *Space and Place: The Perspective of Experience* (Minneapolis: University of Minnesota Press, 1977); Michel De Certeau, *The Practice of Everyday Life* (Berkeley: University of California Press, 1984); Henri Lefebvre, *The Production of Space*, trans. Donald Nicholson-Smith (Oxford: Basil Blackwell, 1974; 1991); and Edward Soja, *Postmodern Geographies: The Reassertion of Space in Critical Social Theory* (London: Verso, 1989).
7. Doreen Massey, *Space, Place, and Gender* (Minneapolis: University of Minneapolis Press, 1994), 2.
8. Laura Gowing, "'The Freedom of the Streets': Women and Social Space, 1560–1640," in *Londinopolis*, ed. Griffiths and Jenner, 131. We will use "place" and "space" interchangeably throughout this introduction. Rather than regarding place as a fixed or bounded site—a conceptualization that rests on a view of space as a static, abstract entity—we view place as a particular articulation of social relations at a particular moment, which may or may not serve to stabilize the meanings of space. See Massey, *Space, Place, and Gender* and Edward S. Casey, "How to Get from Space to Place in a Fairly Short Stretch of Time: Phenomenological Prolegomena," in *Senses of Place*, ed. Steven Feld and Keith H. Basso (Santa Fe, New Mexico: School of American Research Press, 1996), 13–53.
9. In keeping with the scholarship of those who have historicized the differences within each gender, as well as those between genders, such as Alexandra Shepard, John Tosh, Alan Bray, and Michael S. Kimmel, our authors show that the social practice of manhood was diverse, contingent, and contradictory. Alexandra Shepard, *Meanings of Manhood in Early Modern England* (Oxford: Oxford University Press, 2003), 1. See also Michael S. Kimmel, "From Lord and Master to Cuckold and Fop: Masculinity in Seventeenth-Century England," *University of Dayton Review* 18.2 (1986–1987): 93–109; John Tosh, "What Should Historians Do with Masculinity? Reflections on Nineteenth-Century Britain," *History Workshop Journal* 38 (1994): 179–202; and Alan Bray, "To Be a Man in Early Modern Society:

The Curious Case of Michael Wigglesworth," *History Workshop Journal* 41 (1996): 155–65.

10. Shepard, *Meanings of Manhood*, 1.
11. For characterizations of early modern London as feminine see Lawrence Manley, "From Matron to Monster: Tudor-Stuart London and the Languages of Urban Description" in *The Historical Renaissance: New Essays on Tudor and Stuart Literature and Culture*, ed. Heather Dubrow and Richard Strier (Chicago: University of Chicago Press, 1988), 347–74. Studies that code urban transgression in terms of female subjectivity include Elizabeth Wilson, *The Sphinx in the City: Urban Life, the Control of Disorder and Women* (Berkeley: University of California Press, 1991); Judith Walkowicz, *City of Dreadful Delight: Narratives of Sexual Danger in Late-Victorian London* (London: Virago Press, 1992); Janet Wolff, "The Invisible Flâneuse: Women and the Literature of Modernity," *Feminine Sentences: Essays on Women and Culture* (Oxford: Oxford University Press, 1999), 34–50; Gowing, "The Freedom of the Streets," in *Londinopolis*, ed. Griffiths and Jenner, 130–51; and D. L. Parson, *Streetwalking the Metropolis: Women, the City, and Modernity* (Oxford: Oxford University Press, 2000). *Masculinity and the Metropolis of Vice* is in direct dialogue with work of those queer historians who have demonstrated the importance of the urban, notably, Randolph Trumbach's work on the eighteenth-century molly-houses and studies like George Chauncey's *Gay New York: Gender, Urban Culture, and the Making of the Gay Male World, 1890–1940* (New York: Basic Books, 1995) and Frank Mort's *Cultures of Consumption: Masculinities and Social Space in Late-Twentieth Century Britain* (London: Routledge, 1996).
12. Thomas A. King, *The Gendering of Men, 1600– 1750, Volume 1: The English Phallus* (Madison: University of Wisconsin Press, 2004), 5. Several scholars have addressed the contradictions of manhood in the early modern period, like Bruce R. Smith who reminds us that "masculinity is a matter of contingency, or circumstance, or performance." *Shakespeare and Masculinity* (Oxford: Oxford University Press, 2000), 4. Jennifer Low asserts, "notions of masculinity per se were, for the majority of the early modern population, exactly that: vague thoughts, unexamined assumptions"; and Jennifer C. Vaught has recently pointed out that "there are multiple kinds of masculinities, instead of several hegemonic categories, and that these male as well as female gender roles are cultural constructions that are performative and even masquerades." See Low, *Manhood and the Duel: Masculinity in Early Modern Drama and Culture* (New York: Palgrave MacMillan, 2003), 5 and Vaught, *Masculinity and Emotion in Early Modern English Literature* (Aldershot: Ashgate, 2008), 7.
13. Robert Withington, "The Ancestry of the 'Vice,'" *Speculum* 7.4 (1932): 525.

14. "Vice," *n*.1 *The Oxford English Dictionary*, 2nd ed. 1989, *OED Online*, Oxford University Press, October 29, 2008. http://0-dictionary.oed.com/cgi/entry/50277200.
15. Smith, *Shakespeare and Masculinity*, 42.
16. Todd W. Reeser, *Moderating Masculinity in Early Modern Culture* (Chapel Hill: North Carolina Studies in the Romance Languages and Literatures, 2006), 22. Michel Foucault traces this definition of masculinity back to ancient Greece, where "self-mastery" was closely linked to masculinity: it "affirmed…the 'viril' character of moderation…Self-mastery was a way of being a man with respect to oneself." See Foucault, *The Use of Pleasure: Volume 2 of the History of Sexuality*, trans. Robert Hurley (New York: Pantheon Books, 1985), 83. See also Russell West-Pavlov, *Bodies and Their Spaces: System, Crisis and Transformation in Early Modern Theatre* (Amsterdam and New York: Rodopi, 2006), 111.
17. Reeser, *Moderating Masculinity*, 14.
18. See Manley, *Literature and Culture in Early Modern London*, Part II, "Fictions of Settlement," 123–56 and Peter Lake, "From Troynouvant to Heliogabulus's Rome and back: 'Order' and Its Others in the London of John Stow," in *Imagining Early Modern London: Perceptions and Portrayals of the City from Stow to Strype, 1598–1720*, ed. J. F. Merritt (Cambridge: Cambridge University Press, 2001), 217–50.
19. Griffiths, *Lost Londons*, 9.
20. Tim Cresswell, *In Place/Out of Place: Geography, Ideology and Transgression* (Minneapolis: University of Minnesota Press, 1996), 21.
21. Peter Stallybrass and Allon White, *The Politics and Poetics of Transgression* (Ithaca, NY: Cornell University Press, 1986), 5
22. Rob Shields, *Places on the Margin: Alternative Geographies of Modernity* (London: Routledge, 1991), 6.
23. Lupton qtd. in Griffiths, *Lost Londons*, 67; John Twyning, *London Dispossessed: Literature and Social Space in the Early Modern City* (New York: St. Martin's Press, 1998), 4.
24. Shields, *Places on the Margin*, 7.
25. A. L. Beier and Roger Finlay, "The Significance of the Metropolis," in *London 1500–1700*, ed. Beier and Finlay, 11–15. E. A. Wrigley and R. S. Schofield demonstrate that as part of the population surge in England between 1550 and 1650, in which the entire population went from approximately three million to over five million, from 1576 to 1621 there was a marked increase in the number of young men in London. See *The Population History of England and Wales, 1541–1871: A Reconstruction* (Cambridge: Cambridge University Press, 1981), 215–19, 443–50.
26. John Gillis refers to second, third, and fourth sons as the "superfluous" or "surplus" children of the elite. He notes that in periods of

population growth, such as between 1550 and 1630 (when the population of England doubled), younger sons suffered the most since demographic pressures resulted in stricter settlements on inheritance and greater competition for limited resources. See his *Youth and History: Tradition and Change in European Age-Relations, 1770 to the Present* (New York: Academic Press, 1981), 21.

27. Thomas Dekker, *The Guls Horne-booke*, 1609, ed. R. B. McKerrow (London: De La More, 1904), 8; Thomas Dekker, *Work for Armorours*, in *The Non-Dramatic Works of Thomas Dekker*, ed. Alexander B. Grosart, vol. 4 (New York: Russell & Russell, 1963), 120; and John Earle, *Microcosmography*, 1628, ed. Alfred West (Cambridge: Cambridge University Press, 1920), 70.
28. Keith Thomas, "Age and Authority in Early Modern England," *Proceedings of the British Academy* 62 (1976): 1–46; Ilana Krausman Ben-Amos, *Adolescence and Youth in Early Modern England* (New Haven, CT: Yale University Press, 1994); Anthony Fletcher, *Gender, Sex, and Subordination in England, 1500–1800* (New Haven, CT: Yale University Press, 1995); Paul Griffiths, *Youth and Authority: Formative Experiences in England, 1560–1640* (Oxford: Oxford University Press, 1996); Paul Griffiths, Adam Fox, and Steve Hindle, eds., *The Experience of Authority in Early Modern England* (New York: St. Martin's Press, 1996); Marjorie Keniston McIntosh, *Controlling Misbehavior in England, 1370–1600* (Cambridge: Cambridge University Press, 1998); and A. L. Beier, "Social Problems in Elizabethan London," *Journal of Interdisciplinary History* 9 (1978): 204–5.
29. Earle, *Microcosmography*, 3.
30. Ibid.
31. Griffiths, *Youth and Authority*, 34.
32. Anonymous, *The English Courtier and the Country Gentleman, or Civil and Uncivil Life*, 1586, in *Inedited Tracts: Illustrating the Manners, Opinions, and Occupations of Englishmen during the Sixteenth and Seventeenth Centuries*, ed. W. C. Hazlitt (London: Roxburghe Collection, 1868), 15.
33. Griffiths, *Youth and Authority*, 174.
34. John Wharton, *Wharton's Dream* (London, 1578), sig. A3.
35. Derek Keene, "Growth, Modernisation and Control: The Transformation of London's Landscape, c. 1500–c. 1760," in *Two Capitals: London and Dublin, 1500–1840*, ed. Peter Clark and Raymond Gillespie (Oxford: Oxford University Press, 2001), 11.
36. Lawrence Manley, Introduction, *London in the Age of Shakespeare: An Anthology*, ed. Lawrence Manley (University Park: Pennsylvania State Press, 1986), 2.
37. See R. W. Connell, *Masculinities*, 2nd ed. (Berkeley and Los Angeles: University of California Press, 2005), esp. chap. 8, "The History of Masculinity," 185–203.

Part I

Redefining Urban Masculinity: Taverns, Universities, and Gaming Houses

Chapter 1

Manly Drunkenness: Binge Drinking as Disciplined Play

Gina Bloom

Shakespeare's *The Taming of the Shrew* opens with what appears to be a straightforward condemnation of the vice of excessive alcohol consumption, as a lord, finding a drunken tinker passed out before an alehouse, exclaims in disgust: "O monstrous beast, how like a swine he lies!"[1] The lord's outrage is not surprising from the perspective of early modern moralist discourse, which, associating drunkenness with idleness and disorder, figures it as dehumanizing and, thus, emasculating. Thomas Young defines drunkenness as "a vice which stirreth up lust, griefe, anger, and madnesse, extinguisheth the memory, opinion, and understanding, maketh a man the picture of a beast, and twise a child, because he can neither stand nor speake."[2] Excessive consumption of alcohol compromises reason and bodily control, traits thought to distinguish men from beasts as well as from other ostensibly less rational creatures, such as children, women, and men of low status. Sir Walter Raleigh's advice to his son triangulates drunkenness, beastliness, and emasculation when it warns that wine not only "transformeth a man into a Beast" but also "wasteth the naturall heate and seed of generation."[3] For those who aspire to the kind of "patriarchal manhood" Raleigh espouses—where manhood is achieved through the demonstration of self-control, power over dependents, and ability to produce heirs, among other things—drunkenness is necessarily unmanly.[4] Sharing Raleigh's social status and investments in patriarchal masculinity, Shakespeare's lord frames his condemnation of Sly in similar terms.

Far more surprising than the lord's initial response is his subsequent decision to engage Sly in an elaborate game of make believe where the tinker plays a nobleman. Theodore Leinwand convincingly argues that the context of the alehouse is crucial to understanding the rationale for the jest. Observing that early modern alehouses brought into contact men of very different social status, Leinwand views the lord as anxiously working to figure out his relationship to the beggar; the jest is "a form of containment by which one turns one's threatening opposite into one's double."[5] This social friction was aggravated, I would add, by the fact that the alehouse—a fixture not just of the countryside where Shakespeare's scene is set but also, indeed especially, of the urban landscape—was a site for men's excessive drinking. At alehouses men like Sly could witness men of higher status like the lord suffer the socially debilitating effects of drink. To be sure, alehouses could level social differences by bringing out the beast in men of all social positions and contravening commonplace views of drunkenness as solely a lower-class problem. But as bounded, purposeful spaces for recreational pleasure, they also held out ways to reframe excessive drinking as sociable sport, even for elite men. Such establishments, I want to suggest, were part of a larger urban drinking culture that produced a *recreational discourse* of binge drinking, a discourse that competed with moral condemnations of the vice to provide an alternate view of the relationship between excess and masculinity.

To begin to understand the cultural and social work performed by this recreational discourse, and, thus, how the lord's jest comprises a response to Sly's drunkenness, we need to reconsider the claim frequently advanced by scholars that in the early modern period excessive drinking, because of its association with disorder, was considered unmanly. This critical commonplace, an echo of early modern moralist discourse, conflates two problematic assumptions about excessive drinking that this chapter aims to disarticulate and query: one, that for early modern writers, drunkenness necessarily effeminizes and, two, that heavy drinking is always associated with disorder.[6] The first assumption, that heavy drinking effeminizes, has been importantly challenged by Alexandra Shepard, who, like Amanda Bailey in her work on ostentatious dress, points out that early modern manhood was more variegated in its forms than many scholars have presumed. Self-mastery and moderation may have been central to the formation of patriarchal masculinity, but for men disenfranchised by a patriarchal system—particularly working men of lower or middle status and youths who were flooding London in the sixteenth and seventeenth centuries—disorderly behaviors like heavy drinking could constitute a bid for an antipatriarchal, countercode of masculine conduct.[7] From this perspective the drunken Sly is not so easily dismissed, for by embracing drunken disorder as a sign of manliness, he threatens the lord's logic of privilege. But to see how the lord's jest mitigates this threat, we need to reconsider the second assumption—which undergirds Shepard's argument—that drunkenness is unruly.

The lord's jest, I would argue, involves Sly in a more orderly, disciplined form of drunken revelry. In this elaborate game of pretend, Sly's drinking takes the shape of elite recreation. By the lord's rules of play, Sly is restricted to certain kinds of drink (sack, or strong wine, not cheap "small ale" [ind. 2.1]), particular activities to do while drinking (watching a play as opposed to a "Christmas gambold or a tumbling-trick" [ind. 2.129]), and more noble drinking company (ladies and lords, instead of "Old John Naps of Greet,/ And Peter Turf, and Henry Pimpernel" [ind. 2.88–89]). In effect Sly's drinking is transformed into what play theorist Roger Caillois has called *ludus*: convention-bound, calculated, disciplined play. All games, Caillois argues, fall on a continuum between *ludus* and *paidia*, which he defines as improvisational and disorganized free-play.[8] At stake in the tension between *ludus* and *paidia* is more than the categorization of play, however, for, particularly when set in an early modern context, these forms of play are inflected by gender and class differences. By framing Sly's drinking as part of a rule-bound game, the lord imposes some degree of order and self-control onto Sly's otherwise unruly, transgressive behavior, attempting to bring it into alignment with codes of patriarchal manhood.[9]

Before exploring further binge drinking as disciplined play and the ways the city encouraged what I am calling a *recreational discourse* of binge drinking, it will be helpful to define more carefully what I mean by patriarchal versus antipatriarchal manhood. According to Shepard, early modern men laid claim to patriarchal manhood by demonstrating "strength, thrift, industry, self-sufficiency, honesty, authority, autonomy, self-government, moderation, reason, wisdom, and wit" and depending on the man, any one of these might be stressed more than another.[10] Of the five models of ideal manhood Bruce R. Smith identifies in *Shakespeare and Masculinity*, four reflect these attributes with different degrees of emphasis. The "chivalrous knight" embodied by Bolingbroke in the beginning of *Richard II* exhibits strength and authority while still upholding the social and political order that gives him his aristocratic status. The "Herculean hero," of which Coriolanus is an example, shows similar physical prowess and courage as the knight but, wedded to his own standard of ethics, he emphasizes autonomy. The "humanist man of moderation," a model to which Duke Vincentio in *Measure for Measure* aspires, exhibits wisdom, reason, and the capacity for self-government and moderation. The "merchant prince" figured by Basanio in *Merchant of Venice* and most common in city comedies shows thrift, self-sufficiency, and honesty, diligently working to achieve economic success.[11]

Drunkenness would seem to undermine the execution of all of these forms of ideal manhood. Indeed, at the start of *The Taming of the Shrew*, Sly resembles the model Smith calls the "saucy Jack," a figure who flouts conventional standards of masculinity, parodying the aforementioned patriarchal ideals.[12] First, Sly slurs his way through a claim to noble genealogy; tracing his descent from "Richard [instead of William the] Conqueror" (ind. 4), he defends his status with far less elegance than Bolingbroke. Second, Sly presents himself as a kind of Herculean hero, making a case for principled retribution against the alehouse's hostess; his cause is, of course, more specious than Coriolanus's, and he is clearly too inebriated to carry out his threats the way the great warrior does. Third, Sly's drunkenness and temper underscore his lack of moderation; unlike Duke Vincentio, who rightly condemns Angelo for lacking self-control, Sly hardly appears a convincing voice of moral judgment when he calls the hostess "a baggage" (ind. 3), slang for prostitute. Finally when Sly refuses to pay—"not a denier" (ind. 7)—for the glasses he has broken, he exhibits stinginess instead of the thrift characteristic of citizen heroes. In his send-up of popular models of patriarchal manhood, Sly exposes their insufficiency and incoherence, reminding the audience that they are, as Smith writes, "what a man *might be*, not . . . what he *is*."[13] The lord's jest subverts that critique by recasting Sly's drunkenness as the fulfillment of, rather than a disqualification from, gentlemanly status. At the lord's house Sly continues to become inebriated—so drunk that he passes out and is able to be carried back to the alehouse where he was found—but at the same time practices moderating his pleasures and executing authority over a household.

Insofar as *The Taming of the Shrew* is invested in the ways men claim patriarchal manhood through the controlled performance of excess (in violence, dress, and speech, among other things), the play as a whole undoubtedly would benefit from a more sustained reading in the context of my argument. In this chapter, however, I am interested in how the lord's jest points to a wider early modern recreational discourse that rescues drunkenness from associations with effeminacy as well as low status by underscoring, through the frame of gaming, the discipline and order involved in excessive drinking. My focus will be the drinking games represented by a set of understudied early modern texts with decidedly urban and elite roots: Richard Brathwaite's *The Law of Drinking* (1617), a burlesque of Inns of Court life by a writer more widely known by scholars for authoring serious conduct books; and ornate drinking vessels known as "wager cups" that, manufactured in a number of early modern European cities, including London, were designed for games of competitive inebriation.[14]

In their emphasis on the rules of binge drinking, Brathwaite's treatise and the wager cups were positioned in tension with, though not in direct conflict against, the early modern discourses on drinking most scholars have discussed: moralist, medical, political, and hedonist.[15] Though drinking games, like medical treatises on the health benefits of alcohol and royalist injunctions supporting festive drinking customs, defend drinking from moralist condemnation, they do so not by recommending moderate or functionalist indulgence. Rather, drinking games accept inebriation as part of the purpose of drinking. And yet drinking games do not flout moralist discourse entirely or present the activity as careless abandonment to hedonist pleasure. Rather, the games figure binge drinking as an organized and measured activity, subject to rules. In drinking games pleasure is derived, in fact, from following rules as much as from becoming inebriated.

Early modern London had an instrumental role in promoting this recreational discourse of binge drinking. For one thing, London had a higher concentration of public drinking establishments than other English towns, creating the institutional conditions for recreational drunkenness. In the 1590s one German visitor marveled, "I have never seen more taverns and alehouses in my whole life than in London."[16] Although men did not need public houses to drink to excess, these were spaces of sociality, encouraging heavy drinking as a form of social play. Of course, the city held no monopoly on games and recreations involving alcohol. Excessive drinking was a vital part of English countryside festivities such as those held on May Day and Shrovetide Tuesday. Yet as Leah Marcus and others have shown, the recreational pleasures of the countryside were often exports of the city and/or the court.[17] Binge drinking games were no exception. Moralist Richard Young, though he observes drinking games being played throughout the countryside, still links the vice of binge drinking to the city, calling drunkenness the "Metropolitan City of the Province of vices." Even as he laments the spread of drinking houses through English villages, he reserves his harshest rebukes for the city, where the horrors of binge drinking are repackaged as acceptable social behavior. Young raves that "there are in London Drinking Schooles: so that Drunkennesse is profesed with us as a liberall Art and Science."[18]

Young may exaggerate London's institutional support for binge drinking play—perhaps parodying what Jean Howard has identified as a growing London market for instruction in recreations of bodily comportment[19]—but he is not completely off the mark. Drinking games may not have been an official "science" taught alongside fencing and dancing at Academies of Manners or the Inns of Court, but binge drinking was an integral part of university and Inns of Court life. So integral that law student libertine turned moralist Richard Brathwaite, upon leaving Grays Inn, translated and published a German treatise entirely about student drinking culture. Appropriately titled *A Solemne Joviall Disputation, Theoreticke and Praticke; Briefly Shadowing the Law of Drinking*, Brathwaite's burlesque of the law seems intended to amuse its student audience with a demonstration of how their legal knowledge could be applied to a subject as vulgar as binge drinking. The book's popularity among learned readers (several Latin translations were published in England after the English edition appeared) suggests that though it takes as its subject German student drinking practices, the book resonated powerfully with men affiliated with England's patriarchal institutions of higher learning.[20] Indeed, despite English nationalistic rhetoric that linked excessive drinking with the Germans and Dutch, English university men, as Laurie Ellinghausen shows in the next chapter, were just as likely as their foreign counterparts to overindulge in alcohol.[21] Brathwaite's treatise fulfills Young's worst nightmares about the ways these and other Londoners sanctioned binge drinking, turning it into a gentleman's game by framing the activity as disciplined play.

DISCIPLINED BINGE DRINKING IN BRATHWAITE

We can get some sense of the discipline inherent in drinking games, ironically, from Young's own account of a game called "drinking for a muggle." The game involves six men who

> have determined to trie their strengths who could drinke most glasses for the muggle. The first drinks a glasse of a pint, the second two, the next, three, and so every one multiplyeth till the last taketh sixe. Then the first beginneth again, and taketh seven; and in this manner they drinke thrice a peece round, every man taking a glasse more then his fellow: so that hee that drank least, which was the first, dranke one and twenty pintes, and the sixt man thirtie sixe.[22]

Participants in such a game would be under pressure not only to drink their apportioned share without "loosing their witts," but also, in attempting to keep track of how many glasses had been consumed by their neighbors, they would have to remain mathematically dexterous in the face of increasing inebriation. Young identifies an array of similar such games and associates them with London's gentlemen: "He is a man of no fashion that cannot drink *super naculum*, Carouse the Hunters Hoope, quaffe Upse-freese crosse, Bose in Permoysant, in Pimlico, in Crambo, with Healthes, Gloves, Numpes, Frolickes, and a thousand of such dominiering inventions; as by the Bell, by the Cards, by the Dye, by the Dozen, by the Yard." The London neighborhood Pimlico appears here as one site for fashionable drinking games, some of which are, to Young's further consternation, of non-English origin: to "quaffe Upse-freese cross" means to drink with arms laced in the Dutch or German manner.[23] But even as he condemns such games for promoting the (supposedly) foreign vice of binge drinking, Young underscores the games' emphases on precision and discipline: "and so by measure, wee drinke out of measure."[24]

Brathwaite's own English rendering of German drinking games captures this paradox of measured chaos, though the role of discipline in his portrayal of binge drinking is easy to overlook. *Law* seems, at first, to represent heavy drinking as a sign of disorder and abuse, the kind of activity that, if it does not emasculate drinkers, will certainly demean them socially. It describes, for instance, a group of drinkers whose members become so inebriated that they vomit all over each other. In another story of debauchery, a drunk man, not wanting to get up from the table to relieve his bladder, proceeds to "pulling out his yard and making water in his boots, which reached up to his belly."[25] Just at that moment, a toast is drunk to him, compelling him to stand up, at which point his "shamelesse thing burst out, having till then laie hid under the table, and presented it selfe." The scene devolves into utter chaos as the maids at the table, "shreeked out aloud, no otherwise then Geese are wont to doe, ta, ta, ta, what a thing is this?"[26]

Heavy drinking, these examples illustrate, leads to significant disorder as men lose control over their bodily functions. What should remain contained and hidden—one's genitals and half-digested food—is involuntarily exposed, with embarrassing social repercussions.

However chaotic such scenes may be, they must be interpreted within their fuller context, for they are used, ultimately, to lay out the measured rules that bring drinkers into conformity with some of the very standards of patriarchal manliness Brathwaite later outlines in his sober advice book *The English Gentleman*. The urination incident, for example, is offered as the answer to a question about whether a man ought to "hold [his] water" if drinking in the company of maids.[27] The unfortunate result of doing so demonstrates that this is never a good idea, no matter the company. The shared vomiting episode is also used to test the limits of, and thus teach, civility and manly comportment. *Law* introduces the incident by marveling at the degree to which many drunks, who ought to have lost "use of reason and memorie," still manage to maintain "sound and rententive thoughts," something "which wee observe to bee most punctually performed by some of ours; who are not forgetfull of any treatie or discourse offered, even then, when they cast up their gobbets and goblets, and one guest requites another with like payment."[28] Even as these drinkers seem to violate the very essence of decorum by throwing up on each other, they continue to exercise reason and, as good gentlemen, remain mindful of their promises and conversations. Brathwaite's euphemism for the vomiting epidemic—each guest "requites" his neighbor with "like payment"—reframes the chaotic behavior as civilized, social grace, a display of equity and fairness. In fact, other early modern writers use these very terms to describe the manly sparring done on a battlefield or in a duel, where the most honorable conflict is that between equally matched fighters. *Law* reiterates these analogies to honorable conflict when it commends the vomiting drinkers, who are "as men triumphing in the atchievement of so great a victorie" and when it advises on how best to respond after throwing up on a neighbor: obtain some water, wash off his face, and then carry on with the drinking bout.[29]

To transform binge drinking from an effeminizing and ignoble vice into a performance of patriarchal manliness, *Law* represents the activity as a game. Like other games, binge drinking includes its own language and particular scripts for participants. *Law* provides a dizzyingly long list of different kinds of pledges, or healths, each with a particular name and requiring a complex set of maneuvers. Among these is the "health-cup," where everyone stands bareheaded in a circle; the participants proffer wishes of health as a communal cup is sent around, each participant drinking in order of where he is sitting. In the "cup of brotherhood," one man drinks a pledge to another, perhaps to reconcile with him after a fight.[30] To perform successfully in such a pledge, the drinker follows a script, beginning modestly with "*Sir, if I who am but a young man should not seeme altogether unworthy of so high an honour...*" The ceremonial and dignified language continues as the cup is passed between the two speakers, after which, "having used some eare-whisperings one to another, their mutuall request is that this *Brotherhood* may be strengthened with mutuall visitations."[31]

As in any game, maneuvers of play have specialized names. Among the many ways to drink one's pledge are "*Partiall*" measures and "*totall*" (drink the entire cup). The "totall" can be performed "*dis-continuately*" or "*continuately*, when at one draught the whole pot is emptied." In a further refinement of the "continuate" drinking move, the text describes how it may be done "*haustically*, when after the usual manner all is drunke up without taking breath" or, as when the drink is consumed in one gulp, "*florically*," so named because this causes "reflection or refluxion whereof sendeth forth some little bubbles, which our countrey-men call *flowers*."[32] With this etymology for "florical" drinking, *Law* transforms the uncontrollable and uncouth burp that inevitably follows from gulping one's drink into a genteel and pleasant expression. The presence of virtuoso moves, many of which also have names, further provides a sense of stylistic form to binge drinking, emphasizing as well the physical agility and grace needed for the sport:

> it pleaseth some to lift up the glass unto their mouth. Others hang downe their lippe, that they might drink with their heads inclining downward. Some joyne two cups one upon another, and drinke them together. Others take not up the Cup in their hand, but enwreathe it in the crooke of their arme. There are, who set the glasse to their brow, that by little and little it might descened downe by their nose as by a Conduit to their mouth.[33]

There is nothing lazy or idle about this manner of consuming alcohol. To the contrary, such maneuvers require the kind of strength and manual control characteristic of a swordsman or athlete.

It is not only by codifying terminology and establishing rules that *Law* stylizes drinking play, but also by envisioning the consequences for participants who violate the rules. Notably, this violation is presented as a kind of loss of valor. For instance, the text considers what might happen if someone begins to drink "florically" (all contents consumed in one gulp) and "perchance one among all the rest could not performe the same." In this case the rules are flexible, allowing everyone to drink according to his ability. The rules are less lenient when a man cannot drink off "haustically" (typical drinking but without taking a breath), a manageable feat that ought to be learned simply by watching others: "That is a great fault not to know that which all observe. Which is compared to a solecisme or fallacie: and consequentlie admits no excuse. Let him drinke therefore till his eyes water."[34] Insofar as watering eyes announce a man's inability to control his body—which, if secreting fluid, exhibits the excess of moisture Galenic physiology associated with women and children—the cost of losing the drinking wager is appropriate. He who is unable to keep up with his fellow drinkers must then reperform his unmanly shamefulness through tears. But as Brathwaite's later book *The English Gentleman* will do, *Law* draws a fine line between manly excellence and problematic pride. In his sober conduct book, Brathwaite warns, "Now *Gentlemen*, you, whose better parts aime at more glorious ends, so confine your desires to an equall meane, that mounting too high bring you not to an irreparable fall."[35] *Law* offers similar advice about manly modesty when it condemns grandstanding novices who attempt risky maneuvers for which they are not trained. If a man starts to drink florically but cannot, Brathwaite insists that he start again and should not try something he does not know how to do.

As in any game, there are also penalties for those who interfere in the game's proper functioning. And *Law* admits that a certain degree of violence is excusable when policing drinking play. It describes, for instance, how to handle a fellow drinker who has become quarrelsome. First, fellow participants should implore that person to be quiet, then threaten him to be quiet, and then join together to "cudgel" him and eject him from the establishment.[36] Brathwaite intimates, however, that while it is important to contain outbreaks of overly aggressive behavior, some violence is part and parcel of recreational binge drinking. Indeed, this penchant for violence justifies the sport's gendered exclusivity. *Law* maintains that though women are certainly allowed to be present when men binge drink, they should be prepared to put their chastity at risk, for "a Drunkard hath no purpose or disposition to offend, seeing he is forced by a kind of violence to offend."[37] The text goes on to justify men touching a woman who is dressed provocatively or who does not rebuke other men for touching her. Brathwaite's drinkers, even as they engage in excessive alcohol consumption, thus take it upon themselves to manage the excesses not only of themselves, but also of the women around them.

In sum, *Law* rewrites unruly drunkenness as proper recreation for the gentleman, imagining ways to consume immeasurable amounts in a measured fashion. This disciplined play preserves values of patriarchal manhood, such as order, honor, and even modesty. Brathwaite alludes, albeit ironically, to the chivalric potential of drinking games when he calls drinking "a valiant combat or encounter with the pot."[38] It may be the case that the text simply mocks its student subjects for claiming there are rules for what is, in truth, rowdy drunken behavior. Perhaps Brathwaite's very decision to translate the German text constitutes a typically English mockery of Germans for their drunken excesses. But regardless of Brathwaite's aims and wherever the intended satire of the text lies, *Law* participates in and contributes to a wider recreational discourse on the manliness of binge drinking games. Such a discourse confers patriarchal masculinity by attributing to men's binge drinking an aesthetic sensibility and stylized form akin to what Adam Zucker finds in many seventeenth-century representations of gambling. The effect is that stylized drinking similarly pits gender against class. As Zucker points out, the figure of the "true sportsman" conceals social and economic inequities behind the façade of "social style and cultural competencies."[39] In a comparable way, as game rules and virtuoso moves fashion excessive drinking into a demonstration of patriarchal masculinity, they reinforce status differences between men, placing those who get drunk in a disciplined manner above those who do not.

FANTASIES OF MANHOOD IN WAGER CUPS

This link between the disciplinary function of early modern drinking games and the production of patriarchal manliness is nowhere more apparent than in "wager cups." Originating in sixteenth-century Nuremberg, but produced also in London and other European cities, wager cups assume a variety of forms. The mount on one vessel contains a die, so that the cup is meant to be shaken before it is filled, the number on the die denoting how many cups of wine the game participant must then consume. Another version, the pass glass or peg tankard, features notches, or "passes," along its length. The drinker consumes in one gulp down to the next notch before passing on the cup. The cost of failure is drinking down to yet another pass. Very little has been written about these cups and the conditions of their use, but the ornate design and precious materials of surviving cups suggest that they were owned by wealthy families, perhaps brought out only on special occasions. The *jungfrauenbecher* or maiden cup was (and sometimes still is) used for drinking wagers at wedding celebrations in Germany as well as in drinking rituals by London's Worshipful Company of Vintners, which still owns two of the surviving cups (figure 1.1). Less expensive versions of these cups may have been available in more public spaces, as is suggested by Dutch paintings that depict groups of men drinking from pass glasses in taverns or inns. Whatever the history of their use, the cups are of

Figure 1.1 Wager Cups. On left: silver; maker's mark is WF (possibly William Fowler). London (1682–1683). On right: silver-gilt; maker's mark is possibly TI (Thomas Jenkins). Possibly London (c.1680). Reproduced by permission of the Worshipful Company of Vintners.

interest for the way they contribute, like Brathwaite's pamphlet, to a recreational discourse on binge drinking, one that imposes order on excess by inviting men who can afford access to such objects to consume alcohol in a certain way, within a prescribed amount of time, or in a measured amount. Moreover, insofar as the designs of the cups suggest imaginative connections between the drinking act and other (less compromised) cultural performances of manliness, they further illustrate how a recreational discourse on binge drinking worked to shore up displays of patriarchal manhood.

The Dutch puzzle or mill-cup, originating in the seventeenth-century Netherlands and produced well into the nineteenth century (see figure 1.2), is mounted with a windmill whose vanes turn in response to breath blown through a tube attached to the cup.[40] To win the drinking wager, a player must consume the contents of the cup before the windmill ceases spinning. Most versions of the cup include a penalty dial that, after being spun, sets the consequences for losing the wager: the participant must drink the number of cupfuls indicated on the dial. The drinker who is well skilled and practiced in chugging will avoid the penalty. But the cup also rewards the player who simply works hardest during the game, for the best way to avoid the penalty is to keep the vanes spinning as long as possible so as to allow the drinker time to finish the cup's contents. And that is accomplished by sheer respiratory labor.

But to understand the ideological and cultural work of these vessels, we need to attend not only to the rules of play invoked by their structure, but also to what ludologists would call their *gameworld*, the cups' material/semiotic design.[41] The gameworlds of wager cups often invoke fantasies of ideal patriarchal manhood. In the case of the mill-cup, the fantasy is that of pastoral manly industry, for the cup spatially links the drinker's labor with that of the workers who produced the beverage being consumed. Affixed to the side of the mill is a ladder on which are two figures of millers carrying sacks of grain. The drinker's blowing tube is positioned parallel to the ladder and, in some seventeenth-century versions, the tube intersects with the ladder at the place where the blower would place his mouth. Were the cup to be filled with beer, the narrative of communal labor would be elegantly complete: the millers bring the grain into the mill, the drinker provides the energy needed for the windmill to process the grain, and the result is the beer consumed. Of course, the drinker's labor is far more genteel than that of the figures represented on the cup, allowing him, even if a denizen of the city, to indulge in this pastoral fantasy of manly industry without breaking a sweat.

Figure 1.2 Windmill cup. Silver. Probably German (c.1880). Reproduced by permission of Billy Schmerling Sender, Pasarel Ltd.

Whereas the mill-cup invites urban drinkers to participate in an imaginary pastoral scene, where they may bond with each other over shared labor, the maiden cup offers drinkers the opportunity to manage the sexual excesses of an imaginary female body. The vessel takes the form of a woman who wears a billowing skirt that, when turned over, is revealed to be a cup.[42] She holds above her another cup attached to her hands by a swiveling mechanism, so that the cup can swing completely around. Structurally, the vessel challenges its drinkers to consume the contents of both containers without spilling a drop, a task all the more challenging as the drinker becomes increasingly inebriated. The design of the cup's gameworld casts this drinking wager in erotic terms. To consume the larger cup, the participant must turn over the maiden's skirts, looking into and drinking from the space where a woman's legs and genitalia would be. The maiden figure herself is explicitly eroticized. In the German version she is dressed in ornate Venetian fashions, with a low-cut bodice and elaborate hairdo (figure 1.3). The figure of the English cup (figure 1.1) wears more modest attire, her hair restrained beneath a cap. And yet there is an erotic valence to the maiden's innocence. Indeed, when the cup was used by London's Worshipful Company of Vintners—with liverymen drinking a toast to the company from the main skirt cup and a toast to the Company's Master from the small cup—the ritual was called "kissing the maid."[43] Some later versions of the cups recognize these erotic dimensions. Two nineteenth-century cups owned by the Metropolitan Museum, virtually identical to their seventeenth-century predecessors, add engraved inscriptions on the maiden figures' aprons, as if issued directly from their laps: "Hands of[f] I pray you Handle not me / For I am blind and you can see / If you love me lend me not / For fear of breaking bend me not."[44] Though on one level this is merely a warning to handle the cup with care—not unlike curses owners of books wrote in their covers[45]—it works also, especially in combination with the maiden's dress, as erotic provocation. Like the women present in the scenes of drinking Brathwaite's pamphlet describes, the maiden of the cup is to be treated as an erotic object, regardless of her protests. And the drinker's successful control of the unwieldy cup, whose contents may easily spill out, becomes symbolic of his ability to manage female sexual excess.

Such symbolism could have material effects, at least according to the account provided by a witness in an early seventeenth-century legal case, who describes how a group of inebriated men at an English inn used drinking game tropes to structure their sexual assault of a female servant. As if enacting the fantasy of the maiden cup, the men

Figure 1.3 Meinrad Bauch, the elder. Kleiner Jungfrauenbecher (small maiden cup). Gold-plated silver, with turbo snail shell. Nuremberg (c.1603–1609). Reproduced by permission of Staatliche Kunstsammlungen Dresden, Grünes Gewölbe. Photo credit: SLUB Dresden / Deutsche Fotothek.

are described as having taken turns "one after another [to] lift her clothes up to her girdle" in order to "feel her privities and look upon them."[46] Their assault takes the explicit shape of a drinking game when the men, with beers in hand, pretend to be chivalric heroes:

> After which done Jay (who named himself the knight of the castle) sat upon a bench, taking and holding Edith between his legs, placing a stool before her face, and holding her arms fast. And then and there drawing their wicked rapiers and laying them upon the table made proclamations in these or the like words viz: "Oyes, whosoever dareth to break down the walls of grimcunt castle let him approach."[47]

As each man comes forward pretending to be a knight, he lifts up the servant's skirts and proceeds to fondle and then throw a beer at her genitals. The connection to the kinds of drinking games I discussed earlier becomes even more evident when one of the men, who tells the maid that he is more "honest" than the others, declares he "would not break the walls of the castle but would drink a health unto it and so drunk up the glass of beer."

It is not surprising that an inn, the most upscale of English public drinking establishments, provides the setting for this disturbing drinking game. The servant who delivers the testimony notes that the men involved had been drinking beer in an upper chamber of the inn for several hours, consuming 2s. 8d. worth of alcohol, before they descended into the kitchen to commit the assault. These details underscore not only the men's level of inebriation but also their socioeconomic status, for the private chambers of inns and taverns were more exclusive and expensive places to drink. In other words, these are the kind of men who ought to be socially disgraced by abandoning themselves to their sexual desires and chasing a mere servant girl around public premises. Their descent from the patriarchal arena of the upper chambers into the feminized and lower-status arena of the kitchen represents that social degeneration in spatial terms. By stylizing their drunken sexual assault as a game, however, specifically a game of chivalric pretend, the men—like the student drinkers in Brathwaite's *The Law of Drinking* and the users of wager vessels such as the windmill or dice cups—translate otherwise animalistic, socially debasing behavior into organized sport, a performance of not antipatriarchal but patriarchal masculinity.

The episode raises questions about the methodology I have employed throughout this chapter. For one thing, what counts as a "drinking game"? In this category I have included toasts like those

Brathwaite describes or those performed using wager cups in rituals by the Worshipful Company of Vintners; pranks such as that of Shakespeare's lord; a sexual assault framed as a game; as well as more easily definable binge drinking play, such as that involving windmill wager cups. In moving across such disparate sources, I am relying on the well-established link anthropologists and sociologists have theorized between ritual and play. But I am also strategically associating these disparate activities and texts in order to think more broadly about the early modern recreational discourse that London, metropolis of vice, helped promote. In putting such a range of texts into conversation, I am not suggesting that the wager cups offer extra-literary, "historical" support for my reading of more recognizably "literary" texts like Brathwaite's *Law* and Shakespeare's induction to *The Taming of the Shrew*. As I have argued elsewhere, along with other scholars of material culture, historical objects we can touch do not give us access to some stable realm of the real, some privileged account of "how it was."[48] Rather, my goal has been to think about these items as part of a larger recreational discourse that, whether or not engaged through actual practices of play, did a certain kind of cultural work: it transformed binge drinking from an emasculating or plebian vice into a forum for the performance of patriarchal manhood.

This is not to say that the patriarchal manhood produced was stable and robust. The work of blowing into a tube attached to the mill-cup is far from commensurate with the kind of labor involved in producing the beverage in the cup. Similarly, the successful manipulation of a maiden cup by no means testifies to a man's ability to handle the bodies of real women in his life. And, to return to *The Taming of the Shrew*'s Sly, pretending to be a drunken lord does not make a tinker into an aristocrat who commands a household. These are, after all, simply games. As such, the masculinity they produce and the class distinctions they reinforce are provisional and fleeting, even fantastical. This is not to suggest that such fictions are inconsequential, however, as is demonstrated by the legal testimony as well as by the story of Sly. In a closing scene that may have been performed for early modern audiences of *The Taming of the Shrew*, Sly awakens from his drunken slumber to reflect on the play about shrew-taming that he has seen at the lord's house as part of the lord's elaborate drinking game. From having witnessed the dramatization, Sly is confident that he "know[s] now how to tame a shrew" (153) and, like the drunk men who commit sexual assault in the inn, he is ready to practice his knowledge on a real woman, his wife. Nevertheless, given how poorly Sly fares in his conflict with the alehouse hostess earlier in the play, his threat to discipline his wife appears less than convincing. Even the tapster is doubtful, offering to accompany Sly home to confront his angry spouse. Drinking fantasies provide Sly, like other early modern men, an imaginative forum through which to negotiate the challenges of masculinity that cannot be so easily managed in reality, where disciplining bodies—one's own and those of others—is not always such a pleasure.

NOTES

For their helpful comments on earlier versions of this chapter, I thank Amanda Bailey and Roze Hentschell as well as my UC Davis drafts group: Seeta Chaganti, Fran Dolan, Margie Ferguson, Noah Guynn, and Claire Waters. Thanks also to Stephen Freeth, Natalie Giannini, and Libby Otto for their research assistance.

1. William Shakespeare, *The Taming of the Shrew: Texts and Contexts*, ed. Frances E. Dolan (Boston: Bedford Books of St. Martin's Press, 1996), induction, 1.30. Further references to the play appear in my text.
2. Thomas Young, *England's Bane, or the Description of Drunkenness* (London, 1634), sig. D2r.
3. Sir Walter Raleigh, *Sir Walter Raleigh's Instruction to his Sonne: and to Posteritie*, 3rd ed. (London, 1633), 82, 87.
4. I borrow the phrase from Alexandra Shepard, *Meanings of Manhood in Early Modern England* (Oxford: Oxford University Press, 2003), discussed further below.
5. Theodore B. Leinwand, "Spongy Plebs, Mighty Lords, and the Dynamics of the Alehouse," *Journal of Medieval and Renaissance Studies* 19.2 (1989): 159–84, esp. 172.
6. On drunkenness as effeminizing, see Karen Britland, "Circe's Cup: Wine and Women in Early Modern Drama," in *A Pleasing Sinne: Drink and Conviviality in Seventeenth-Century England*, ed. Adam Smyth, Studies in Renaissance Literature (Cambridge: D. S. Brewer, 2004), 109–25. On the tavern as an effeminizing space, see Jean E. Howard and Phyllis Rackin, *Engendering a Nation: A Feminist Account of Shakespeare's English Histories*, Feminist Readings of Shakespeare (New York: Routledge, 1997), esp. chap. 11. On drunkenness and drinking establishments as linked to disorder, see David Underdown, *Revel, Riot and Rebellion: Popular Politics and Culture in England 1602–1660* (Oxford: Oxford University Press, 1987); Paul Griffiths, "Masterless Young People in Norwich, 1560–1645," in *The Experience of Authority in Early Modern England*, ed. Paul Griffiths, Adam Fox, and Steve Hindle (New York: Macmillan, 1996), esp. 159; A. Lynn Martin, *Alcohol, Sex, and Gender in Late*

Medieval and Early Modern Europe (New York: Palgrave Macmillan, 2001), esp. chap. 6.

7. Shepard, *Meanings of Manhood.* Amanda Bailey, *Flaunting: Style and the Subversive Male Body in Early Modern England* (Toronto: Toronto University Press, 2007). For an exploration of how Dutch youths' excessive drinking constituted a form of manly display, see Benjamin Roberts, "Drinking Like a Man: The Paradox of Excessive Drinking for Seventeenth-Century Dutch Youth," *Journal of Family History* 29 (2004): 237–52.
8. Roger Caillois, *Man, Play and Games*, trans. Meyer Barash (Urbana: University of Illinois Press, 2001[1958]). There are obvious limitations to this schema, which introduces a problematic binary. In fact, improvisation and "free-play" are governed by rules, though these may be implicit or internalized by participants. To be fair, however, even Caillois uses this schema primarily as a heuristic device.
9. There has been interesting work on the relationship between drinking, male homosociality, and status. See Stella Achilleos, "The *Anacreontea* and a Tradition of Refined Male Sociability," in Smyth, *Pleasing Sinne*, 21–35; Cedric C. Brown, "Sons of Beer and Sons of Ben: Drink as a Social Marker in Seventeenth-Century England," in Smyth, *Pleasing Sinne*, 3–20; Michelle O'Callaghan, "Tavern Societies, the Inns of Court, and the Culture of Conviviality in Early Seventeenth-Century London," in Smyth, *Pleasing Sinne*, 37–51; B. Ann Tlusty, *Bacchus and the Civic Order: The Culture of Drink in Early Modern Germany* (Charlottesville: University Press of Virginia, 2001); Patricia Fumerton, "Not Home: Alehouses, Ballads, and the Vagrant Husband in Early Modern England," *Journal of Medieval and Early Modern Studies* 32.3 (2002): 493–518. Much of this work has focused, however, on different spaces and contexts for drinking (inns vs. taverns vs. alehouses; particular male societies) or different kinds of drink (wine vs. beer vs. ale). In my focus on the relationship between social status and *techniques* of consumption, I pursue a less widely developed angle, so far discussed only in relation to pledge drinking. On the latter, see Anna Bryson, *From Courtesy to Civility: Changing Codes of Conduct in Early Modern England* (Oxford: Clarendon, 1998), esp. 92–94; and Tlusty, *Bacchus.*
10. Shepard, *Meanings of Manhood*, 247.
11. Bruce R. Smith, *Shakespeare and Masculinity*, Oxford Shakespeare Topics (Oxford: Oxford University Press, 2000), 44–54.
12. Ibid., 54–57.
13. Ibid., 63.
14. Brathwaite's book appeared in English as Blasius Multibibus, *A Solemne Joviall Disputation, Theoreticke and Praticke: Briefly Shadowing the Law of Drinking* (Oenozphthopolis [i.e., London], 1617). Despite its popularity in its own day, the book has been

virtually ignored by scholars, even as Brathwaite's conduct books *The English Gentleman* (London, 1630) and *The English Gentlewoman* (London, 1631) have assumed centrality in an emerging canon of seventeenth-century advice literature. The exception is O'Callaghan, "Tavern Societies." Similarly, wager cups have received very little scholarly notice and virtually none by scholars of literature and history. The few collectors and museum curators who consider the cups either treat them as amusing historical novelties or emphasize their expert craftsmanship and precious materials. The exception is Roberts, "Drinking Like a Man," who discusses Dutch versions of the cups as evidence of the centrality of drinking to early modern Dutch youth culture.

15. The bulk of criticism on excessive drinking emphasizes early modern religio-moralist discourses. See, for example, Charlotte McBride, "A Natural Drink for an English Man: National Stereotyping in Early Modern Culture," in Smyth, *Pleasing Sinne*, 181–91; Mack P. Holt, "Europe Divided: Wine, Beer, and the Reformation in Sixteenth-century Europe," in *Alcohol: A Social and Cultural History*, ed. Mack P. Holt (Oxford: Berg, 2006), 25–40; Smyth, "'It were far better to be a *Toad*, or a *Serpant*, then a Drunkard': Writing About Drunkenness," in Smyth, *Pleasing Sinne*, 193–210. Smyth includes one pro-drinking text in his discussion but focuses on the ways this text "picked up and responded to established condemnations of drunkenness" (193). Several scholars have observed that early modern medical discourse links moderate alcohol consumption with good health. See Ken Albala, "To Your Health: Wine as Food and Medicine in Mid-sixteenth-century Italy," in Holt, *Alcohol: A Social and Cultural History*, 11–24. The best work on what I call a hedonistic discourse of drinking is Joshua Scodel, *Excess and the Mean in Early Modern English Literature*, Literature in History (Princeton, NJ: Princeton University Press, 2002), which explores the ways seventeenth-century poets adapt ancient symposiastic drinking poetry, celebrating the pleasures of excessive wine drinking as an escape from daily cares.
16. Qtd. in Peter Clark, *The English Alehouse: A Social History, 1200–1830* (London: Longman, 1983), 49. This is not to say that all drinking in public houses lead to drunkenness. With alcohol being cheaper and more accessible than clean water, it (and especially ale) was widely consumed for more than recreational purposes. Nevertheless, city authorities regularly complained about male drunkenness at taverns, alehouses, and, to a lesser extent, inns. On the different functions of alehouses, taverns, and inns, see R. F. Bretherton, "Country Inns and Alehouses," in *Englishmen at Rest and Play: Some Phases of English Leisure 1558–1714*, ed. Reginald Lennard (Oxford: Clarendon, 1931), 147–201. And on the urban inn in particular,

Alan Everitt, "The English Urban Inn, 1650–1760," in *Perspectives in English Urban History*, ed. Alan Everitt (London: Macmillan, 1973), 90–137.

17. Leah S. Marcus, *The Politics of Mirth: Jonson, Herrick, Milton, Marvell and the Defense of Old Holiday Pastimes* (Chicago: University of Chicago Press, 1986). On the extent to which London tastes impacted the design and furnishings of English country houses and the recreational pursuits of their female dwellers, see Alice T. Friedman, "Inside/Out: Women, Domesticity, and the Pleasures of the City," in *Material London, ca. 1600*, ed. Lena Cowen Orlin (Philadelphia: University of Pennsylvania Press, 2000), 232–50.
18. Young, *England's Bane*, sig. D3v.
19. Jean Howard, *Theater of a City: The Places of London Comedy, 1598–1642* (Philadelphia: University of Pennsylvania Press, 2006), esp. chap. 4.
20. O'Callaghan, "Tavern Societies," nicely situates Brathwaite's work within an urban elite tavern culture. An account of *Law*'s publishing history and relation to its German source can be found in Matthew Wilson Black, "Richard Brathwait: An Account of His Life and Works" (Doctoral Thesis, University of Pennsylvania, 1928), esp. 101–5.
21. George Evans Light, "All Hopped Up: Beer, Cultivated National Identity, and Anglo-Dutch Relations, 1524–1625," *Journal X* 2.2 (1998): 159–78, discusses English efforts to "blame their own perceived national inebriety" (160) on other nations, especially the Dutch.
22. Young, *England's Bane*, sig. E8v–F1r.
23. Thomas Nashe's *Summer's Last Will and Testament* uses the term, apparently referring to the German tradition of "drinking *Brüderschaft*": "A vous, monsieur Winter, a frolick upsy freese: cross, ho! Super nagulum." Qtd. in Karl Elze, *Notes on Elizabethan Dramatists: With Conjectural Emendations of the Text* (Halle: M. Niemeyer, 1880), 32. It is possible (and, if so, all the more interesting given the connection between urban culture and drinking games) that Pimlico refers to the name of a game, like Crambo and other terms in this list.
24. Young, *England's Bane*, sig. D3v.
25. Richard Brathwaite, *The Law of Drinking*, ed. W. Brian Hooker (New Haven, CT: Tuttle, Morehouse & Taylor, 1903), 71.
26. Ibid., 72.
27. Ibid., 71.
28. Ibid., 69.
29. Ibid., 70. One might argue that this tension between Brathwaite's rhetoric of civility and the riotous activities he describes supports Smyth's point that even pro-drinking literature that offers elaborate rules for drinking in an effort to represent it as an elite art reveals the

disorder behind all the ordered rules. But I would suggest that it is worth our while investigating more closely the productive work these rules of drinking play perform.

30. Brathwaite, *Law*, 41, 44.
31. Ibid., 45.
32. Ibid., 38–39.
33. Ibid., 53.
34. Ibid., 39.
35. Brathwaite, *The English Gentleman*, 37.
36. Brathwaite, *Law*, 65.
37. Ibid., 78.
38. Ibid., 34.
39. Adam Zucker, "The Social Stakes of Gambling in Early Modern London," in *Masculinity and the Metropolis of Vice*, 73.
40. No English versions survive, but given how much of seventeenth-century English drinking culture was influenced by the Dutch—the most obvious example being the shift from ale to beer—it is not hard to imagine that these objects traveled to England. If so, they would necessarily have come through the port of London.
41. Espen Aarseth, "Genre Trouble: Narrativism and the Art of Simulation," in *First Person: New Media as Story, Performance, and Game*, ed. Wardrip-Fruin and Pat Harrigan (Cambridge, MA: MIT Press, 2004) argues that the gameworld is the most "coincidental" (48) of the elements of game design (e.g., chess will be the same game whether one plays with pieces shaped like chivalric warriors or abstract pegs). I follow other theorists of games, however, in arguing that the gameworld's design is highly significant to the experience of game-play.
42. The most useful of sources on maiden cups is Yvonne Hackenbroch, "Wager Cups," *The Metropolitan Museum of Art Bulletin* 26.9 (1968): 380–88.
43. Sophia Lee, *The Worshipful Company of Vintners: A Catalogue of Plate* (London: Vintners' Company, 1996), 37.
44. The dating of these particular cups is uncertain. The Metropolitan Museum has long dated them to the middle of the seventeenth century, but a recent appraiser suspects they may have been produced in the nineteenth century, when there was a minor vogue for copies of maiden cups. In any event they seem designed to resemble their seventeenth-century counterparts.
45. William H. Sherman, "What Did Renaissance Readers Write in Their Books?," in *Books and Readers in Early Modern England: Material Studies*, ed. Jennifer Andersen and Elizabeth Sauer (Philadelphia: University of Pennsylvania Press, 2002), 119–37.
46. G. R. Quaife, *Wanton Wenches and Wayward Wives: Peasants and Illicit Sex in Early Seventeenth Century England* (New Brunswick, NJ: Rutgers University Press, 1979), 170. I am grateful to Fran Dolan for bringing this text to my attention.

47. Ibid.
48. Gina Bloom, *Voice in Motion: Staging Gender, Shaping Sound in Early Modern England*, Material Texts (Philadelphia: University of Pennsylvania Press, 2007). See also, Natasha Korda, *Shakespeare's Domestic Economies: Gender and Property in Early Modern England* (Philadelphia: University of Pennsylvania Press, 2002).

Chapter 2

University of Vice: Drink, Gentility, and Masculinity in Oxford, Cambridge, and London

Laurie Ellinghausen

The early modern universities of Oxford and Cambridge might be imagined as hermetically sealed bastions of learning and piety, because of their historical role as training grounds for clergy. However, this pastoral image runs aground on the fact that scholars actively participated in urban pastimes—and with growing populations, notable increases in building activity, active city councils, and thriving craft guilds, as well as crime and poverty, late sixteenth-century Oxford and Cambridge certainly offered an urban experience, if on a smaller scale than that of London.[1] Noting the regularity with which historians separate the university from its urban environs, Victor Morgan argues that the two should be examined in relation to each other and to the larger spheres of which they are a part:

> There is, perhaps, a temptation to conceive the relationship between a university and its urban context simply as bipartite.... I suspect that the relationship is rarely as simple as this. To borrow a phrase of the anthropologists, universities and their urban environs are almost always "part societies," and the relationship between these two particular constituent elements can only be fully understood within the larger context.[2]

The concept of the "part society" suggests that cultural spaces, and the behaviors and people associated with them, are always hybrid creations to some degree. Economic relationships, among other things, make such crossovers possible. This heterodox blending of locations, behaviors, and identities appears in drama and prose written by university men in the 1590s, where the prestige and entitlement of university education meet not only economic and social dislocation, but also a predilection for urban pleasures, such as the intoxication of drink and the enjoyment of alehouses and taverns. Just as the putatively separate spheres of gown and town ultimately mingle, so do elite men and common experiences.

As Amanda Bailey and Roze Hentschell argue in this volume's introduction, early modern ideas of masculinity depend greatly on the politics of cultural space. Here I analyze drinking practices among early modern university men with special attention to the socioeconomic complexities of these relationships, which emerge from the sizeable gap between ideology and lived experience. College administrators, many of whom operated under the influence of Puritan doctrine, strained to impose sobriety on an increasingly diverse body of men. At both universities, officials tried to stem the "notorious and incorrigible" drunkenness of their scholars, which they viewed as exhibiting a level of excess contrary to good religious and civil conduct.[3] These attitudes mirror a larger sphere of moralistic discourse concerning the evils of drinking. Some commentators saw drink as a form of contamination by the Dutch, due to the wars in the Low Countries. Some blamed the devil, and others blamed the alehouse for encouraging people to get drunk.[4] Moralists like Christopher Hudson fulminated against the common drinking establishment: "Alehouses are nests of Satan where the owls of impiety lurk and where all evil is hatched, and the bellows of intemperance and incontinence blow up." The Northhamptonshire preacher Robert Bolton declared, "we lift up our voices loud against drunkenness and it is high time, for it grows toward a high tide and threatens—a lamentable inundation to the whole kingdom."[5] Such pronouncements were conditioned in part by assumptions concerning drinkers' gender and class. While many writers presumed women to be disorderly by nature, excessive drink was thought to *create* disorder in men—that is to say, drinking was encoded as "male" activity, despite women who also partook.[6] As for the class of drinkers, the relationship between drink and identity depended heavily on the notion of "civility," a concept that originated in Italy with the idea that the city was for the well bred. Civility also implies peace, order, and "quietness," as well as characteristics suggestive of elite status: well bred, courteous, and gentle, with their opposites being barbarous, wild, or rude.[7] Drunkenness was a lowly state, as "bills against drunkenness attributed the vice especially to 'the worst and inferior people' "[8]—a description that aligns the "worst" behavior with the natural "inferiority" of society's lowest members, the notorious overindulgence of the court notwithstanding.

The presumed elision between drinking, masculinity, and lowly status becomes a model ripe for exploration for Cambridge graduate and London satirist Thomas Nashe, who infused his own contributions to moral discourse with gritty urban realism and a predilection for the grotesque. In doing so, he frames drinking behaviors in a way that pays heed to the economic realities that he experienced as both a graduate and a denizen of London's competitive economic landscape—realities that moralism, with its neat distinctions of status and behavior, tended to ignore. By examining his writings on drink in tandem with the *Parnassus* plays, a group of vernacular comedies staged at Nashe's alma mater in the economically troubled 1590s, I will highlight some instances in which actual drinking practices, which yoked participants into a shared socioeconomic matrix, could confound simplistic distinctions between the learned and the common, the town and the gown, and the pious and the profane. In doing so, I will also suggest ways in which London can be conceived as a cultural space related to other metropolitan cultures in the realm—that is to say, I aim to offer a view of "London" that reflects the diverse backgrounds of its new arrivals as well as those born and bred there. First, I will detail the prominence of drink at the universities, tracing how the *Parnassus* plays circumvent patriarchal logic to link drinking to the failed promise of university education. Then, I will show how Nashe's later writing puts this particular angle on drink into practice by introducing diversity, contingency, and economic realism into moral discourse surrounding drink in the London metropolis. Taken together, these writings remind readers that drinking is not simply the devil's work, but a social custom that brings seemingly incongruous identities together into a multiplicity of relationships.

Drinking at the University: The Socioeconomics of Vice

Despite its elite image, the university population exemplified a segment of society highly likely to drink. Only men inhabited the university, making it literally a "male" space. With respect to class, the population contained a mix of nobility and lower orders: one could find propertied aristocrats hoping to enter government, the second sons of noblemen preparing to earn a living, the sons of prosperous middle-class parents, or "sizars" on scholarship. When university men drank, they fraternized with men of different backgrounds, thus embodying the idea of the drinking space as "ambiguous territory," where people who might not normally associate come together under the banner of "good fellowship."[9] In addition, the youth of these men requires us to consider the politics of age, for drink was often classed with gaming, dancing, and bawdry as part of ribald youth culture. In the revels at Oxford and Cambridge, young men negotiated between the giddy pleasures of youth and conduct-book versions of sober manhood. Speculating that most young people experimented at both extremes, Paul Griffiths describes youth as a "contested territory" in early modern English society, one in which transitions from childhood to maturity were neither linear nor smooth.[10] While moralists tended to characterize youthful behavior in terms of either its pious ideal or its profane opposite, festive drinking fellowships tested this duality, which rested on the assumption that gentility and vulgarity were consistent, permanent, and mutually exclusive character traits. Drink-induced intoxication, in combination with the socially "ambiguous" nature of the drinking space, exposes the malleability of distinctions like young versus old and pious versus profane.[11]

Anecdotal evidence supports this theoretical picture, showing that drunken riot was not the exclusive preserve of the lowest orders. Then as now, university students loved their drink. Seventeenth-century historian Arthur Wilson claimed that he never drank more in his life than he did among "the greatest bachelors of divinity" at Oxford; one foreign visitor found Oxford men to be proud, pedantic, and over all, massively devoted to beer. Several period commentators even report drunkenness among the dons, tutors, and proctors, despite some colleges' reputations for Puritanism.[12] Both towns, growing rapidly during the late sixteenth century, were replete with inns, taverns, and alehouses. As local residents, scholars were not simply gentlemanly "bachelors of divinity," but *drinkers* whose behavior necessarily brought them into contact with the city outside of the university walls.

These real habits produce several sets of competing significations—for example, the meaning of honorable masculinity and its relationship to drinking. On the one hand, drinking constituted a major social ritual and the refusal to join one's friends in the tavern could be construed not only as antisocial, but also as placing one's masculinity into question—alcohol was "one of the primary lubricants of young men's fraternal bonding," as demonstrated by its use in toasting of comrades, the striking of bargains, or the mending of quarrels.[13] But to have a reputation as a drunk stained one's honor, whether defined as gentle lineage or gentle conduct. University authorities condemned group drinking as an activity that compromised gentility and the masculine ideal of self-control. As Alexandra Shepard writes, rowdy scholars

> embraced precisely the kinds of behavior—violent disruption, excessive drinking, illicit sex—condemned by moralists as unmanly, effeminate, and beast-like.... While such critiques were often levelled at youthful miscreants, who in addition risked severe punishment for their misdeeds, the governors of the university and of other institutions charged with the socialization of young men more frequently condemned their behavior as "common" or undignified, implicitly ranking codes of manhood according to distinctions of social status.[14]

These paraphrases intermingle class discourses and the languages of masculinity—"excessive drinking" is distinctly the realm of the "common." Moreover, these characterizations call the drinker's very masculinity into question ("unmanly" and "effeminate") and even his humanity ("beast-like"), placing him on a downward progression from reason to sense, head to body, urbane to rustic.[15]

Thus university life, as one bastion of formative manhood, exemplifies how urban pleasures induced young men to hedge and sometimes cross the line of self-control. This sociological challenge to moralistic piety is buttressed by the fact that the universities themselves had a clear economic stake in urban drinking cultures. Struggles for control of licenses and taxation formed the heart of town-gown conflicts, including taxation of the elite classes, responsibility for slums and poor relief and, most pertinent here, the licensing of alehouses and taverns.[16] These disputes indicate that, while the universities promoted an image of themselves as a world apart (and by implication, superior), they viewed the surrounding nonacademic environment as essential for its economic functioning.

Thus while university administrators condemned drunken festivity for its scholars, the university itself had economic ties to the town's drinking establishments. Moral and economic agendas appear to contradict, leaving us to wonder how this paradox played out in the lives of the drinkers themselves. Although authoritarian reactions to drunkenness are well documented, the scholars' *own* attitude toward drink invites further speculation as to how they perceived its place in their lives. University drama offers one set of clues, linking the embrace of drink to social and economic disappointment. The *Parnassus* plays embed drink in a contemporaneous story of loss, one told from the young men's perspective and not found in idealistic moral prescriptions regarding gentlemanly behavior. These vernacular plays revel in the farcical and the grotesque, conditioned in part by the penury and disrespect that many graduates found upon leaving the university. Although university education had traditionally been the province of second sons training for the clergy, the late sixteenth century witnessed an influx of young men into Oxford, Cambridge, and the Inns of Court. As a result, the universities produced far more graduates than could attain preferment and many graduates found themselves schoolmastering, serving as lecturers in local parishes, or taking up other positions associated with drudgery and occupational displacement.[17] Thus while administrators monitored students' behavior as a way to preserve their gentlemanly status, many scholars' social prestige foundered on economic changes beyond their own control. The *Parnassus* plays call attention to the fate of these scholars by casting the vicious behaviors of university men not as the folly of undisciplined youth but as a reflection of the painful gap between nominative privilege and real hardship.

Taken as a sequence, the three plays dramatize this experience by moving from an articulated standard of moral purity to a "realistic" perspective in which scholars drink in response to economic disappointment. The first play, *The Pilgrimage to Parnassus*, allegorizes the path to knowledge by depicting two scholars, Philomusus and Studioso, traveling to Parnassus hill. Along the way they receive guidance from the fatherly Consiliodorus, who advises them to maintain sobriety: "Consorte not in the waye with graceless boys / That feede the tavern with their idle coyne / Till there learne purses starve at last for foode" (69–71). The scholars follow this advice, even when they meet Madido, a drunken lover of Horace. Studioso advises Madido to substitute "the poetes boule" (194) for drink, suggesting that the pleasures of poetry do not need alcoholic enhancement. Madido's arguments to the contrary represent a major temptation that the two boys manage to evade successfully. As a whole, *Pilgrimage* rewards moral purity through the idealized rewards of learning, which are presented as ends in themselves.

Despite its idealism, *Pilgrimage* does not entirely avoid the mention of economic hardship. But scholarly penury becomes merely one temptation—signifying cynicism or despair, perhaps—on the way to the mountaintop. Through a wisecracking character named "Ingenioso," the boys receive ample warning that scholarship is not the path to riches. Ingenioso, a figure based largely on the famous fellow graduate Nashe, warns the boys that "Parnassus is out of silver pitifullie, pitifullie" (576–77).[18] At the end of his scene, where we witness him attempting to sell verses to a patron, all three of the men declare devotion to learning despite poverty:

> *Studioso.* Muses adewe, longe may youre groves growe greene,
> Thou you to us too, too unkinde have beene.
> *Philomusus.* Farewell Appollo, ere will I adore thee,
> Though thy poore hands not able to relive me.
> *Ingenioso.* Youe beutuous nimphes of Hellicon adew:
> How ever poore, yet I will worship youe. (441–46)

The scholars' impending poverty, like drink, becomes an obstacle to be conquered and ultimately dismissed. Although economic experience receives ample space and consideration in the play, the ideal of scholarship ultimately subsumes it in favor of learning itself.

The first scene of the second play offers a very different approach to the tribulations of scholarship, one that treats those things that seem incongruous with scholarly purity—money, criminality, and drink—as complex realities rather than simplistic "temptations." In *The Return from Parnassus, Part I*, Consiliodorus fears that the boys "have burnt out the suns faire torch / In foolish riot and regardless plaie" (80–81). His suspicion proves to be true. The trilogy shifts from allegory to satire as the boys fall into ruin: in this play and in *Part II*, the boys and their friends find nothing but poverty, underemployment, and public scorn for all of their learning. Consiliodorus's suspicion is confirmed when we learn from a local tapster that the boys have "overrune the reckoninge" at the local alehouse, in addition to other unpaid debts (*1 Returne*, 469–566). In contrast to the image that many university men had of townsmen as bumbling antagonists, *1 Returne* casts the townspeople as sympathetic figures who incur economic hardship at the hands of university men, so widespread has riotous living become among the scholars. The playwright emphasizes the point by having the boys join forces with Luxurioso, a drunk of "waterie wit" (402) who turns ballad-peddler. In Luxurioso, excessive drinking signifies his lowliness as a hawker of cheap printed street literature—the very kinds of texts that scholars, like Nashe himself, habitually disdained.[19]

Unlike the writings of fellow graduate Robert Greene, who relates his past as an indulgent drinker with great detail, the *Parnassus* plays offer no prodigal narrative, nor do they revere learning as an institution that transcends everyday hardship. Instead, the characters embrace drink as part of their status as disappointed scholars, thus infusing drink with an economic rationale. Furthermore, the ability to withstand economic hardship with vicious behavior—and an even more vicious wit—becomes a badge of masculine bravado. When Ingenioso and his friend Judicio take an inventory of contemporary poets, they dismiss Michael Drayton as lacking "one true note of a Poet of our times" and that is that "hee cannot swagger it well in a Taverne, / nor domineer in a hot-house" (*2 Returne,* 249–51). However, a well-known affinity for tavern "swaggering" does not rescue Ben Jonson from scorn; this "wittiest fellow of a Bricklayer in England" is dismissed for his slow composition, which the scholars feel suits him better for "his old trade of Bricklaying" (293, 297). To be sure, the ability to "swagger" and "domineer" suggests masculine control over others, reorienting the graduates' lowly status in a way that attempts to recapture a sense of supremacy. But the example of Jonson also reveals a distinct elitism in this particular articulation of mastery, for the swaggerer must also possess education, ready wit, and poetic capability. Accordingly, the scholars commemorate Nashe for both his numerous "faultes" and his "mother witt" (314, 318). Nashe comes off as a swaggerer indeed, one who is admired for the deadly use of a wit honed by learning—and by an intimate familiarity with vice, as opposed to the avoidance of it, which Ingenioso and Judicio take as evidence of an effete disposition.

By dramatizing a downward slope from hope to despair, the *Parnassus* plays interrogate the moralistic model of drink as sin by assigning drink a supporting role within a larger story of loss. Recent scholarship links drinking to economic hardship by framing alehouses as "alternative societies" that offered an escape from—even a challenge to—marginalization. Peter Clark describes the alehouse as "a refuge for craftsmen, labourers and vagrants affected by difficult economic competition" where drink served "primarily as an anaesthetic against a harsh, oppressive world." Similarly, Patricia Fumerton argues that alehouses enabled "vagrant" men to experience an alternative home, one better suited to the "detached or 'free' subjectivity" wrought by vagrant experience than the traditional identifying structures of family and trade.[20] But as the *Parnassus* plays suggest, vagrancy and poverty are not restricted to the nominal underclass; indeed, university men's own experience of dislocation leads them to the solace of drink and drinking circles. This is not to suggest that scholars would have regarded themselves as the equals of laborers and craftsmen—the palpable elitism of the *Parnassus* plays and Nashe's writings dictates otherwise. However, the scholars' embrace of drink puts pressure on any easy alignment between drink and "lowly" status, asking moralists whether—in a contemporary climate where the high expectation of privilege meets deep disappointment—the connection between vicious conduct and social status is really as simple as that.

Drinking in London: Nashe, Antitheatricalists, and Urban Vice

In addition to their perspective on drink, the stylistic affiliations of the *Parnassus* plays offer an important link between academic culture and the metropolitan culture of London. With their liberal use of satire and humoral comedy, the last two *Parnassus* plays more closely resemble public plays on the London stage than earlier forms of university drama, which were performed in Latin and Greek as recitation exercises for students. One scene in *2 Returne* depicts Philomusus and Studioso auditioning for acting jobs in front of Will Kempe and Richard Burbage, who taunt the boys for their pride (4.3). If the appearance of Burbage and Kempe is any indication, the *Parnassus* playwright was familiar with the London stage.[21] Despite the universities' attempts to ban traveling companies and prohibit scholars from attending plays outside the university walls, it seems that many university men were open to the kinds of performative experimentation that one finds in urban theatrical culture. One account from Oxford describes men of Brasenose College dancing at the local Mitre Tavern with a townsman's daughter "in boy's apparel." Another period of especially hard drinking among the heads and fellows of Oxford coincided with a trend toward effeminate dress—petticoats, face paint, and scented clothing.[22] For men accustomed to such extracurricular play, an attraction to the London stage—with its propensity to dislocate categories of gender and class through performance—does not require a large cognitive leap. Fittingly, London's first group of professional playwrights, who inhabited the notorious suburbs of Bishopsgate and Shoreditch, came largely from Oxford and Cambridge.

The scene of cross-gendered revelry at the Mitre Tavern offers the kind of composite picture that moralists liked to paint for their readers—one in which drink plays a prominent role among other sins. London's most widely read antitheatricalists specifically link the evils of the theater to drinking and tavern culture. To the common argument that plays can provide morally healthful examples, Philip Stubbes replies,

> If you will learne to deride, scoffe, mock and flowt, to flatter & smooth: if you will learn to play the whore-maister, the glutton, Drunkard, or incestuous person: if you will learn to become proude, hawties, & arrogant; and finally, if you will learne to contemne God and al his lawes to care neither for heaven nor hel, and to commit al kinde of sinne and mischief, you need to go to no other schoole, for all these good Examples may you see painted before your eyes in enterludes and playes.[23]

Here the "Drunkard" is merely one example, rhetorically interchangeable with the "incestuous person" and the "glutton," of the "al kinde of sinne" that playgoing promotes. For Stubbes, the institution of the theater encompasses all sins and encourages them through staged examples. For William Prynne, writing more than forty years later, the play itself becomes one of these sins, the "chief" of all "sinful lusts of the flesh" that include "dancing, dicing, [and] health-drinking."[24] In these antitheatrical tracts, the stage becomes a bad parent or a misleading teacher, steering helpless souls into drunkenness and other vices. Drinking, bawdry, dancing, and playgoing comprise a set of sinful activities that antitheatricalists never bother to disentangle, except perhaps to suggest that the cessation of plays might stop all the rest. Moreover, the antitheatricalists' religious imperative ignores any need to contextualize these sins as part of city life, where the businesses that promote these alleged vices compete with each other and engage the city's denizens as economic agents.

Nashe and the "university wits," a group of writers who have been defined in part by their predilection for the shocking and the grotesque, lived and wrote in London while this kind of moralistic antitheatrical discourse was very much in play.[25] Their stints at Cambridge and Oxford exposed them to the kinds of vices they would observe and write about in the metropolis. Greene relates: "at the Universitie of Cambridge, I light amongst wags as lewd as my selfe, with whom I consumed the flower of my youth" (*Repentance* 19). A barber-surgeon at Trinity College remembered Nashe as a troublemaker who "fell into divers misdemeanors" and "flourished in all impudencie toward Schollers, and abuse to the Townsmen; insomuch that to this daye the Townes-men call everie untoward Scholler of whome there is great hope, *a verie Nashe*."[26] Thus the infamous vice of the university wits was not strictly a London phenomenon, but one that was nurtured by university life and later cultivated by the metropolis. Moreover, the penury they claim to have suffered as writers in the market for cheap print lends their own well-publicized drinking, like that of the *Parnassus* characters, an air of social and economic disillusionment.

Although these satirical writings reflect the ills of urban society, Greene's cony-catching pamphlets and Nashe's prose tales also assume the form of firsthand accounts. Thus these texts may be read as "fiction" with a "documentary core"[27] that maintains an awareness of the plenitude of London life—the panoply of different individuals and occupations, the variety of places, and the ways in which economic systems locate these people and places within hierarchies and even condition behavior. Eschewing the rigid categorical imperatives that govern the writings of Stubbes and Prynne, *Pierce Pennilesse* both patterns itself after and destabilizes moralistic discourse on drinking, representing drunkenness in a way that allows for a level of contingency and nuance unavailable in more polemical writings. Nashe's fictionalizing represents one response among many to be found in popular literary culture that, as Lawrence Manley writes, posed an "alternative response" to "the language of crisis and the literal sense of 'monstrosity' in which [preachers] typically portrayed the anomalies, disruptions, and innovations of London's burgeoning life as portents of impending doom, shakings in the very foundations of civilized life."[28] In the mouth of the archetypal preacher, "doom" provides the major organizing principle for all moral aberrations, painting a picture of social life that is organized around sharp polarities of pious goodness and incipient damnation. Like other Elizabethan pamphleteers, Nashe grounds his prose in this very discourse, but as a writer of fiction, he disrupts these dualistic codes to allow new circumstances, new images, and thus new ways of thinking about the diverse ways in which the city's dwellers interact with the urban economic landscape.

We see this dynamic of confirmation and disruption in his famous defense of plays, where he begins like the antitheatricalists, naming drunkenness as one of several social evils:

> Whereas some Petitioners of the Counsaile against [plays] object, [plays] corrupt the youth of the Cittie, and withdrawe Prentises from theyr worke; they heartily wishe they might bee troubled with none of their youth nor their prentises; for some of them (I meane the ruder handicrafts servants) never come abroade, but they are in danger of undoing: and as for corrupting them when they come, thats false; for no Play they have, encourageth any man to tumults or rebellion, but layes before such the halter and the gallowes; or praiseth or approoveth pride, lust, whoredome, prodigalitie, or drunkennes, but beates them downe utterly.[29] (I: 213–14)

As he asserts that plays in no way "praiseth" drunkenness, Nashe begins his argument according to the cultural logic of moralists who condemn drink. By acknowledging "youth" and "prentices" to be of primary concern, Nashe supports the perception that drunkenness is a problem chiefly among young urban males of the artisanal class, particularly those in the "ruder" trades. Once again, men are the problem here—rowdy young men of a certain lowly degree who merely affirm their gendered and social proclivities when they drunkenly riot against all good order. By recalling this particular version of masculine misconduct, Nashe confirms the widespread suspicion that drink goes hand in hand with other forms of "rebellion" that threaten the social order by making the drinker forget his place.

But whereas the moralistic writings of the Tudor period frequently treat playgoing, prostitution, pride, and drunkenness as all of a piece—under the general rubrics of "rebellion" or "damnation"—Nashe does not remain with this model. The pamphlet may be full of "second-hand morality,"[30] but in keeping with the subversive dynamism that Lorna Hutson and other critics have noticed, *Pierce Pennilesse* modifies the sharp polarities of moral discourse by extracting plays from other vices and separating the remaining vices from each other. Nashe dismantles the monolith of "rebellious" activities to allow for degrees of better and worse sins, or even some necessary evils. In this revision, drink figures not as a *moral* activity per se, but as a feature of the social and economic landscape that must be dealt with as such. Drawing on the knowledge of the city's diverse commercial landscape that he demonstrates throughout the text, Nashe notes that apprentices who wish to drink in fact have *options*, each with its own set of consequences:

> As for the hindrance of Trades and Traders of the Citie by them, that is an Article foysted in by the Vintners, Alewives, and Victuallers, who surmise, if there were no Playes, they should have all the companie that resort to them, lie bowzing and beere-bathing in their houses every after-noone. Nor so, nor so, good brother bottle-ale, for there are other places besides where money can bestow it selfe; the signe of the smock will wipe your mouth cleane: and yet I have heard yee have made her a tenant to your tap-houses. (214)

By distinguishing "Vintners, Alewives, and Victuallers" from the "signe of the smock" (i.e., the brothel), Nashe informs his audience that drinking and prostitution are not in collusion, but in competition. This awareness of commercial reality is one way in which Nashe demonstrates his difference from Elizabethan critics who, in the words of G. R. Hibbard, "had no eyes at all for what was actually going on around them."[31] The metropolitan cultural landscape is not reducible to sober obedience (the legitimate "Trades and Traders" that master unruly young men) versus evil rebellion (drink, prostitution, and plays all comprising one seedy portrait). Rather, theaters play a distinct role as a provider of relatively innocuous distraction among other distractions.[32] Nashe accepts that apprentices likely *will* drink and indeed may pose a threat to civic peace (at least as long as they remain men of humble origin). Yet he responds by asking not how drink may be prevented, but how the drunkard might best be occupied once he has done the deed:

> But what shall hee doo that hath spent himselfe? where shall hee haunt? Faith, when Dice, Lust, and Drunkennesse, and all have dealt upon him, if there be never a Playe for him to goe too for his pennie, he sits melancholie in his Chamber, devising upon felonie or treason, and howe he may best exalt himselfe by mischiefe. (214)

Even when the apprentice has "spent himself" on all available sins, he needs a place to go. The theater provides such a place precisely because it is *not* an alehouse, nor a brothel—the theater will offer him entertainment rather than letting him ponder rebellion. Nashe thus advises the reader to look beyond representations that lump all of these establishments together toward what each actually offers.

In similar fashion, *Pierce Pennilesse* relativizes drinking behaviors themselves by insisting that there are not just two kinds of drinkers, but eight different kinds. To be sure, Nashe gives drunks no quarter—they come across as merely ridiculous. But even so, his comic taxonomy of drunken types allows for different stages and degrees:

> The first is Ape drunke, and he leapes, and sings and hollowes, and daunceth for the heavens: the second is Lion drunke, and he flings the pots about the house, calls his Hostesse whore, breakes the glasse windowes with his dagger, and is apt to quarrell with any man that speaks to him: the third is Swine drunke, heavy, lumpish, and sleepie, and cries for a little more drinke, and a fewe more cloathes: the fourth is Sheepe drunke, wise in his owne conceipt, when he cannot bring foorth a right word: the fifth is Mawdlen drunke. (207)

The passage names three more types: the "martin," the "goat," and the "fox." In keeping with the common belief that drunkenness induces an animal state, nearly all of Nashe's eight types resemble animals. But again, Nashe adopts terms from moralistic discourse while complicating the effects of drunkenness on the imbiber: he may be merry, violent, sleepy, proud, or melancholic, for example. Notably, none of these types appears politically rebellious, even when violent or deceptive. This absence may be due to the fact that, with the exception of the pronoun "he," the drinkers are not as clearly labeled by gender and class as they are elsewhere in *Pierce Pennilesse*. By breaking the state of drunkenness down into a wide variety of different "types," Nashe introduces a diversity of circumstances into dualistic moral codes, thus making room for more complex way of regarding human behavior. As Hutson writes, Nashe's texts "pit the changing discourses of moral and social values inconclusively against one another, making the moment of social transformation itself available for contemplation."[33] Nashe subjects drink to the same "contemplation" by exploring its actual role in social life and its effects on individual drinkers.

While I have focused my analysis so far on urban environments, it is worth noting—in the spirit of bridging putatively separate spheres—that Nashe's interest in the social contexts of drink extends beyond the urban environment to the country, as we see in his only surviving play, *Summer's Last Will and Testament.* Hibbard views the play as an achievement separate and distinct from Nashe's pamphlet writing: "[The play's] author had abilities as a dramatic craftsman that his activities as a pamphleteer would hardly lead one to expect."[34] Not only does this remark fail to acknowledge the skill in colorful depiction necessary for success in both genres, but it also ignores a thematic link between Nashe's pamphlets and his play: the place of drink in social life, particularly among the cultures of the nonelite. In *Summer's Will,* questions of drinking's role in local culture are treated with respect to hospitality and festivity, a set of traditions on the wane everywhere, but particularly in the city. This entertainment, staged for the Archbishop Whitgift at his palace in Croydon, enacts the ancient theme of the passing of the seasons. Drink, which here appears in a pastoral setting, figures in the play as part of a confrontation between festivity and stern patriarchal admonition, which prohibits drink and all other youthful enjoyments.[35] As the aging "Summer" faces his demise (the play was staged around October 1592), he summons members of his kingdom to account for themselves. The four seasons (Summer, Winter, Autumn, and "Ver") are joined by Bacchus, Orion, Harvest, and Christmas as well as satyrs, nymphs, morris-dancers, and other pastoral figures. Throughout, the clownish "Will Summer" (modeled on Henry VIII's court fool) observes the proceedings.

Will Summer is a Bakhtinian character who ponders everything he hears regarding drinking, feasting, hospitality, wealth, and other forms of enjoyment. Exhibiting "engagingly 'idle,' irresponsible casualness," Will's ridiculousness conceals a genuinely thoughtful disposition.[36] Inviting the actors to bring out "a rundlet of Renish wine, disputing of the antiquity of red noses," he initially appears as a figure of overindulgence.[37] Like *Pierce Pennilesse*, Nashe's comedy pays heed to the polarities of moral discourse: Will opines that all vices are "conversant" in a "cup of wine," even as he admits his fondness for it, while the dying patriarch Summer condemns drunkenness (624, 1070). Once again, overindulgence is linked to forgetting one's place, as when the festive spendthrift Ver refuses to live "within [his] bounds," arguing that being an "unthrift" is the best way to happiness (242, 284). About halfway through the play, the deformed figure of Bacchus appears to sing the praises of wine for everyone, including the scholar:

> Give a scholler wine, going to his booke, or being about to invent, it sets a new poynt on his wit, it glazeth it, it scowres it, it gives him *acumen*. Plato saith, *vinum esse fomitem quendam, et incitabilem ingenij virtutisque*. Aristotle saith, *Nulla est magna scientia absque mixtura dementiae*. There is no excellent knowledge without mixture of madnesse. And what makes a man more madde in the head than wine? (988–95)

Bacchus, a learned character who draws on classical sources in his defense of drink, voices a familiar concept: that drink can induce "mad" genius and "excellent knowledge," polishing a scholar's wit. But the priggish Summer and his cohort find no virtue in that, again consigning drink to the lowliest individuals: Winter pronounces scholars a "thriftles kind of men" and calls poets "drunken parasites" (1253, 1268). Each articulation of enjoyment meets its moralistic answer in the mouth of the patriarchal Summer.[38]

As Summer repudiates each of his prodigal subjects, sober virtue meets extreme versions of vice. But unlike the one-dimensional figures of excess typically found in antimasques, Will responds thoughtfully and critically to these moral polarities. Moreover, Will exists not merely to comment, but also to test the different behaviors on display—as C. L. Barber writes in his analysis of this festive play. Will, like Shakespeare's Touchstone, "looks with a lackluster eye at festive enthusiasm—and yet dryly acknowledges his own share in folly."[39] Will's status as both observer and participant bridges the discursive polarity between sober judge and animalistic drunk, offering spectators a figure who moderates between two extremes and whose enjoyment does not necessarily constitute an abandonment of reason. When Bacchus appears onstage, he draws Will into the action by having him get on his knees and quaff ale. Will responds by rejecting drunkenness: "No more of this, I hate it to the death. / No such deformer of the soule and sence, / As is this swynish damn'd-borne drunkennes" (1072–74). Although a lowly figure, Will is no Caliban: he tries the drink while maintaining his wits and judgment, recognizing that any more drink will compromise his manhood by making him "swynish."[40]

Nonetheless, Will defies moralistic prescription by refusing to abstract his own rejection of drink into a commandment for everyone. Instead, he deliberately refrains from judging others: "I am a sinner as others: I must not say much of this argument. Everie one, when hee is whole, can give advice to him that are sicke" (1135–38). When Will recognizes everyone as a "sinner," then drinkers merely *resemble* swine momentarily—they are not an actual subhuman species, cut off from the whole of humanity. In this empathetic light, the play's debate over the social function of drinking and feasting (as promoted by Harvest, an advocate for the old practices of hospitality) takes on new terms. Drink and its related "sins" are no longer universally good or bad—they emerge instead as behaviors subject to the inclinations of the individual while still being tied to the fabric of social life.[41] This emphasis on community and festivity also counters the image of the drinking fellowship as dangerous and volatile masculine group, separate from and destructive to mainstream society. As he suggests in *Pierce Pennilesse*, this more expansive outlook on drinking may be applied to the city as well, which represents much more than just a den of iniquity.

Thus Nashe intervenes in moralistic discourse not by denying that drink is a "sin," but by complicating the moral significance of drink by embedding it in socioeconomic life. The cultural awareness he imparts in *Summer's Will*, that drink represents an important part of local festivity, extends into the putatively more sinful city, where Nashe also intimates ways in which drink occupies an important role in local culture. Given this widespread application, the idea of the drinking establishment as "alternative society" must be applied with caution, because while it offers a useful account of the importance of such spaces for marginalized individuals, it can also confirm conceptions of drink as "low" activity by ghettoizing it to "low" spaces. As the case of the university demonstrates, drink represented an important aspect of social bonding in "high" as well as "low" cultures and urban as well as pastoral settings, although the significance of drink can vary among them. Nashe, as Cambridge graduate and London pamphleteer, both sees and *shows* drinking practices in their complex "real world" manifestations.

Conclusion

It is a commonplace of Tudor pedagogical writing that women could be "ruined" by too much education. The abundant drinking we witness in the *Parnassus* plays and in writings of Nashe initially suggests a less common idea—that men could be corrupted by learning as well.[42] The orthodox moralistic strains of *Summer's Last Will and Testament* impugn scholars in particular by linking learning, knowledge, and "contemplation" to the practice of vice (1389); books are deemed "Poyson wrap up in sugred words" (1419) that lead young men to ruin. Curiously, this description of books echoes Nashe's defense of plays as "sower pils of reprehension, wrapt up in sweete words" (*Pierce Pennilesse* 213). Their similar wording reminds us that books, drama, and learning itself—as well as many other pleasures, such as drink—can exert either a salutary or a destructive influence, depending on culture and individual inclinations. This fact also holds true from the opposite perspective, which maintains an idealized moral superiority for men of learning: learning does not exempt a "gentleman" from vice after all, any more than it exempts him from the experience of social dislocation and economic hardship.

The embedding of drink in social and economic context highlights the fact that social degrees, cultural spaces, and behaviors are not truly reducible to moral polarities. The "part society" model, when applied to Nashe and other university-educated writers who struggled within the London literary market, helps illuminate the urbanity of university life, which so many college officials strained to keep "pure" of drink, excessive dress, and the influence of popular culture. Although these writers did not all know each other while at their respective universities, they seem to have gotten something out of the experience besides formal education. The pleasures of the university setting may well have played an important role in the university wits' own notoriety, which they themselves strategically cultivated in London and translated to readers as firsthand urban experience. The viewpoints imparted in their texts, informed by both university culture and London, expand the image of London to include other urban cultures and influences that the late sixteenth-century influx of outsiders brought into a newly adopted city.

Notes

1. For a detailed account of Oxford's growth, see "Early Modern Oxford," *A History of the County of Oxford: Volume 4, The City of Oxford* (1979), 74–180, URL: http://www.british-history.ac.uk/report.aspx?compid=22804, date accessed: July 25, 2008. An overview of Cambridge's civic structure may be found in Victor Morgan, *A History of the University of Cambridge, Volume II* (Cambridge: Cambridge University Press, 2004), 241–45. Of particular note is the influx of the poor into Cambridge (247), showing that widespread urban poverty was not only a "London" problem.
2. Morgan, *Cambridge*, II: 241.
3. Qtd. in Charles Edward Mallet, *A History of the University of Oxford*, vols. I–III (New York: Barnes & Noble, 1924, rpt. 1968), II: 48. Restrictions on drinking were often part of a general program of Puritan-leaning reform; see II: 88, 118, 120, and 166. For drinking-related incidents and official responses to them at Cambridge, see Alexandra Shepard, *Meanings of Manhood in Early Modern England* (Oxford: Oxford University Press, 2003), 103–13.
4. Peter Clark, *The English Alehouse: A Social History, 1200–1830* (New York: Longman, 1983), 109.
5. Hudson and Bolton are quoted in Jessica A. Browner, "Wrong Side of the River: London's Disreputable South Bank in the Sixteenth and Seventeenth Century," *Essays in History* 36 (1994): 34–72, 48 and 50, respectively.
6. See Susan Dwyer Amussen, "The Gendering of Popular Culture in Early Modern England," in *Popular Culture in England, c. 1500–1800*, ed. Tim Harris (New York: St. Martin's Press, 1995), 48–68, 51, 63–64. Amussen cites a representative sample of petitions in which only one woman stands accused of a drinking-related offense, as opposed to one-third (38.7 percent) of men (see 62).
7. For an overview of definitions of "civility," see Peter Burke, Brian Harrison, and Paul Slack, introduction to *Civil Histories: Essays Presented to Sir Keith Thomas*, ed. Peter Burke, Brian Harrison, and Paul Slack (Oxford: Oxford University Press, 2000), 1–30. For more on civility as applied to speech, see Burke's essay in the same volume: "A Civil Tongue: Language and Politeness in Early Modern Europe," 31–48.
8. Clark, *English Alehouse*, 109.
9. On the social fluidity of the drinking establishment, see Barbara A. Hanawalt, *Of Good and Ill Repute: Gender and Social Control in Medieval England* (New York: Oxford University Press, 1998), 105 and Alan Everitt, "The English Urban Inn, 1560–1760," in *Perspectives in English Urban History*, ed. Alan Everitt (New York: Barnes and Noble, 1973), 91–137.

10. Paul Griffiths, *Youth and Authority: Formative Experiences in England* (Oxford: Clarendon Press, 1996), 232.
11. In the preceding chapter, Gina Bloom analyzes drinking games with a similar goal in mind: to account for drinking spaces as spheres in which the participants enact "fantasies of manhood" that rework patriarchal ideals. In particular, I share Bloom's wish to complicate overly general notions of "early modern masculinity" in favor of a more complex discourse in which different forms of masculinity emerge and even compete in recreational settings.
12. Christopher Hill, "Appendix—a Note on the Universities," *Intellectual Origins of the English Revolution* (Oxford: Clarendon, 1965), 301–14, 306–7; Mallet, *A History*, II:143.
13. Shepard, *Meanings of Manhood*, 100–101. See also Bloom's analysis of the wager cups used in drinking games.
14. Ibid., 94.
15. Ibid., 95.
16. See "Early Modern Oxford" and Mallet, *A History*, 108, 313.
17. See Mark Curtis, "The Alienated Intellectuals of Early Stuart England," *Past and Present* 23 (1962): 25–43; David Cressy, "A Drudgery of Schoolmasters: The Teaching Profession in Elizabethan and Early Stuart England," in *The Professions in Early Modern England*, ed. Wilfrid Prest (London: Croom Helm, 1987), 129–53; Hugh Kearney, *Scholars and Gentlemen: Universities and Society in Pre-Industrial Britain, 1500–1700* (London: Faber and Faber, 1970), 15–33. For a fuller treatment of contemporaneous writers' responses to graduates' displacement, with a particular focus on Nashe, see chap. 2 of my *Labor and Writing in Early Modern England, 1567–1667* (Aldershot, UK: Ashgate, 2008).
18. J. B. Leishman details the resemblances to Nashe in the introduction to his edition, *The Three Parnassus Plays* (London: Ivor Nicholson & Watson, 1949), 71–79. All passages from the plays are cited from this edition.
19. For one of Nashe's clearest dismissals of the vulgar professional who writes for the print market, see his "Preface" to Greene's *Menaphon*, addressed "To the Gentleman Students of Both Universities."
20. Clark, *English Alehouse,* 15, 111; Patricia Fumerton, "Not Home: Alehouses, Ballads, and the Vagrant Husband in Early Modern England," *Journal of Medieval and Early Modern Studies* 32.3 (2002): 493–518, 512.
21. Frederick S. Boas, *University Drama in the Tudor Age* (New York: Benjamin Blom, 1914), 343–44.
22. Mallet, *A History*, 15, 422. On the link between clothing and dissolute behavior, see also Curtis, *Transition*, 54–55 and Charles Nicholl, *A Cup of News: The Life of Thomas Nashe* (London: Routledge and Kegan Paul, 1984), 27. On the presence of "cosmopolitan diversions"

at Cambridge, see E. S. Leedham-Green, *A Concise History of the University of Cambridge* (Cambridge: Cambridge University Press, 1996), 63–64. Morgan's assessment of excess in dress at Cambridge leads him to conclude that the "situation in the university towns was no doubt similar to that in London" (*Cambridge,* II: 140).

23. Philip Stubbes, *The Anatomie of Abuses*, ed. Margaret Jane Kidnie (Tempe, AZ: Renaissance English Text Society, 2002), 204.
24. William Prynne, *Histrio-mastix* (London, 1633), titlepage, sig. B2.
25. For these authors' roles in cultivating the literary grotesque in late Tudor London, see Neil Rhodes's *Elizabethan Grotesque* (London: Routledge and Kegan Paul), 1980.
26. Qtd. in Nicholl, *Cup of News*, 28.
27. Ibid., 46.
28. Lawrence Manley, *Literature and Culture in Early Modern London* (Cambridge: Cambridge University Press, 1995), 300.
29. Thomas Nashe, *Pierce Penniless His Supplication to the Devill*, in *The Works of Thomas Nashe*, vol. 1, ed. Ronald B. McKerrow (Oxford: Basil Blackwell, 1958), 214. Subsequent references will be cited in text by page number.
30. Lorna Hutson, *Thomas Nashe in Context* (Oxford: Clarendon, 1989), 172.
31. G. R. Hibbard, *Thomas Nashe: A Critical Introduction* (Cambridge, MA: Harvard University Press, 1962), 78.
32. Furthermore, as Hutson points out, the putatively legitimate trades hardly escape satirical condemnation in *Pierce Pennilesse* (*Nashe*, 189–90). Like other recent critics, I do not seek to confirm what post-structuralist critic Jonathan V. Crewe calls the "Nashe problem"—that Nashe's rhetoric consciously and deliberately confounds the "logocentric" reader's search for a stable "meaning" (*Unredeemed Rhetoric: Thomas Nashe and the Scandal of Authorship,* Baltimore and London: Johns Hopkins University Press, 1982, 1–20). Rather, I merely wish to call attention to how Nashe complicates simplistic "good vs. evil" moral discourse by introducing plurality and nuance into as many urban institutions as possible.
33. Hutson, *Thomas Nashe in Context,* 83.
34. Hibbard, *Thomas Nashe*, 87.
35. Whitgift was a former vice chancellor at Cambridge. It is possible that the play takes its concern with the abolition of revels from something both Whitgift and Nashe would have been familiar: the traditional role of the festive calendar in educational settings. See Marie Axton, "*Summer's Last Will and Testament:* Revels' End," *The Reign of Elizabeth I: Court and Culture in the Last Decade*, ed. John Guy (Cambridge: Cambridge University Press, 1995), 258–73.
36. Peter Holbrook, *Literature and Degree in Renaissance England: Nashe, Bourgeois Tragedy, Shakespeare* (Newark: University of Delaware Press, 1994), 65.

37. Thomas Nashe, *Summer's Last Will and Testament*, in *The Works of Thomas Nashe*, vol. 3, ed. Ronald B. McKerrow (Oxford: Basil Blackwell, 1958), 434–35. Subsequent references will be cited in text by line number.
38. For a reading of the play as an anti-Puritan affirmation of festivity, see Stephen S. Hillard's *The Singularity of Thomas Nashe* (Lincoln: University of Nebraska Press, 1986), 48–61.
39. *Shakespeare's Festive Comedy: A Study of Dramatic Form and Its Relation to Social Custom* (Princeton, NJ: Princeton University Press, 1959), 65.
40. Elizabeth Cook offers a different, but compatible, take on the social realism of this scene. Cook reads the drinking episode as an "inclusive moment" that reaches out to the spectators by staging characters of varying status in the very social act of drinking. Drink's status as "real" experience is underwritten further by the actor whose physicality is on display: "the barriers between the various levels of being which the show contains are momentarily broken down in this communal act. That this act should be drinking—an act which is not just bodily but social—is also significant" ("'Death proves them all but toyes': Nashe's Unidealising Show," *The Court Masque*, ed. David Lindley, Manchester: Manchester University Press, 1984, 17–32, 29). Pushing even further the implications of Will's festive role, Holbrook sees Will as downright antagonistic to elite modes, calling Will an "adversary" who "brings the mythmaking" of elite art "down to earth" (*Literature and Degree*, 66–67).
41. I see Nashe's nonjudgmental stance toward drink as compatible with Hutson's take on the play, which emphasizes themes of work and leisure: "There is no hint of the meritocratic doctrine of simultaneous moral and social improvements implied by a distinction between good and bad uses of time, profitable and unprofitable servants" (*Nashe,* 171). The play's empathy toward festive indulgence and human imperfection nicely fits its broader theme of humility in the face of certain death. See Cook's "Nashe's Unidealising Show," esp. 19–20, 21–22. In keeping with my focus on the gap between ideals and practice, the play's active questioning of moral discourse can be seen as an "unidealising" move in its own right.
42. Some historians assert that the university was not about studying at all, but about outfitting young men with enough instrumental "learning" to gain or preserve an esteemed station. See Hill's response to Mark Curtis in "Appendix," 301–14.

Chapter 3

The Social Stakes of Gambling in Early Modern London

Adam Zucker

> Even when play turns about a money prize, it is not the prize, which indeed could be won in many other ways, which is the specific point of the play; but the attraction for the true sportsman lies in the dynamics and in the chances of that sociologically significant form of activity itself. The social game has a deeper meaning—that it is played not only in a society as its outward bearer but that with its help people actually "play" "society."[1]
>
> —Georg Simmel, "Sociability."

Simmel's concept of "play" positions sociable behaviors such as gambling and flirting as abstract enactments of society's "serious relationships." Flirting, Simmel suggests, is a strictly formal, or "play" version of sex; gambling, in turn, is a "play" version of the economy. Gambling's structures of profit and loss, of risk and reward, echo and indeed depend upon the practices that compose the "real" economy, but the point of gambling itself is essentially social; that is to say, gambling is communicative, interactive, full of struggle and pleasure and sorrow, and its purpose is rooted in these qualities. For Simmel, the sociability of gambling far outweighs its financial elements: "the true sportsman" is never really in it for the money.

Even setting aside the overwhelming role the "gaming industry" has played in our modern leisure-based economy, I am sure there are countless gamblers who would disagree with Simmel's claim. It seems nearly impossible to separate wagering on matters of chance or skill from the stakes of the wager itself. In fact, the figure of the "true sportsman," as I argue at more length below, masks a complex range of material relations that put pressure on Simmel's formalizing logic. That said, the printed textual records of early modern London society reveal a notion of gambling that bears a close resemblance to Simmel's. The meanings and purposes of betting, gamesters, and "money prizes"—meanings and purposes that compose the social utility of wagering—are a regular preoccupation of all kinds of writers in the sixteenth and seventeenth centuries, including (but far from limited to) moralizing protestant social critics, chorographers, satirists, courtesy writers, and the special focus of this chapter, dramatists. London's theaters were closely linked both in material and in cultural space to popular forms of wagering, and drama offers a useful lens through which to inspect the elements of gambling that made it an overdetermined object of scorn and pleasure in the period. Drama, to put it as Simmel might, reveals the "dynamics" of gambling's "sociologically significant form" in sixteenth- and seventeenth-century London. It does so by staging gambling's links to social and economic practice in the period and extracting a useful narrative device from the serious field of commerce: the mystifying force of chance profit.

The diversification of commerce in London at the turn into the seventeenth century meant that more and more people from all ranks of society were coming to find their places within increasingly abstract networks of production and exchange. More and more people were moving to the city and, in turn, being exposed to the risky ventures of merchant capital, to the interest-based profits and losses of credit finance, and to the notion of hazard as a potentially crucial generator of economic profit. Games of chance and debates about them—their playful enactments, their contingent discourses, their pleasures, and their dangers—were crucial, symbolic elements within the intensely incorporative social relations that accompanied the rise of commercial society in early modern London. As I explore in more detail below, individuals had the option to position themselves "for" or "against" gambling as a matter of morals or political pragmatism. But rather than seeing the more or less negative responses to gambling as indications of either a conservative reaction against risk and commercial expansion or a progressive trend toward the development of a merchant class in London, I argue that playwrights and other authors turned to the social stakes of gambling to examine a definitive and seductive cultural field in early modern London, a field oriented by the figure of "the gallant" and productive of increasingly stylized modes of fashionable masculine urbanity.

THE SPACE OF THE BET

Theater historians often encounter the interplay between gambling and drama in Tudor and Stuart England through the screeds of antitheatrical writers, most of who turn out to have been thoroughly anti-dicing, as well. The full title of John Northbrooke's infamous 1579 tract is "A Treatise wherein Dicing, Dauncing, Vaine plaies or Enterludes with other idle pastimes, &c. commonly used on the Sabboth day, are reproved, by the authoritie of the worde of God and auncient Writers"; and Phillip Stubbes's *Anatomie of Abuses*, which calls gaming houses "the very seminaries, and nurseries of all kynd of abhomination,"[2] expends nearly as much ink decrying gambling as it does drama. These kinds of correlations continued to make appearances in the seventeenth century, as in Thomas Taylor's expansive list of men taken in the "snare of the devil," which sketches out a familiar matrix of player, rogue, vagrant, Papist, and cheat:

> they must liue in an vnlawfull calling, wherein they be slaues and drudges to euery mans sinne: such as are Players, Iesters, Wisards, Tumblers: such are schollers, who for preferment runne into Popish countries, and betake themselues to Seminaries, & so become traytors. Yea those that haue no calling, must liue too: but how? by filching, stealing, or begging, as idle and roguish vagrants; and those at home whose extreame idlenes brings pouerty vpon them as an armed man. Or els by gaming, cheating, and by their wits. The whole course of all which, is but a prentiship to the deuill.[3]

If playing games could easily be linked with playing plays as idle, evil pastimes by those who disapproved of both, the two were even more tightly bound together by those who made their living in and through the theater. The ties created by sermonizers and moralists were mainly rhetorical or discursive in nature, but those created by Tudor and Stuart playwrights, actors, theater-builders, and audience members were practical, spatial, and material. John Stow's brief reference to theaters in the *Survay of London* gives us some sense for this deep connection, as he describes the shift from the transitory space of miracle play performance to the emergence of secular, commercial playhouses:

> Of late time in place of those Stage playes [i.e., miracle plays], hath beene used Comedies, Tragedies, Enterludes, and Histories, both true and feigned: For the acting whereof certain public places have been erected. Also Cocks of the game are yet cherished by diverse men for their pleasures, much money being laid on their heads, when they fight in pits, whereof some be costly made for that purpose.[4]

Stow's quick move from theater-going to cock-fighting reminds us of the ways in which different kinds of playing spaces in London, spaces of pleasurable vice and commercial entertainment, bordered on and overlapped with one another. Though it was not yet built when the *Survay* was first published, Beeston's Cockpit theater had been an actual cock-fighting arena. The bloody spectacle of bear-baiting that took place at the Hope and presumably other outdoor theaters was meant to be bet upon. And the appearance of men wagering in and of itself could be an entertaining sight on the early modern stage: "Before the Play begins, fall to cards," Dekker orders in *The Gull's Hornbook*,[5] mocking those who would draw attention to themselves by misbehaving from the onstage stools in London's indoor theaters. The space of the theater was often quite literally the space of the bet.

It may be unsurprising, then, that Tudor and Stuart playwrights fit wagers and gambling into their plays with remarkable frequency.[6] (Though such tallies can only tell us so much, it seems worth noting that 167 of the 1,116 plays first performed between 1500 and 1642 currently indexed in the Early English Verse Drama database use the word "dice"; 112 use the word "gamester.")[7] A small sampling of the many examples of gambling references and scenes reveals a diversity of purpose and situation: Sirs Francis Acton and Charles Mountford, in Heywood's *A Woman Killed with Kindness*, fly into homicidal rages arguing about a bet on the sparrow-catching abilities of their hawks, setting into motion the play's secondary plot; the doomed husband of *A Yorkshire Tragedy* turns his sword on his sons and wife after losing his fortune playing dice (a plot that secularizes—and makes horrifically violent—the morality tradition of staging the waywardness of allegorical Youth through dice games, as in *The Enterlude of Youth* [1565] and *Nice Wanton* [1560]); Puntavarlo, in Jonson's satire of travel insurance in *Every Man Out of His Humour*, plans to bet 5,000 pounds at five to one odds that he, his wife, his cat, and his dog will all survive a journey to Constantinople and back; Castruchio wagers

100 ducats with Pioretto that he will be able to break the spirit of the unflappable merchant Candido in Dekker and Middleton's *1 The Honest Whore*; the action of *Cymbeline* is forced forward by Iachimo and Posthumus's bet on Innogen's chastity; and in the last scene of *Hamlet*, the Prince of Denmark dies with Claudius's wager on him still hanging in the balance. For the sake of brevity, I will simply point out that each of these examples serves a purpose, both in the narrative sequence of its respective play and in the world imagined within it, that far exceeds the distribution of money or financial gain. Political intrigue, masculine aggression, social aspiration, nationalist fantasy, and moral castigation mark off the force of these scenes and others like them. It may be difficult to think of Claudius, Laertes, and Hamlet as "true sportsmen," but it is clear that they are playing at something far removed from the "six Barbary horses" and the "six French rapiers and poniards" that are the literal stakes of what Hamlet calls "this brother's wager" in the moments before his death.

References to wagering and money-prizes in general are particularly concentrated in Jacobean and Caroline city comedies, which often straightforwardly intensify the commercial significance of gambling by staging merchants, usurers, gallants, and gulls taking on risk in the form of loans, investments, and the burgeoning practices of credit finance more generally. This is often the pattern in the comedies of Middleton and his collaborators.[8] Plays that thematize the exigencies of merchant capital—most famously, *The Merchant of Venice*, but also plays like Phillip Massinger's *The City Madam*, Rowley's *A New Wonder: A Woman Never Vext*, and Heywood's *2 If You Know Not Me*—often explicitly liken "venturing" to gambling: Old Foster in *A Woman Never Vext*, for example, bemoans "The merchants casualty: / We alwayes venture on uncertaine ods."[9] These "uncertain ods" extended to a diversifying range of commercial projects in Tudor and Stuart England—not least of all the publication of playbooks. As Douglas Bruster, Jean-Christophe Agnew, and the recent Blayney v. Farmer and Lesser debate in *Shakespeare Quarterly* have shown us,[10] city comedy's representations of the risks of local commerce and long-distance trade are in some sense self-reflexive visions of theater's own dependency upon the uncertain outcomes of London's literal and cultural marketplaces with which it was engaged.[11]

The Jonsonian tradition of city comedy, however, with its explicit interest in elite masculinity, shifts attention away from the analogy between gambling and merchant commerce to refract practical risks and serious relationships into social games based around cultural competencies related to tastefulness and wit.[12] Take, for example, these lines from John Cooke's *Greene's Tu Quoque* (1614) spoken by Staines, a witty impoverished gentleman who is in the process of gulling Bubbles, his oafish former servant. Bubbles, in a strange turn of events, has become Staines' master after inheriting his estate from an uncle who happens to have been the usurer to whom Staines was in debt. As he schemes to regain his lands, Staines promises Bubbles to instruct him in the ways of tasteful gallant-hood, and does so here with a satirical lesson about gambling:

> if you will be a true Gallant, you must bear things resolute, as this sir, if you be at an Ordinary, and chance to loose your money at play, you must not fret and fume, tear cards, and fling away dice, as your ignorant gamester, or country-Gentleman does, but you must put on a calm temperate action, with a kind of careless smile, in contempt of Fortune, as not being able with all her engines to batter down one piece of your estate, that your means may be thought invincible, never tell your money, nor what you have won, nor what you have lost: if a question be made: your answer must be, what I have lost, I have lost, what I have won, I have won, a close heart and free hand, makes a man admired.[13]

Though it is meant as a joke, this passage displays a familiarity with a social logic of play that closely resonates with Simmel's. The "careless smile" Staines invokes works to distance its wearer from the force of Fortune, and a tautological dismissal of the stakes of the game—"what I have lost, I have lost"—takes the place of an actual engagement with money. The reasons for gambling in the first place become bound to the sociable act of laying a bet, not to the outcome of the event wagered upon. Staines's advice to "never tell your money" in essence draws a boundary between gambling and its putative substance, or, at least, it refocuses our attention on a different substance, on the material performance of *sprezzatura* bound up in a disdain for all those who actually consider money to be the point of a bet. Only the "ignorant gamster" would believe it to be so.

The position of tasteful gambler that Staines mocks recalls one of the foundational concepts of Pierre Bourdieu's sociology of manners in *Distinction*: "the aesthetic disposition," the basis of which is an "elective distance from the necessities of the natural and social world."[14] Bourdieu elaborates,

> The aesthetic disposition...tends to bracket off the nature and function of the object represented and to exclude a "naïve" reaction—horror at the horrible, desire for the desirable, pious reverence for the

> sacred—along with all the purely ethical responses, in order to concentrate solely upon the mode of representation, the style, perceived and appreciated by comparison to other styles[. It is] one dimension of a total relation to the world and to others, a life-style, in which the effects of particular conditions of existence are expressed in a "misrecognizable" form.[15]

Bourdieu's analysis deepens Simmel's observations about sociability by arguing that there can be something pernicious about "playing society." The aesthetic disposition—the disposition of the "true sportsman"—masks oppressive relations of power that create and maintain differences in class or rank, and indeed that make the truth of the sportsman knowable at all. As a result, what Simmel might call "real" differences become "misrecognized" as functions of social style and cultural competencies; the role of economic capital is obscured (and reinforced) by symbolic or cultural capital; and the transmission of wealth through society remains restricted and uneven. The social stakes of gambling are, for Bourdieu, essentially economic—regardless of the money prize explicitly at risk.

Bourdieu's ideas stem from his analysis of French society in the 1960s, and we should be wary about flatly importing terms from his sociology back into the early seventeenth century. Class relations and the accumulation of capital in Stuart London, though they were increasingly trending toward modern structures, were far from identical with those organizing Bourdieu's subjects. But it seems clear that the rudimentary modes of sociological analysis that took place in the period's favored satirical genres—dramatic comedy of course, but also the Theophrastan character sketch and the closely related verse epigram, which I explore in a later section of this chapter—had begun to define and simultaneously to critique something resembling the aesthetic disposition within the field of urban culture.[16] The figure of the gallant in city comedy is the epitome of this sociological vision. Characters like Laxton, Greenwit, and Jack Dapper in Middleton and Dekker's *The Roaring Girl* and Clerimont, Truewit, and Dauphine in Jonson's *Epicoene* all strive toward a distant, style-obsessed perspective on the staged cities through which they move. This distance, however, necessarily collapses upon itself under the analysis of the social functions of fashion, wit, and tastefulness more generally that comedy and other satirical genres enacted. Stuart London's represented forms of style were never simply abstract suggestions, especially in printed and theatrical satire, written to appeal to a paying audience who would both recognize and influence the forms themselves. They were part of broader urban system of commerce and exchange that ordered flows of power and capital in increasingly modern ways.

Gambling became a rich signifier in city comedy for the ways in which the London gallant's imagined position in social space presumed an impassable distance from the mundane realities of urban commerce upon which it depended. This is especially true in Ben Jonson's *Bartholomew Fair*, a play that focuses intently upon the intricate hierarchies and social pleasures that compose the fabric of marketplace culture. In act four, as the play's characters meander through its imagined fairground, the well-dowried Grace Wellborn decides to choose between two prospective mates, the gentlemen Winwife and Quarlous, both of whom she barely knows. Each of the men writes a word down upon a ledger (they choose "Argalus" and "Palemon," names famous for their romance associations), and the first stranger who comes by is asked to select one. Grace agrees beforehand to wed the man attached to whichever name is chosen. Quarlous and Winwife are essentially betting Grace's fortune on the toss of a coin. But, crucially, the money prize attached to Grace is not in and of itself socially definitive in *Bartholomew Fair*. Both Winwife and Quarlous have already hit the play's jackpot before the coin is even tossed. Grace is willing to play this ludicrous game in the first place because she is able within an hour of meeting them to determine that her two gallant suitors are exactly the same: "You are both equal and alike to me yet... For you are reasonable creatures; you have understanding and discourse" (4.3.33–37).[17] "Understanding and discourse" are Grace's terms for competency, for wit, or taste, all qualities entirely lacking in Bartholomew Cokes, her unwanted, puppet-obsessed fiancé. With this structuring classification in mind, the form of the wager set up to differentiate between Winwife and Quarlous in fact traces out a completely empty distinction between the two of them, asserting their shared status as witty gallants, but obscuring the source of the true generative division in Jonson's imagined London between the tasteful suitors and all those who never get a chance to write a name in Grace's ledger: the gallants' privileged position in the world of the play as educated Londoners is taken entirely for granted. For audience members invested in a logic of cultural competencies that makes *them* sophisticated viewers of Jonson's imagined fair—and this includes many scholars over the course of the twentieth century[18]—the gallants become stand-ins: observers, not participants; true sportsmen, not greedy aspirants to the crass profits and pleasures sought after by Cokes, Ursula, and the clownish peddlers of the fair. Making their love-lives (and their finances) directly subject to an exaggerated moment of chance—rather than to the frantic whirl of buying and selling that surrounds them—helps Jonson to produce this illusion of distance. The manner in which, as Simmel might put it, Quarlous and Winwife play at courtship (and indeed at fair-going) makes abstract their connection to the accumulation and restricted flow of money in Jonson's comic market.

But wit, like the form of the wager, is never an entirely abstract, culturally isolated practice. The gallant's aesthetic dispositions may depend upon profits that appear to arise from substanceless acts of play, but there is always a material, historical context for the social stakes of gambling. In *Bartholomew Fair*, that context is, of course, the fair itself. By the end of the play, Quarlous, the more successful of the two gallants, is shown to be a creature of the fair as much as Littlewit or Knockem is. He achieves Dame Purecraft's hand in marriage and wins control over Grace's fortune not by flipping a coin or rolling the dice, but by manipulating the very substances of the fair so many critics assume he has abjured (including Trouble-All's clothes, Justice Overdo's warrant, and a "nest of beards" to which he has access, mysteriously enough). The social stakes of Winwife and Quarlous's wager—the ways in which chance profit is seemingly shaken free from the "real" practices of the early modern economy staged in Jonson's fair—can make their integrated status difficult to see. The narrative form of the bet, in other words, helps carve out a comic space in Bartholomew Fair in which wit and gallantry momentarily appear to be distinct or separate from the materials and economic relations that guarantee them.

The Gamester

We can further chart out the shifting social stakes of gambling in early Stuart London if we link Jonson's gallants to a wider discourse of wagering in the period, just as he himself made sure to do: Quarlous, in the first edition of *Bartholomew Fair*, is designated in the dramatis personae as "A Gamester."[19] The term would come to have a particularly long life on the London stage: first James Shirley in 1635, then Susannah Centlivre in 1705, and finally Edward Moore in 1753 each wrote plays entitled *The Gamester*.[20] Clearly, the resonance of gambling and of financial play in general held a lasting appeal for dramatists and theater-goers drawn to the suspenseful effects of chance outcome. Popular playwrights noticed the entertainment value of the figure of the Gamester, and we should approach it with this in mind: in Stuart England especially, "The Gamester" was a magnetic type more than an actual person, a usefully imagined position in social space, such as "The Gallant" or "The Usurer," rather than a single historical individual. As such, it served as a touchstone for a community that constantly toyed with the symbolic resonance of gambling alongside other leisurely pursuits.

In the early decades of the seventeenth century, "The Gamester" usually referred to a dedicated, habitual gambler—though, as we have already begun to see, it had a wider set of meanings in the culture of urbane gallantry. Even in materials written for a presumably sympathetic audience, there was often a less-than-ambiguous hint of disparagement attached to the term. The Gamester could be seen as an addict, as in Thomas Wilson's *Saints by Calling*: "We see the Gamester never well but when he is at dice, or cardes, or other game."[21] He could be imagined as a poor choice of husband who loses himself in the pleasure of play, as in Patrick Hannay's early modern self-help tract in pentameter couplets, *A Happy Husband, Or Directions for a Maide to Choose her Mate*:

> No Gamester let him be…
> Some in lesse time unto some Art attaine,
> Then others spend in Play; somes pleasing vaine,
> Will seeme so mild, in this deare double losse,
> They outwardly not take it for a crosse.[22]

In the style of Middletonian city comedy, he could be used to ring the changes of mercantile commerce, as is the case in several books of satirical Theophrastan characters sketches, like I. H.'s *The House of Correction* ("A Gamester at Irish is a Merchant Aduenturer"),[23] and in Richard Brathwaite's *Whimzies* ("A Gamester Is a Merchant-Venturer, for his stocke runnes alwaies upon hazard").[24] Or, harkening back to the moralizing energies of Stubbes and Northbrooke, the Gamester could be called out as a garden variety sinner, as he is in the character sketch in John Stephens's *Satyres*: "The seven deadly sinnes sleepe in his pocket, and he never drawes money but the noise awakes them."[25]

Different kinds of texts needed different kinds of Gamesters to do their work, but most references to the figure in Jacobean texts link him to a kind of seductive wastefulness. Take, for example, Epigram 176 in John Davies' 1611 collection *The Scourge of Folly*—a book that, with its verse tributes to Shakespeare, Marston, Jonson, and Fletcher alongside Inns of Court members and various noblemen, clearly stakes out its editor as an urbane, play-going cultural critic.

"What a Common Gamester is Like" sees gambling as a paradoxically destructive means of support:

> A Gamester's like the Ivy on a Wall;
> Which creepes into the joynts, unjoyning it:
> But when, unjoynted so, it's like to fall,
> The joynts together it doth (tottering) knit:
> A Gamster so, undoes a sound estate
> With Gaming much; but, even as he sincks,
> With Tricks he learnes in Game (which Truth doth hate)
> He (staggering) is upheld to purse some Chincks :
> *Then, they that fall to plaie to end their Stay,*
> Pray God they fall to worke; the end of play.[26]

This is a familiar castigation of the Gamester and of gambling more generally. The kinds of "play" that Simmel reads as essentially substanceless are given a serious practical weight when held in apposition with "worke; the end of play"; and the conceit of the ivy vine neatly encapsulates the sense that gambling might weaken solid finances even as it seems to hold the promise of keeping things together. The moralizing tone of earlier writers like Stubbes and Northbrooke shapes the bias of the poet, though it does so with a decided lack of protestant hyperbole. "Truth" may hate the tricks the Gamester has mastered to keep the walls of his estate from crumbling, but God seems to have little to say on the matter. Indeed, the trouble from the perspective of the epigram—and this is also true of Hannay's advice to his husband-seeking readers—is the poor economic prospect of wagering itself. Gambling is set out as an unreliable, dangerously invasive support. But as one might expect in a fashionable collection like *The Scourge of Folly*, the Gamester is not castigated for being a sinner. "Playing" is set out here as something other than simply vice: instead, it is figured as a kind of wasteful profession, or a terrible choice of occupation.

By the 1630s, an even softer analysis of the Gamester and gambling in general had begun to appear in London's printed matter. George Whetstone had tried frantically to convince Inns-of-Court students in the 1580s to "use your handes, to the managynge of Armes, and not your Fyngers to the trippynge of Dice, a Pastyme, so villanous, that (notwithstandynge) the losse be doubtfull, the dishonour is certaine."[27] Samuel Ward's sermon "Woe to Drunkards" was advertised with a clever visual version of Whetstone's warning on its title page (figure 3.1). The signifiers of status for wealthy young men in London—at least for the purposes of Ward and his publishers—were

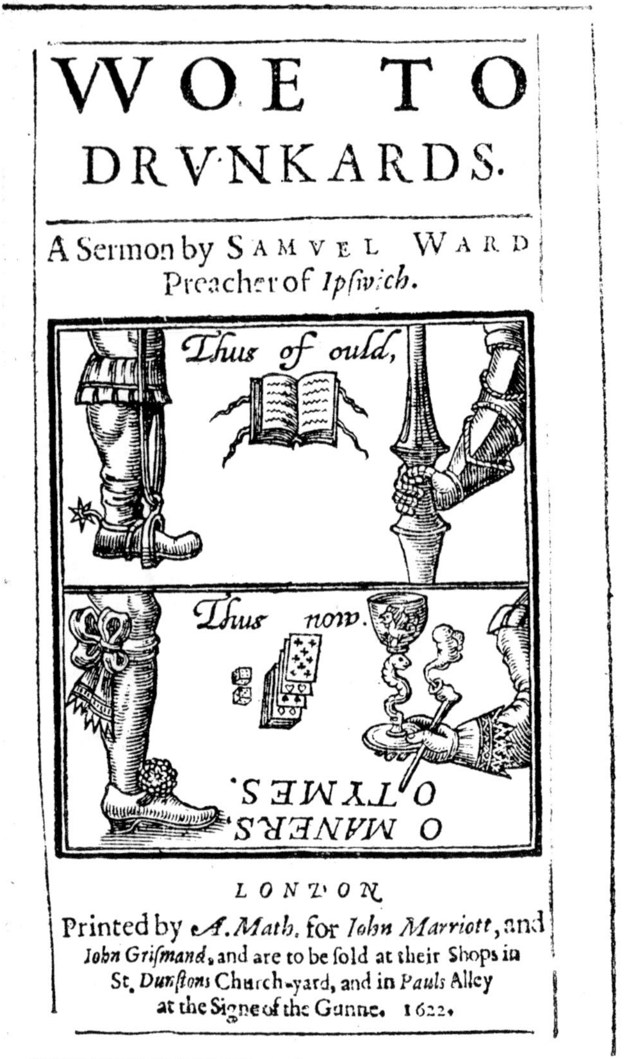
WOE TO
DRVNKARDS.
A Sermon by SAMVEL WARD
Preacher of Ipſwich.

LONDON,
Printed by A. Math. for Iohn Marriott, and
Iohn Griſmand, and are to be ſold at their Shops in
St. Dunſtons Church-yard, and in Pauls Alley
at the Signe of the Gunne. 1622.

Figure 3.1 Title page from Samuel Ward, *Woe to Drunkards* (1622). Reproduced by permission of the Mortimer Rare Book Room, Smith College.

drifting away from feudal markers of studious chivalry and toward ribbons, smoke, and dice. Compare, on the other hand, Richard Brathwaite's mild reference to young gentlemen in 1631: "It is no great matter to play at dice, but it is a great error to make dice their dayes-taske. Let it be their pastime, not their practice."[28] What

Whetstone, Ward, and others desperately feared seems to have come to pass: gentility—that sturdily conservative iteration of gallanthood and tastefulness—had begun to encompass a range of urban pleasures and behaviors that included gambling.[29]

The notion that playful pursuits could be reasonable pastimes rather than sinful, wasteful vices is one of the foundational premises of Richard Brome's, Thomas Nabbes's, and especially James Shirley's Town comedies of the 1630s.[30] Bornwell, the beleaguered husband of Aretina, the eponymous character in Shirley's *The Lady of Pleasure*, gets to the heart of the decade's interrogation of the proper place of recreation as he complains to his wife, "You make play / Not a pastime but a tyranny, and vex / Yourself and my estate by it" (1.1.109–11).[31] By the end of the play, as is often the pattern in Shirley's comedies, the excessive desires of Aretina have been checked. She sees the error of her ways when Bornwell mirrors her own obsessively wasteful behaviors in a charade of Townish hedonism. He pretends to lose huge sums of money dicing and responds to those losses in the same exaggeratedly careless manner as the character ridiculed in Cooke's *Tu Quoque*:

> I had rather lose a thousand more, than one
> Sad thought come near my heart for it. Vex for trash?
> Although it go from other men like drops
> Of their life blood, we lose with the alacrity
> We drink a cup of sack, or kiss a Mistress.
> No money is considerable with a gamester,
> They have souls more spacious than Kings. Did two
> Gamesters divide the Empire of the world,
> They'd make one throw for it all, and he that lost
> Be no more melancholy than to have played for
> A morning's draught. Vex a rich soul for dirt,
> The quiet of whose every thought is worth
> A Province? (5.1.38–34)

As in Cooke's play, the careless, or as Bornwell would have it, the "quiet" aesthetic disposition of the gallant Gamester comes in for some ridicule here. But while the potential for play to shade from pastime to tyranny is often lambasted in Shirley's Town comedies, gambling in and of itself is not necessarily a problem. Two scenes of *Hyde Park*, for example, are taken up entirely by a foot-race and a horse-race, both of which are accompanied by a frenzied rush of bets placed and wagers matched by nearly every character in the play, men and women alike. The play features a lascivious Lord Bonville who is chastized and, like Aretina, reformed by the end of act five, but his intense love for betting on horses is never called into question.

The same pattern holds true for *The Gamester*, in which Shirley goes so far as to make the gambler Will Hazard the play's ethical centerpiece. *The Gamester* has three distinct narrative lines (one of which was apparently suggested by King Charles);[32] the relevant one for this discussion deserves a brief summary. Wilding, an appropriately named lecher, believes that he has arranged an assignation with Penelope, his wife's young cousin who is also his ward. At the agreed upon moment for the tryst, however, Wilding is in the midst of a losing streak in a high-stakes dice game. Hoping to recoup his losses, he sends Hazard (who has just won hundreds of pounds) to sleep with Penelope in his place, assuming that in the dark she will not notice the difference. Later, Wilding's wife tells him that she knew of the assignation and, in the dark, slept with him in her cousin's place. Wilding is distraught, imagining that he has made himself a cuckold, and schemes to marry Penelope (and her substantial dowry) to Hazard in the hopes that the Gamester will keep the tryst a secret in order to make an honest woman of his betrothed. At the end of the play, it is revealed that Wilding's wife and Penelope, hoping to shame Wilding into honest living, were waiting for him in a lit room when Hazard arrived to take his place, and they recruited him to play the ensuing trick. Hazard and Penelope are married. Wilding is persuaded to be a better husband. But, *nota bene*, no one is in any way persuaded to stop gambling. The play's last line, spoken by Hazard—"May never Gamester have worse fate than I"—does little to suggest that he has changed in any way.[33] Wilding has been made unwild, sexually; but Hazard is still Hazard.

In some ways, Hazard ends up an even more perfect version of himself than he was when the play began. As he gets richer and richer over the course of the play, we discover that he is a Lord divorced from his lands by his debts, and that each dicing triumph keeps alive his hope that "I may live to be a land-lord agen" (sig. F3). Strangely enough, it happens. By the end of the play, the dice have brought him 2,000 pounds. This is the *exact amount*, the audience goes on to learn, of Penelope's dowry, over which Wilding reluctantly cedes control when she marries Hazard. The precise symmetry here should not be surprising. A comic world dominated by a Gamester is one in which the transfer of wealth between men through the networks of marriage and familial inheritance—a dominant subject of early modern comedy—is mirrored by the homosocial comic relations of the gaming table: the site, as *The Gamester* puts it, of "deepe playe" (sig. E4).

In this version of Shirley's intricately imagined West End world, the status of the landed gentry becomes legible as equally dependant on the structured economics of marriage contracts and on the chance profits of stylized urbanity.

But *The Gamester* does not read as the story of a profitable marriage. The play is not, after all, called *The Suitor*, or *The Dowry-Winner*. The financial symmetry of the play's romantic outcome is unbalanced by the social stakes of gambling, or, in other words, by the entertaining demands of the dice upon our attention. The distracting, occlusive power of the bet is at the center of gambling's relationship with the early modern stage, even from the very beginning of the period under consideration in this book. A wager makes Quarlous and Winwife appear momentarily to exist outside of the world of the fair, despite being in the midst of it. Cooke's careless gamester, simply by gambling, shows that he has nothing to do with the financial relations that, in the end, make his wager possible—he has simply lost what he has lost. Even the early Tudor *Enterlude of Youth* gives voice to this power of play to distract us from serious relationships through a vice figure named Riot. He hopes with the following offer to convince the play's protagonist to abandon the company of Charity and Humility:

> Syr I can teache you to play at the dice
> At the quenes game and at the Iryshe
> The Treygobet and the hasarde also
> And many other games mo
> Also at the cardes I can teche you to play
> At the triunph and on and thirtye
> Post, pinion, and also aumsase
> And at an other they call dewface
> Yet I can tel you mor & ye wyll con me thanke
> Pinke and drinke and also at the blanke.[34]

Gambling, in the final analysis, is distracting. Dewface and the Queen's Game and the Treygobet and Hazard—these all sound a good deal more entertaining than Charity and Humility. But we should not let ourselves be distracted by the social stakes of laying a bet. The textual history of the Gamester, the gallant, and of gambling more generally in early modern London suggests that thinking of "play" or "vice" in isolated, strictly formal terms can obscure the ways that material relationships help produce and are shaped by the simple possibilities of play itself. The satirists and playwrights of Jacobean and Caroline London were far from blind to the ramifications of this set of facts. In the end, they articulate the diverse stakes of a wager—its pleasures, its rewards, and its sad, blinding effects—in ways far more revealing than those who would castigate gambling as an immoral, invasive, idle vice.

Notes

For their time spent with drafts of this chapter and for their valuable suggestions, I owe a debt of gratitude to Mary Bly, Natasha Korda, the editors of this volume, the anonymous reader for the press, and the members of the "London and Beyond" seminar at the 2008 meeting of the Shakespeare Association of America

1. Simmel, "Sociability," in *On Individuality and Social Forms*, ed. Donald Levine (Chicago: University of Chicago Press, 1971), 134. Recent work that delves into the idea of "play" in early modern England includes Louis Montrose, *The Purpose of Playing* (Chicago: University of Chicago Press, 1996), esp. 1–99 and Anna Nardo, *The Ludic Self in Seventeenth-century English Literature* (Albany: State University of New York Press, 1991), esp. 1–14.
2. Phillip Stubbes, *The Antomie of Abuses* (London, 1581), sig. O8. Cf. Thomas Elyot's pithy claim in *The Boke named The Governour* (1531) that "there is nat a more playne figure of idlenesse than playinge at dise." Ed., Ernst Rhys, Everyman Library (London and New York: J. M Dent, 1907), 108 and George Whetstone's rather more elaborate version of the sentiment in the dedication of *A Mirour for Magestrates of Cyties* (London, 1584):

   O, how happie were it for your Posterytie, if, the Innes of the Court, were farre from Dicying-houses, or Dicing-houses, with their Originall, the Deuill. But, if you can not be thus separated, this little Booke, wyll (with regarde) guide you as safe, as the Clue of threede did Theseus, in the Laberinth. These Houses (outwardly) are of the substance of other Buildinges, but within, are the Botches and Byles of Abbomynation: they are lyke unto deepe Pittes, couered with smooth Grasse, of which, men must be warned, or els, they can hardly auoide that thie eye cannot discouer. (sig. ¶1v–¶2r)
3. Thomas Taylor, *Christs Combate and Conquest: or, The Lyon of the tribe of Iudah* (Cambridge, 1618), sig. F8v. See also Epigram 7 from Samuel Rowland's *Humour's Ordinary* (London, 1605), which links drinking, theater-going, bawdry, and gambling as like pursuits:

   Speake Gentlemen, what shall we doe to day·
   Drink some braue health vpon the dutch carous,
   Or shall we to the Globe and see a play,
   Or visit Shore-ditch for a bawdy-house?
   Let's call for Cardes or Dice, and haue a game;
   To sit thus idle, is both sinne and shame.

4. John Stow, *The Survay of London* (London, 1598), sig. G7r-v.
5. Thomas Dekker, *The Guls Horne-Book* (London, 1609), sig. E4.
6. For recent work on the subject, see Linda Woodbridge, "He beats thee 'gainst the odds": Gambling, Risk Management, and Antony and Cleopatra," in *Antony and Cleopatra: New Critical Essays*, ed. Sara Munston Deats (New York: Routledge, 2004), 193–211; Luke Wilson, "Drama and Marine Insurance in Shakespeare's London" in *The Law in Shakespeare*, ed. Constance Jordan and Karen Cunningham (New York: Palgrave Macmillan, 2007), 127–42. See also Delmar E. Solem, "Some Elizabethan Game Scenes," *Educational Theatre Journal* 6.1 (1954): 15–21.
7. Statistics valid as of February 12, 2007. Early English Verse Drama Database accessed via Chadwyck-Healy's "Literature Online" site.
8. See, for example, *Your Five Gallants*, which contains an extended dice-playing scene; *Michaelmas Term*, with its commodity swindle set up by dicing losses used by Short-yard and Quomodo to rob Sir Richard Easy of the title to his estate; and William Rowley's *A New Wonder: A Woman Never Vext* (London, 1632), which features a dicing reprobate who falls under the powers of the never-vext woman and immediately gives up gambling for book-keeping.
9. Rowley, *A New Wonder*, sig. A2v. On "venturing" and its connections to risk, see Theodore Leinwand, *Theater, Finance, and Society in Early Modern England* (Cambridge: Cambridge University Press, 1999).
10. Jean-Christophe Agnew, *Worlds Apart: The Market and the Theater in Anglo-American Thought, 1550–1750* (Cambridge: Cambridge University Press, 1986); Douglas Bruster, *Drama and the Market in the Age of Shakespeare* (Cambridge: Cambridge University Press, 1992); Alan B. Farmer and Zachary Lesser, "Structures of Popularity in the Early Modern Book Trade," *SQ* 56.2 (2005): 206–13 and "The Popularity of Playbooks Revisted," *SQ* 56.1 (2005): 1–32; Peter Blayney, "The Alleged Popularity of Playbooks," *SQ* 56.1 (2005): 33–50.
11. Writers on commerce itself were also interested in forms of gambling. Gerald Malynes's *Consuetudo, vel Lex Mercatoria* (London, 1622) contains a chapter "Of Merchants Wagers, Stipulations, or Conventions" (sig. S3r–S4r) that treats the legality and social codes guiding various kinds of bets. Among the other helpful guidelines: "A Wager laid who shall eate or drinke most is unlawfull" (sig. S3v).
12. I have argued these points at more length in Adam Zucker, "The Social Logic of Ben Jonson's *Epicoene*," in *Renaissance Drama* 33 (2004): 37–62; see also Bruce Boehrer, *The Fury of Men's Gullets: Ben Jonson and the Digestive Canal* (Philadelphia: University of Pennsylvania Press, 1997), 42–79; Richard Dutton, *Ben Jonson: Authority: Criticism* (London and New York: St. Martin's and Macmillan,1996), esp. 1–19; Kathleen McLuskie, "Making and Buying: Ben Jonson and the Commercial Theatre Audience," in

Refashioning Ben Jonson: Gender, Politics, and the Jonsonian Canon, ed. Julie Sanders, Susan Wiseman, and Kate Chedgzov (London and New York: St. Martin's and Macmillan, 1998), 134–54; Janette Dillon, *Theatre, Court and City, 1595–1610* (Cambridge: Cambridge University Press, 2000), 124–36.

13. John Cooke, *Greene's Tu Quoque* (London, 1614), sig. D3v. Cf. Thomas Dekker's bad advice in *The Guls Horne-Booke*: "You must not sweare in your dicing: for that Argues a violent impatience to depart from your money, and in time will betray a mans need. Take heed of it. No! whether you be at Primero or Hazard, you shall sit as patiently (though you loose a whole half-years exhibition) as a disarmed Gentleman does when he's in the unmerciful fingers of Serjeants" (sig. E1v).
14. Pierre Bourdieu, *Distinction: A Social Critique of the Judgement of Taste*, trans. Richard Nice (Cambridge, MA: Harvard University Press, 1984), 5.
15. Ibid., 54.
16. Recent investigations of this and related developments include Amanda Bailey, *Flaunting: Style and the Subversive Male Body in Early Modern England* (Toronto: University of Toronto Press, 2007); Anna Bryson, *From Courtesy to Civility: Changing Codes of Conduct in Early Modern England* (Oxford: Oxford University Press, 1998); and, in a slightly later moment, Mark Dawson's *Gentility and the Comic Theatre of Late Stuart London* (Cambridge: Cambridge University Press, 2005). The idea of the detached pleasure-seeker obtained in mercantile contexts as well: Malynes reports, "Wagers between Merchants are many times more done for sport and recreation than for gaine: for over great wagers are against good manners, and may concerne a Merchant much in reputation and credit" (*Consuetudo, vel Lex Mercatoria*, sig. S4).
17. *Bartholomew Fair*, ed. Suzanne Gossett, Revels Student Editions (Manchester: Manchester University Press, 2000).
18. On the separateness or distance of Quarlous, Winwife, and Grace from the Fair, see, for example, Jonathan Haynes, *The Social Relations of Jonson's Theater* (Cambridge: Cambridge University Press, 1992): "Grace and Winwife's marriage and Quarlous' fortune are made possible by the Fair, yet they never really participate in it" (126); and John Gordon Sweeney III, *Jonson and the Psychology of Public Theater* (Princeton, NJ: Princeton University Press, 1985): "This extreme self-consciousness . . . allows [Quarlous] to stand outside the fair, to consider it a play to be observed and not enacted" (183).
19. Ben Jonson, *Workes* (London, 1640), sig. A3v; Don Surly is called the same in the dramatis personae of *The Alchemist.*
20. Centlivre's and Moore's plays, though they remain outside of the scope of this chapter and collection, were each immensely popular;

Moore's moral melodrama featured Garrick in the title role and was staged well into the nineteenth century.

21. Thomas Wilson, *Saints by Calling* (London, 1620), sig. Nn1v. The reference occurs during a discussion of the need of the lover for his loved object, even if that object is inappropriate, and the thought continues: "The Fornicator is neuer at rest, vnlesse he bee with his harlot. The Couetous man is best pleased, when he lookes vpon, or fingereth money."
22. Patrick Hannay, *A Happy Husband, Or Directions for a Maide to Choose her Mate* (London, 1619), sig. B5v.
23. I. H., *The House of Correction: or, Certayne satyricall epigrams* (London, 1619), sig. D3v.
24. Richard Brathwaite, *Whimzies: or A Caste of New Characters* (London, 1631), sig. C12.
25. John Stephens, *Satyres* (London, 1615), sig. O1v-2r. See also Francis Lenton's *The Young Gallants Whirligig* (London, 1629), sig. C3.
26. John Davies, *The Scourge of Folly* (London, 1611), sig. G2. Italics in the original.
27. Whetstone, *A Mirour for Magestrates of Cyties*, sig. E1v.
28. Brathwaite, *Whimzies*, sig. D2.
29. See, Dawson, *Gentility*, and Jean Howard, *Theater of a City: Places of London Comedy, 1598–1642* (Philadelphia: University of Pennsylvania Press, 2006), 162–208. This is not to say that the campaign against gambling as a vice disappeared: John Philpot's *A Prospective Glasse for Gamesters*, for example, appeared in 1646, warning the "young men and apprentices of London" to whom it was dedicated against the "unbecommingnesse of so sensuall a vice" (sig. A2r-v).
30. See Martin Butler, *Theatre and Crisis, 1632–1640* (Cambridge: Cambridge University Press, 1984).
31. James Shirley, *The Lady of Pleasure*, ed. Ronald Huebert, *The Revels Plays* (Manchester: Manchester University Press, 1986).
32. We know as much from Henry Herbert's records: "On thursday night the 6 of Febru. 1633, The Gamester was acted at Court, made by Sherley, out of a plot of the king's, given him by mee; and well likte. The king sayd it was the best play he had seen for seven years." Ed. Joseph Quincy Adams, *The Dramatic Records of Sir Henry Herbert: Master of the Revels, 1623–1673* (New Haven, CT: Yale University Press, 1917), 54–55. There is much to be gleaned from this brief note about the networks of communication between playwrights and their royal patron, about the role of the Master of the Revels as a potential conduit between them, and most of all, about Charles's rather predictable taste for his own inventions. But it is difficult to know which element of the play Herbert is referring to. The convoluted bed-trick at the center of the Hazard/Wilding narrative seems to have been inspired by a tale in Marguerite de Navarre's *Heptameron* (or, at least, by one of the versions of the fabliaux that inspired the tale).

See Robert Stanley Forsythe, *The Relations of Shirley's Plays to the Elizabethan Drama* (New York: Columbia University Press, 1914), 357–65.

33. James Shirley, *The Gamester* (London, 1637), sig. K2v.
34. Anon., *The Enterlude of Youth* (1513?, London, pr. 1565), sig. C3.

PART II

Sexualizing the City: Cathedrals, Brothels, and Barbershops

Chapter 4

Carnal Geographies: Mocking and Mapping the Religious Body

Mary Bly

Cathedrals map the loftiest human ambitions onto the urban landscape. St. Paul's Cathedral embodied a wish to celebrate and communicate with the divine; its physical domination of London registered the strength of this desire. "For wee haue a *golden candlestick*, a glorious Church," preached the Bishop of London in 1620, "whereem the light of the Gospell shineth."[1] Paul's gave London spiritual shape, punctuating its cartography with a sacred focal point.

Yet the use-value of that golden candlestick had long been a battlefield: the cathedral was not only on the front line of religious disputes, but its space was also co-opted by those with no interest in the gospel. Throughout the sixteenth and seventeenth century, Paul's alternately housed not only Protestant and Catholic services, but it also housed something of a daily fashion show, a thoroughfare, a market, and a financial exchange. This chapter argues that in the early 1600s Paul's and its attached boys' theater became a platform for flamboyant displays of carnality. Desire for and celebration of the divine were not replaced by desire for and celebration of the corporeal male, but in an odd echo of the erotic aspects of Christianity's emphasis on Christ's body, the cathedral became London's most popular staging ground for male display. Seizing on this potent fracture, the attached theater deployed religious vocabulary in service of some of the most sexually explicit drama written for the early modern stage. The Middleton play *The Puritan* serves as a pointed example of this sort of engagement: it exploits the symbolic coding of the cathedral, turning the Nicene Creed into a paeon of sexual desire for the "quick" male body. As a landmark in the spiritual landscape of London became important to secular geographies, plays performed in its environs reveled in the juxtaposition, turning Puritans to punks.[2]

Thus if the cathedral was designed as a place to aid humans in negotiating relationships with the divine, by the 1600s Paul's was at least as important as a place in which people negotiated relations among themselves. Moreover, the social interactions that occurred in Paul's often seem to have been flagrantly opposed to interaction with the divine—in fact, to be most fertilely human, responding to lust for money, for servants, and for bodies. James Pilkington, Bishop of Durham, writing earlier in the sixteenth century, mapped his disgust onto the structure itself: "The south alley for popery and usery, the north for simony, and the horsefair in the midst for all kinds of bargains, meetings, brawling, murders, conspiracies, and the font for the ordinary payment of money."[3] Yet the cathedral was never considered public space, like a village square. The symbolic economy of the cathedral—its status as a "glorious Church"—was not forgotten in the midst of the transactions taking place at the font or elsewhere in the building.[4] I would argue that location was crucial to those interactions. Financial transactions took place at the font because the site lent authority to the contract. Men paraded Paul's Walk (the middle aisle), displaying the beauty of their costumes and themselves, because the clash between sacred and secular lent a transgressive fillip to that activity.

I am interested in understanding how early modern use of the cathedral, especially as the site of struggle between sacred and secular, may have given a similar clandestine power to plays performed at its small theater.[5] Humanist geographers distinguish between *spaces*, the areas through which we walk, and *places*, areas altered or built by humans, and equally important, given meaning by being interpreted and imagined.[6] Places are spaces that matter, carrying a meaning constructed from "accretional layers of gossip and song, oral history, written history, essays and poems," in Yi-Fu Tuan's words.[7] They are areas to which a person or group has developed an emotional attachment or a sharp awareness, as in a local neighborhood or a so-called home town. It is only through use of the "geographical imagination," in Cara Aitchison's term, and a focus on the symbolic rather than the material, that we are able to articulate what codes define a given place at a given moment.[8] I would argue that the plays performed in Paul's own theater, just through the cathedral's South wall, fed on the coding of the cathedral as an early modern London place, and understanding of the cathedral is crucial to understanding plays written for performance there.

Who controls the transformation of a place? Whose definition rules, turning space to place? The answer as regards English cathedrals seems self-evident: they appear to be defined by the monarchy, along with Anglican high clergy and architects. Even when Paul's served as the fulcrum for religious change during the turbulent 1500s, as royalty mandated services that reflected the current theological inclination, the cathedral's identity was still established by the monarch and implemented by higher clergy.[9] To some extent, the religious identity of the monarch was stamped directly onto the identity of the cathedral itself. As Henry Farley writes in 1616, giving voice to Paul's, "I am *Gods house*" succored by "faire *Eliza*...Full foure and fortie yeeres."[10] Fair Eliza, or Queen Elizabeth, defined the cathedral as a place of Anglican worship; other English kings and queens redefined "*Gods house*" as they pleased. Yet as Henri Lefebvre has argued, social and political forces may well engender a place, but they cannot master it completely.[11]

Paul's certainly defied definition by the queen or high Anglican clergy. Those who used the space did not consider "*Gods house*" to be a constraint. In 1620, the Bishop of London compared the cathedral to "the bodie of the King, a building not made with hands, but shaped of flesh and bloud"; the problem is that a building that metaphoric cannot be constrained by its designated likeness to the king's body.[12] Considered as a body, the cathedral is not encompassed by the body of Christ, or by that of the king; its contours include those who seized the space and made it their own. This chapter borrows a recent term coined by the humanistic geographer, Ronald Davidson: *recalcitrant space*. Davidson invented the phrase to describe an area that resists being turned from a space to a place; he portrays a featureless section of an LA strip as an example of recalcitrant space.[13] I am going to alter his usage to discuss space that is the focus of an official designation—and yet is used in a recalcitrant fashion. The battle that raged among clergy, government, and the people throughout the 1600s regarding use of St. Paul's Cathedral encapsulates the complexities behind creation of *place*: even when designated in a given fashion, literally anointed by the king as a sacred temple, people stubbornly turned the cathedral to other uses, giving it a very different emotional shape.

We see this even—or perhaps particularly—in examining interactions that reverberate with a tension between the sacred and the all-too-human. This experience is not unique to Paul's as a cathedral. Carl Estabrook's thoughtful examination of contested space in English cathedrals came to the conclusion that such battles "dramatically exposed the unsettled boundary between the sacred and the secular."[14] Estabrook is writing of contested aspects of ritual and performance, but his observation applies as well to more informal battles waged in the cathedral. In 1623, John Donne published the sermon he gave on the dedication of a new chapel at Lincoln's Inn. Though he was the Dean of St. Paul's at the time of his sermon, he does not limit his scolding of the "irreuerent manner which hath ouertaken vs in all these places" to the cathedral alone. "*Gods* House," he observes, "is no *Ordinary*...where any man may pretend to doe what he will."[15] I would suggest that although he does not name it, Donne is actually referring to Paul's, which accumulated a plethora of labels referring to "dining" or "breakfasting," a direct imbrication of an ordinary (or tavern) and the part of the cathedral known as the middle aisle, or Duke Humphrey's walk. As Samuel Speed put it in his *Legend of Duke Humphrey,* "Open is his Table unto all, / To those that come without, or with a call!"[16]

The phrase "to dine with Duke Humphrey" refers to the monument of Sir John Beauchampe (died 1358), believed at the time to be a monument to Humphrey, Duke of Gloucester, who was actually buried in St. Albans. The middle aisle of Paul's was nicknamed after Humphrey, and the term seems to have referred in general to the public space of Paul's. Edward Sharpham says that "through wante of meate many times they walke out their dinner in Duke Humfrey his Allie, or else fetch a sleep vnder a pillar in Powles, onely to beguile hunger."[17] Gabriel Harvey bluntly defines the practice as going "to seek his dinner in poules with Duke humfrey: to licke dishes, to be a beggar."[18] Thus Donne's definition of a church as "no *Ordinary*" would have had particular import to his listeners, bringing to mind the unruly and nondevotional crowds who daily walked the cathedral.

The middle aisle, also known as the Mediterranean, was a key hub in fashionable London, where men gathered throughout the day to stroll and gossip, regardless of religious services being conducted.[19] The practice of walking that aisle is referred to in more than twenty plays of the period, staged at public and private theaters; Ben Jonson placed an act of *Every Man Out of His Humor* there, and Middleton did the same with *Your Five Gallants* and *Michaelmas Term*.[20] In addition, Thomas Dekker wrote two pamphlets depicting the aisle: *The Gull's Hornbook*, which instructs his "gull" in making a proper impression in Paul's, and (with Thomas Middleton) *Meeting of Gallants at an Ordinarie*, which recounts a conversation between gallants in the same place. What comes through clearly in these portraits is the stubbornness with which gentlemen seized control of Paul's, although it should be noted that Dekker's *Dead Tearme* describes different classes jostling for that space; his lengthy list includes the knight, the gull, the gallant, the upstart, the gentleman, as well as "the Ruffian, the Cheater, the Puritan, the Cut-throat . . . of all trades & professions some, of all Countreyes some" (51).

Queen Elizabeth did not even attempt to curb the practice as a whole, which reveals the sway the walkers commanded over the aisle. Instead, she fruitlessly attempted to prohibit persons who "walk up and down, or spend the time in the same . . . *during the time of preaching, lecturing, or other divine service*" (my italics). Charles reiterated the injunction, again limiting the prohibition to "the times of Diuine Seruice."[21] As a 1623 Roman Catholic biography had it, "They're [the Protestants'] Sundayes and feastes, how are they neglected, when on these days there are more idel persons walking up and downe the streets and in St. Paule's church (which is made a walking and talking place) than there is on others!"[22] Royal proclamations tried to curb walkers—but they could not force those men to engage in pious activity. In fact, one gains a sense of the church as having a divided population, two audiences who brushed shoulders but rarely mixed. Samuel Speed's *Legend of His Grace Humphrey, Duke of S. Paul's Cathedral Walk* admitted that "Some on devotion come to feed their muse; / Some come to sleep, or walk, or talk of news" (sig. F1v). And Dekker's *Dead Tearme* gives voice to Paul's own steeple, who bitterly complains of being that "whilest deuotion kneeles at her prayers, doth prophanation walke vnder her nose in contempt of *Religion*" (52).

Observers saw the two audiences as sharply distinct. An Elizabethan ballad, "Death's Dance," put the situation bluntly, noting that men go to Paul's "To walke, and not to pray."[23] Sermons often reproached gentlemen for attending Paul's without pious intent, separating the walkers from the prayers. In "The Gallants Burden," a sermon preached at Paul's Cross in 1612, Thomas Adams asks the obvious: are not "the Allies in this Temple often fuller of Walkers, then the Quire of Petitioners?"[24] In 1623, Adams offered a similar assessment at the Cross, reproaching men and women, "ambulatory Christians, that weare out the Pauement of this grate Temple with their feet, but scarce euer touch stone of it with their knees; that are neuer further from God, then when they are nearest the Church."[25]

Amanda Bailey has done an excellent job in *Flaunting: Style and the Subversive Male Body in Renaissance England* of describing the strutting progress of young males who displayed their disposable income, transformed into clothing, in Paul's Walk.[26] The cathedral was home to a gaudy social drama that featured displays of conspicuous consumption. The effect was to create desire not only for magnificent clothing—but also for the bodies within. As she notes, "In *Every Man Out* it seems that one can only view clothes with an acquisitive eye, which leads one to regard the male bodies wearing them as desirable objects that also may be obtained."[27] I want to build on her portrait by focusing on the way in which translation of display to desire both competed with and was strengthened by the sacred coding of the cathedral. The two populations using the church were not, of course, as distinct as the quotations above suggest. Walkers *chose* to throng in a cathedral: whether they prayed or not, the location adds spice to their eroticized flamboyance. Speed identifies walkers who beheld the church as "*Diana's* Temple," and addressed themselves in prayer "to *Venus*...studying a fresh Caress" (sig. F2). Humanist geographers map evidence to create "geographies of prostitution"; just as Paul's punctuated London in a spiritual sense, it should also appear in a sexualized cartography.[28]

John Earle's *Microcosmography,* a series of seventy-eight satirical portraits, offers a good example of how the cathedral's religious affiliation became blurred with a vigorous sense of erotic availability.[29] Earle's portrait turns Paul's Walk into a personage, akin to a "Drunkard" or an "Insolent Man." In essence, Earle does the work of an early modern humanist geographer. He focuses on the clash between sacred and secular: "were the steeple not sanctified," he argues, the cathedral were "nothing liker Babel...The best sign of a Temple in it is that is the thieves' sanctuary" (84–85). He cannot even identify its theological leanings: "It is the general Mint of all famous lies, which are here like the legends of Popery, first coined and stamped in the Church" (84). The implication is that the church itself coins and stamps the lies told in the middle aisle. Earle concludes by labeling the cathedral the "ear's brothel [that] satisfies their lust and itch" (85). Paul's loses its standing as a temple and becomes a brothel.

The easy slide from temple to brothel is not inexplicable, given the ongoing arguments over the boundaries of the sacred resulting from the Reformation, including the familiar association of popery and the Whore of Babylon.[30] But the connection is not only metaphorical. Dekker tells his gallant in *The Guls Horne-Booke* to walk in the aisle so that bystanders may "reioyce to behold his most hansome calfe," and describes singing boys who "buzze" the praises of handsome gentlemen, swarming around them "like so many white butterflyes."[31] There was an elaborate, ritualistic quality to the progress down the aisle. The Paul's scene in Middleton's *Your Five Gallants* depicts a character, Pursenet, lamenting that gallants now salute each other only with one hand:

> Do we salute by halves?
> Are not our limbs at leisure?
> Where's comely nurture, The Italian kiss,
> Or the French cringe?[32]

The erotic quality of a "handsome calf" and an "Italian kiss" speaks to the role that physical beauty played in the stroll down the middle aisle. The act that Thomas Middleton placed in Paul's, the first scene of *Michaelmas Term*, grows from the combined pleasure of watching men stroll the aisle while telling bawdy jokes. For example, Quomodo points out Master Easy to his companion Shortyard and instructs him: "take surely note of him; he's fresh and free . . . flatter, dice, and brothel to him; give him a sweet taste of sensuality . . . drink drunk with him, creep into bed to him, kiss him, and undo him, my sweet spirit."[33]

The implication that one might select a lover from the throng at Paul's is substantiated by references suggesting that sex workers followed young men to the building. It certainly makes sense that prostitutes would throng in arenas in which men, particularly young men, were determined to display their manhood. J. H. in his "Characters" of 1619 describes a courtesan who "many times she repayres thither, especially vnto *the lower end of the Middle Ile*."[34] As in John Earle's *Microcosmography*, J. H. mediates between official use of the cathedral (a place for choristers, or singing boys), and its use by prostitutes. The juxtaposition between sacred and sexual is half the joke; as he says, his courtesan "loues not to stand in a *Surplisse*," or else she would have been "a *Quirrister at Pauls*" (sig. D2v). Similarly, the prostitute Shave'em in Massinger's *City Madam* works in Paul's, and Dekker places an "Appel-squire," or pimp, among those in the walks.[35] Everard Guilpin's satirical view of a "walke in Poules" includes a sex worker who appears to be not only soliciting, but actually working in the cathedral:

> There in that window mistres minkes doth stand,
> And to some copesmate beckneth her hand,
> In is he gone, Saint *Venus* be his speede,
> For some great thing must be aduentured.[36]

The epigram seems to suggest that intimacies of this nature were actually conducted inside the cathedral, perhaps in a recessed window.[37] Fascinatingly, while a "copesmate" is defined as a partner in sexual intercourse or a paramour, a "cope" is a religious vestment worn by ecclesiastics in procession, or at Vespers.[38] Thus "copesmate" brings together sexual and spiritual, implying that Mistress Minkes solicits not only gentlemen but also priests.

Paul Griffiths's study of prostitution in Elizabethan London concludes that bawdy houses operated "as an expression of the sexual vitality and camaraderie of males (especially young males), which overlapped with other items of male consumption."[39] In an arena in which masculinity was being paraded through conspicuous consumption, it makes sense that goods other than clothing would be on offer.

I have found few mentions of ladies walking in Paul's; those few emphasize female desire and availability. Speed, for example, includes "Doxies" in his survey of the cathedral inhabitants, describing "a light-heel'd Girl, / Adorn'd with Ribbons, Paints, and Bastard-Pearl" (sig. G1). Thomas Dekker and John Webster's *Westward Ho* also includes a jest that places sex in Paul's itself; Justiniano makes a bawdy assignation with Mistress Honeysuckle and her friends: "the way—through *Paules*: euery wench take a piller, there clap on your Maskes: your men will bee behind you, and before your prayers be halfe don, be before you, and man you out at seuerall doors."[40] Mistress Honeysuckle's very appearance in Paul's signals her lustful character. Prayers and sex blend in a transgressive mix that suggests significant flirtation (perhaps while masked), if not the actual "manning." Later in the seventeenth century, Ned Ward's description of London includes a visit to Paul's where he describes a "wild and wanton" lady, thinking "more on a gallant than she did on her devotions," and then "a parcel of wenches fit for husbands ... who were full able enough, and I suppose willing, in an evening to help the young workmen home with their tools, if they would venture to thrust 'em into their custody."[41]

Another potent fracture point between sacred and sexualized use of the space was the advertisements posted within the cathedral. Roze Hentschell notes that bills were posted on a "serving man's pillar": "Rather than selling household goods, or cloth, or food, the 'vendors' inside Paul's peddled men and their talents or ideas and relied on the leisurely browser for their living."[42] In the act of Jonson's *Every Man Out of His Humour* set in the aisle, Puntarvolo reads aloud a posted "bill" that barely conceals its sexual import: "If there be any lady or gentlewoman of good carriage that is desirous to entertain (to her private uses) a young, straight, and upright gentleman of the age of five- or six-and-twenty."[43] A gentleman usher was an euphemism for a woman's sexual partner; Puntarvolo and Carlo are depicted as fascinated by the notices, praising this one as "above measure excellent" (3.3.38). The second notice is for a gentleman who professes to teach the "most gentleman-like use of tobacco." Carlo and Puntarvolo promptly twist that to a sexual innuendo:

> *Carlo.* Well, I'll mark this fellow for Sogliardo's use presently.
> *Puntarvolo.* Or rather, Sogliardo, for his use. (3.2.56–57)[44]

Interestingly, there seems to have been more than mere advertisements pasted up in Paul's. In *The Wonderful Year* (1603), Thomas Dekker reprints some verses written on Queen Elizabeth's death. His prologue expresses fear of entering a "sea of censure," where he will be "pressed forth in shops and stalls, / Pasted in Paul's, and on the lawyers' walls, / For every basilisk-eyed critic's bait."[45] Although Dekker's meaning is rather obscure, the prologue seems to suggest that his elegiac verse will be pasted up in Paul's, as well as sold in bookshops. *Pilgrimage to Parnassus* makes a similar reference: Madido maintains that if he had a quart of "burnt sacke," he would be so inspired to write poems that "ere longe not a poste in Paul's churchyard but shall be acquainted with our writings."[46] There might even have been pictures accompanying such placards. In Ben Jonson's *Alchemist,* in the midst of a quarrel between Face and Subtle, Face threatens to "Write thee up bawd in Paul's," with all his tricks "told in red letters; and a face cut for thee, / Worse than Gamaliel Ratsey's."[47] Juliet Fleming in her study of early modern graffiti points out that red ochre is one of the media used in this period for writing on walls; she suggests Face threatens to draw a cartoon of Subtle's face on the walls of Paul's, labeling it bawd.[48] Paul's may not only have been a place to engage sexual favors; its very walls appear to have been adorned with bawdy pictures.

I would argue that everything from bawdy jokes to sexual activity appeared in the cathedral precisely because of the building's sacred coding. The transgressive overlap intensified the erotic quality of these transactions. The same delight lies behind the many early names for sex workers such as "Whitefriars nun" or "Wenches of the old religion."[49] Those who chose to walk in Paul's "to dine on Wit," as Speed has it, preferred their dinner to be a bawdy one, delighting in jests such as his, naming a doxy a "*Seeming Saint*" (sig. F4, G1).

Thus far I have discussed gentlemen battling religious services for control of the middle aisle. But as an emblematic cathedral, Paul's was also a focal point of religious revolution, as various sects tried to expound their views by turning Paul's into a stage. For example, two Quaker women entered the cathedral in 1662, during the service. One of them wore sackcloth, with a blackened face and blood in her hair. She threw blood on the altar, and they both ended up in Bridewell.[50] Quakers were a small minority in early modern England, but the battles that raged over performative aspects of the Anglican rite were far more wide-spread, and St. Paul's was crucial to a public communication of belief, whether the performer was Puritan, Anglican, or Quaker. Indeed, it has been argued that the Reformation began with the determination to redefine sacred spaces.[51]

As is often discussed, "Puritan" is an inadequate word that bunches together a number of factions; but one crucial aspect accepted by scholars is that Puritans were not separatists.[52] In other words, in contrast to those belonging to the Family of Love, Puritans did not seek to set up their own system of worship—and therefore Paul's was as important to Puritans as it was to Anglicans. In both cases, the cathedral was a crucial staging ground for theological belief. Traditional scholarship has argued that a primary concern of the Reformation was actually to "rid particular people, places and things of sanctity and sacred power," though this view has been modified in recent years.[53] I would argue that we should look not for rejection but for transformation. The cathedral offered a sacred sphere whose use was a matter of negotiation and contest, and like other sects, Puritans battled for control of St. Paul's.

In a geographical sense, the cathedral was the eye of the Puritanical hurricane, since Puritans lived around it, and the churches in the immediate vicinity, such as St. Antlings, were known as Puritan strongholds.[54] At the same time, Paul's was the face of the Anglican church, and the Liturgy of the Church of England was conducted daily with majestic emphasis. The fact that Paul's services were accompanied by organ music was feverishly denounced in early tracts. As D. Lupton said in his "character" of Paul's, "Puritaines are blowne out of the Church with the loud voice of the Organs, their zealous Spirits cannot indure the Musicke, nor the multitude of the Surplaces; because they are Relickes, (they say,) of *Romes* Superstition."[55] In fact, after a small fire destroyed the organ pipes, dissenters announced it was a judgment from heaven against the abominable music that defiled the church service.

One of the key sources of controversy was the open air pulpit at Paul's Cross, in the churchyard. Although appointment to that pulpit was made by the Bishop of London, the sermon often served as a vehicle for incendiary polemic. Bishop Sandys complained bitterly of trying to keep "fanatical spirits from the Cross"—and failing.[56] In the 1570s, for example, Edward Dering was appointed by Bishop Sandys to the pulpit, but he argued so fiercely for Puritan supremacy that he was removed in 1573.[57] Similarly, in 1609 William Holbrooke used the pulpit to attack those who would "vex" the godly; a few years later he was censured for nonconformity after a notable sermon in West Ham.[58] By 1625, it appears that the audience in the cathedral courtyard may have actually been actively hostile to non-Puritan preachers. That year Richard Montagu, later a bishop, wrote to John Cosin to dissuade him from preaching at Paul's Cross: "You cannot hold against the faction: strong, fierce, potent, especially there . . . I never came at the Cross. I never will. It should do no good but my body harm, my reputation hazard, my cause hurt. For the City, you know, furioso more calvinisat."[59] Montagu presumably understood that "furioso" well; he had published a pamphlet the previous year that incensed London's Puritan population so much that they complained directly to the king.

Thus if secular users of the cathedral reshaped it as sexualized place, predicated around the flaunting of masculinity, Puritan reformers tried to seize control in an equally powerful reproach of the Anglican church. Sexualized masculinity came into direct confrontation with religious practice. It is this potent combination that I argue echoes through the play, *The Puritan*. The complicated, overlapping codes of Paul's cathedral—as a religious and a sexualized space—overflow into the play, written specifically for the boys' theater attached to the cathedral and performed by them in 1606.[60]

One of the characteristic aspects of the repertory of the Paul's boys' company is its sexual explicitness.[61] The parallel boys' company in the Blackfriars constantly flirted with the danger of offending the very nobility who thronged its audience. But the Paul's boys walked a different kind of edge—a sexually titillating, dangerous edge that,

I would argue, fed from the same transgressive juxtaposition of sex and devotion that characterized the Cathedral itself in the early 1600s. *The Puritan* depicts the streets and churches around the cathedral as morally degenerative, even as they are acknowledged to be the bailiwick of a Puritan population. The play is clearly pitched at the audience walking the middle aisle of "*Gods house*," in that it presents a sharp divide between young, witty characters and those with any sort of religious faith. Paul Yachnin has described Paul's boys' imagined audience as "a version of the sociocultural field, whose high center was urban, gentlemanly-but not courtly-cultural production and reception."[62] Paul's walkers were certainly urban, but not necessarily aristocratic or powerful. In fact, Guilpin's satire on Paul's walk follows the description of Mistress Minkes with a "troupe of puisnes [younger sons, inferiors] from the play, / Laughing like wanton schoole-boyes all the way" (163–64).

The Puritan is tailor-made for young men with a humor for "wanton" jokes. The play opens as Lady Widow-Plus, the Puritan of Watling Street, enters in mourning for her husband, "the sweetest Husband that euer lay by woman."[63] She grieves because "nothing was so hot, nor too deere for mee," and in reverence to the memory of her husband, she swears never again to entertain "the carnall suite of Man" (sig. A4). From the first moment, the play revels in the clash between erotic and religious language. "Carnal" is used here in its sexual meaning, as in Thomas Wilson's 1533 "wedlocke and carnal copulation." But the word frequently occurs in contexts that pit it against a spiritual opposite, as in Milton's description of false fruit as "carnal desire inflaming." The Widow's vow is inflected by the *Oxford English Dictionary*'s specific definition, "not spiritual, in a negative sense."[64]

When the Widow weeps her way home from her husband's funeral, her eldest daughter, Franke, promptly seconds her mother's vow to avoid carnality. But the Widow's younger daughter, Mall, is horrified:

> I lou'd my father well too; but to say,
> Nay now, I would not marry for her death? [*sic*]
> Sure I should speake false Lattin; should I not?
> Ide as soone vow neuer to come in Bed.
> Tut? Women must liue by th'quick, and not by th'dead. (sig. A4v)

Mall's speech is ripe with double entendres: coming in bed, living by the quick (or priapic) rather than by its opposite. Mall later repeats the last pun, reiterating: "when I spend one teare for a dead Father, I could giue twenty kisses for a quick husband" (sig. A4v).

The connections between this speech and the cathedral next door would have been immediately caught by its audience. Mall's speech burlesques the Nicene Creed, explicitly referring to the version contained in the 1559 Book of Common Prayer, which was designated to be read at all services, from Eucharist to morning and evening prayer, by the minister together with the people. This English version was adopted under Edward VI; an example of St. Paul's Cathedral's symbolic weight is the fact that the English service came into use in the cathedral *before* the Act of Uniformity, which decreed use of the Book of Common Prayer and made the use of Latin illegal, was passed in 1549 by Edward's Second Parliament. This brief history is complicated by the fact that the Book of Common Prayer itself was controversial among Puritans preachers, who regularly refused to use sections of it and found themselves in ecclesiastical courts defending their abbreviations or rearranging of the proscribed prayers.[65]

The Creed reads as follows:

> I beleeue in God the Father Almighty, maker of heauen and earth: and in Jesus Christ his onely Sonne Our Lord, which was conceiued by the holy Ghost, borne of the Virgine Mary, suffered vnder Ponce Pylate, was crucified dead and buried, he descended into hell. The third day he rose againe from the dead. He ascended into Heauen, and sitteth on the right hand of God the Father Almighty. From thence he shall come to iudge the quicke and the dead. I beleeue in the holy Ghost, the holy Catholique Chuch, the Communion of Saints, the forgiuenesse of sinnes, the resurrection of the body, and the life euerlasting. Amen.[66]

Mall's speech bursts into parody of the very services taking place in the cathedral. In her hands, "quick" is no theological term for a living body, but a priapic pun aimed at the lively, standing man himself. The speech draws its transgressive force from the conjunction of erotic appreciation of the male body and religious observance, very similar to the kind of effect I have been describing in relation to the middle aisle.

I also find it interesting that the line "where I spend one teare for a dead Father, I could giue twenty kisses for a quick husband" capitalizes Father, although the earlier reference is uncapped. Quite possibly this simply reflects printer carelessness, but it lends itself as support of a reading of the speech as a far more revolutionary intervention into the concept of dead father/undead Father. Yet I would not say that we could read "dead Father" as coterminous with "Father Almighty," no matter how tempting it is to think of nuns "who would not marry for [his] death." Interestingly, later in the play, a character named for a Puritan church refuses to steal "for mine owne Father," with the reference capitalized (sig. C2). *The Puritan* is specifically referred to in a sermon preached from the Cross in 1609; William Crashawe disparages the "continuall prophanesse in their phrases, and sometime Atheisme and blaphemie."[67] But even given that Crashawe was referring specifically to *The Puritan*, variations on his attack appear in other Puritan fulminations against the theater in general. In 1611, for example, Robert Bolton preached a sermon at the Cross that maintained plays contain "Oathes, Blasphemies, Obscenities, and the abusing sometimes of the most pretious things in the booke of God, whereat wee should tremble, to most base and scurrill iests."[68]

Thus rather than overreading the passage, I would suggest that Mall's speech would simply burst on the ear as a cluster of religiously inflected jokes. The question of who is speaking "false Lattin," for example, mocks the religious services next door with the same insolent aplomb with which the Paul's Walkers strolled the middle aisle during a service. Crucially, of course, Latin was the distinctive characteristic of the Catholic Church. Therefore, Catholic prayers were condemned for not being "spirituall," as Andrew Willet wrote in 1602, calling "popish latine praiers" no more than "lip-labour," contrary to the Protestant emphasis on English.[69] Specifically *false* Latin seems to bracket the religiously inflected use of the language (since it remained the language of legal courts and universities). Of course, the Latin Mass prevailed before King Edward's reign, and again during Queen Mary's reign. English was only restored by Queen Elizabeth in 1558. But more importantly, by 1600 religious Latin was a trigger point for both Anglicans and Puritans. It heralded rejection of a religion in which people did not understand the primary language, invoking, as a 1624 sermon had it, "*chanteries* for *superstition* in an *vknowne tongue*."[70]

Significantly, the play mocks Catholic ideas with the same fervency with which it mocks the Creed. The scholar, Pyeboard, comes to the Widow and tells her that due to "certaine spirituall Intelligence," he has discovered that her husband is in Purgatory. The Widow responds with fervor to this Catholic idea: "Purgatorie? tuh; that word deserues to bee spit vpon; I wonder that a man of sober toung, as you seeme to be, should haue the folly to beleeue there's such a place" (sig. D1). But Pyeboard convinces her that his information was gained "Metaphysically, and by a super-naturall intelligence" (sig. D1). To an early modern Englishman, the question of Purgatory and Latin is tied closely together. Willet characterized Catholic doctrine as "fuller of vables and dreames, then any religion in the world beside: so they drame of purgatorie fire" (45).

The Widow protests that her husband kept Church, "and e'en for Religious hast," went ungartered "to get a good seate at an afternoone Sermon" (sig. Dlv). Pyeboard sharply critiques that reasoning: "hee thought it Sanctity ynough, if he had kild a Man, so tad beene done in a Pue... Oh,—a Sermon's a fine short cloake of an houre long, and will hide the vpper-part of a dissembler" (sig. Dlv). Here we have a ruthless destabilization of the "seeming" sanctity of religious practice, particularly that of Puritans: "Church, I, he seem'd al Church, & his coscience was as hard as the Pulpit!" (sig. Dlv). But along with that destabilization, we have a further transference of people *into* churches: "he seem'd al Church."

That "Church" is perplexingly both Catholic and Puritan.[71] After Nicholas steals the Sir Godfrey's chain, for example, Godfrey wails that he "oft told it oeer at my praiers" (sig. D4). The fact that all three thousand links are made of gold ties Catholic prayer with Puritan practice, since the sect was famously criticized for greed. Yet rosaries were outlawed with the Royal Injunctions of 1538, and by the 1590s possession of rosary beads was grounds for imprisonment.[72] At the same time, rosaries were clearly still in use, albeit secretly; the Jesuit Henry Garnet published *The Society of the Rosary* on his own press in 1593. And telling prayers by beads appears to have occurred in St. Paul's Cathedral as well as privately. Samuel Speed notes that "Some with their Beads unto a Pillar croud" (sig. Flv). Anne Dillon argues that it would be a mistake to see references to rosaries in the final decade of Elizabeth's reign as "merely a spiritual remnant of pre-Reformation times." In fact, she argues, the rosary was a "subtle piece of Counter-Reformation social and spiritual engineering."[73] There is nothing subtle about Sir Godfrey's golden rosary. Its spiritual engineering, so to speak, seems to imbricate Puritan and Catholic practice. Later in the play when Godfrey and his nephew are afraid a devil will burst through the door, they strew "Godlies zealous works" [surely Puritan tracts] outside. But the nephew adds, "Ile teare two or three rosaries in pieces, and strew the leaues about the Chamber" (sig. G2v). Again Catholic and Puritans are invoked at once.

Mall's offhand comment about "false Lattin" offers another example of the joint indictment, in its attention to language. Puritans were often criticized for being overly precise in their use of English, a characteristic invoked in a subplot when the Widow's servingman,

Nicholas, agrees to "nim," though he would never "steal" (sig. C1v). Latin is specifically used in the play as a device to dazzle the foolish, as when Captain Oath, pretending to raise a devil, gibbers Latin-like words gathered from Apothecary labels. As Frances Dolan has pointed out, "Latin was the language of witchcraft, incantation, Catholic prayer, and other superstitious and residual practices."[74]

The Widow has three serving-men: Nicholas St. Antlings, Simon St. Mary-Overies, and Frailty. In act one they enter, identified as "*the Widdow Puritaines Servingman*...in black scurvy mourning coates, and Bookes at their Girdles, *as comming from Church* (sig. B2v). Frailty is, of course, a typically Puritan name. But Nicolas and Simon are actually named after Puritan churches. St. Antlings was in Watling Street, a few blocks from the cathedral, and St. Mary Overies was in Southwark (*over* the river). Notably, the Widow is surnamed the "Widow of Watling Street," tying her to the same church, and when she plans to marry in act five, she heads to St. Antlings. St. Antlings was famous for a Puritan lecture series that began in 1599 and daily gathered devout Londoners. Sir William Dugdale called the church a "grand nursery" of "seditious preachers," and Valerie Pearl names it the "most notable Puritan endowment in the City."[75] The parish of St. Mary Ovaries was equally famous for its Puritan preaching. It was later renamed St. Saviour's, and then Southwark Cathedral.

As I noted earlier, the Puritan preacher William Crashawe referred directly to *The Puritan* in a sermon preached from Paul's Cross on December 3, 1609, which condemned the players for bringing "religion and holy things vpon the stage."[76] He seizes on the servants' names as the heart of the play's theological, sexual contestation:

> Two hypocrites must be brought foorth; and how shall they be described but by these names, Nicolas S. Antlings, Simon S. Maryoveries? Thus hypocrisie a child of hell must beare the names of two Churches of God, and two wherein Gods name is called on publikely every day in the yeere, and in one of them his blessed word preached everie day (an example scarce matchable in the world): yet these two, wherin Gods name is thus glorified, and our Church and State honoured, shall bee by these miscreants thus dishonoured, and that not on the stage only, but even in print.[77]

With Nicholas and Simon, we see the literal creation of place from space. The characters *are* churches, a construction that is particularly vivid when their entire name is invoked. For example, on being asked to steal, Nicholas retorts: "no, it shal nere bee sayd, that *Nicholas* Saint Tantlings committed Bird-lime!" (sig. C1). Middleton has taken two

Puritan churches and (with recalcitrant force) transformed the sacred to the sexual, not to mention the dead to the quick. On meeting the servants, Corporal Oath immediately renames them "halfe-Christned *Katomites,* you vngod-mothererd Varlets" (sig. B3). The servants are only *half* Christian, and un-godmothered, which implies unbaptized. Further, they are catomites, or boys kept for the pleasure of men. Oath regularly refers to them with religiously inflected insults such as "Puritanicall Scrape-shoes" (sig. B3) and "Holy-paring, religious outside thou" (sig. B3v). If churches were seen metaphorically as the body of Christ (as cited earlier, in terms of the cathedral), these two churches undergo a transgressive reformulation into sexualized, foolish, males. At the end of the play when Nicholas's theft is discovered, Skirmish's identification seems particularly pointed: "he that will not sweare, but lie, he that will not steale, But rob: pure *Nicholas Saint Antlings*" (sig. H3v).

From the point of view of a humanist geographer, the creation of place as a person is fascinating. The play picks up the tension embodied in the cathedral between spiritual and sexual and reshapes it into an actual character, who is a religious place. Yet if *The Puritan* comments on the bitter tension between Puritans and walkers, to name two factions, it also comments on its own ability to recreate place within the theater. The play takes the "accretional layers of gossip and song, oral history, written history, essays and poems" that make up a place (to quote Tuan once again) and reforms them into a hybrid person/place. The fact that Nicholas refers, apparently, to the preacher of the church he embodies, thickens his likeness to the actual structure: "our Parson railes against Plaiers mightily I can tell you, because they brought him drunck vpp'oth Stage once,—as hee will bee horribly druncke" (sig. C1v).[78]

The theatrical heart of the play is Corporal Oath's conjuration of a sulpherous, Latin-speaking devil from Hell. In one sense, the characters' belief in the devil's presence ridicules religious beliefs of any kind. But on another level, the devil also stands for the theater's ability to control space in a way that Paul's cathedral cannot. Pyeboard specifically instructs Captain Oath to act in a theatrical fashion while "playing" the devil: "haue you neuer seene a stalking-stamping Player, that will raise a tempest with his toung, and thunder with his heeles?" (sig. F2). In the conclusion of *The Puritan,* devils and false Latin are rejected in favor of sober, middle-class matrimony. The Christian framework—whether adhered to by Puritans or Catholics—is ridiculed and dismissed. Earlier in the play, Captain Oath worried whether "in this false coniuration, a true Deuill should pop vp indeed," but

Pyeboard laughed at him: "A true Deuill, Captaine, why there was nere such a one, nay faith hee that has this place, is as false a Knaue as our last Church-warden" (sig. F2v). No devil—or Christian—cannot be created by players, as Frailty tells the Widow about Captain Oath: "if you saw him once, youde take him to be a Christian" (sig. G1v).

But the same is not true of the uncontrollable space of St. Paul's, where the profane walkers brushed shoulders with worshippers, and no one was able to banish them. As King James himself put it on October 28, 1618, "And that he may have nothing elce to feare / Let him walke Pauls, and meet the Devills there."[79]

Notes

1. The Bishop of London, *A Sermon at Paules Crosse, on Behalfe of Pavles Church.* March 26, 1620 (London, 1620), 42. According to the Clergy of the Church of England database, the Bishop of London in 1620 was John King, who served from 1611 to 1621.
2. "Punk" was early modern slang for a female sex worker; the linguistic turn "Puritan turned Punk" comes from *The Isle of Gulls.* This pleasing alliteration led to numerous popular jests along those lines.
3. Enno Ruge makes the argument that Paul's "was the symbol of many things but very probably not of the authority of the Church or its high moral standards." Bishop Pilkington, 1560, qtd. Henry B. Wheatley, *London: Past and Present*, III (London: John Murray, 1891), 64; Ruge, "Preaching and Playing at Paul's: The Puritans, *The Puritaine*, and the Closure of Paul's Playhouse," in *Censorship and Cultural Regulation in the Modern Age*, ed. Beate Müller (Amsterdam: Rodopi, 2004), 43.
4. I would argue that the cathedral's domination of London, in a social and spiritual sense, was not significantly diminished by its deteriorating physical state. The steeple was long gone by 1609, and yet the church remained a focus of royal ceremony and a tourist attraction; Dekker's *"Paules Steeples complaint"* (in *Dead Tearme*) insists that every stranger looks to Paul's but feels no pity "because to them it [the damage] appears sleight, or else it appears to them nothing at all." Dekker, *The Dead Tearme*, in *The Non-Dramatic Works of Thomas Dekker*, vol. 4, ed. Alexander B. Grosart, 5 vols. (New York: Russell & Russell, 1963), 44.
5. The theater was housed in the almonry, the north wall of which was the south wall of the cathedral nave. The playhouse was on the second floor, likely on the north end of the almonry. It was extremely small, even for a private theater. Its early modern history begins in 1550, with singing boys' performances organized by their master, Sebastian Westcott. They began playing publicly in around 1575; their last play was performed in the summer of 1606. See *English*

Professional Theatre, 1530–1660, ed. Glynne Wickham, Herbert Barry, and William Ingram (Cambridge: Cambridge University Press, 2000), 306–19.

6. The distinction is obviously delicate, given that every "space" has seemingly the potential to be a "place." There is a vast bibliography on the subject, much of it stemming from the philosopher Henri Lefebvre's influential work. Humanist geographers have extended and altered Lefebvre's ideas. In addition to the work noted elsewhere in this chapter, I found the following particularly useful: Lefebvre, *The Production of Space*, trans. Donald Nicholson-Smith (Malden, MA: Blackwell, 1991); Linda McDowell, "The Transformation of Cultural Geography," in *Human Geography: Society, Space, and Social Science*, ed. Derek Gregory, Ron Martin, and Graham Smith (Minneapolis: University of Minnesota Press, 1994), 146–73; Susan J. Smith, "Practicing Humanistic Geography," *Annals of the Association of American Geographers* 74 (1984): 353–74; J. Nicholas Entrikin, *The Betweenness of Place: Toward a Geography of Modernity* (Baltimore: Johns Hopkins University Press, 1991).
7. Yu-Fu Tuan, "Language and the Making of Place: A Narrative-Descriptive Approach," *Annals of the Association of American Geographers* 81 (1991): 692.
8. Cara Aitchison, "New Cultural Geographies: The Spatiality of Leisure, Gender and Sexuality," *Leisure Studies* 18 (1999): 19.
9. For an excellent collection of essays on the history of the cathedral, see *St. Paul's: The Cathedral Church of London, 604–2004*, ed. Derek Keene (New Haven, CT: Yale University Press, 2004). Frances Dolan approaches this question from a different direction by asking "how were Catholics the products and producers of distinctive physical, ideological, and symbolic spaces?" Dolan notes that the reformation "fundamentally, shifted the cultural meanings and uses of places." See "Gender and the 'Lost' Spaces of Catholicism," *Journal of Interdisciplinary History* XXXII (2002): 644, 641.
10. Henry Farley, "The Complaint of Pavles, to All Christian Soules" (London, 1616), 21, 27.
11. Lefebvre, *The Production of Space*, 26.
12. The Bishop of London, *A Sermon at Paules Crosse*, 34.
13. Ronald Davidson, "Recalcitrant Space: Modeling Variation in Humanistic Geography," *Journal of Cultural Geography* 25 (2008): 161–80.
14. Carl B. Estabrook, "Ritual, Space, and Authority in Seventeenth-Century English Cathedral Cities," *Journal of Interdisciplinary History* XXXII (2002): 619.
15. John Donne, "The Feast of Dedication, Celebrated at Lincolnes Inne, in a Sermon thereupon *Ascension Day*" (London, 1623), 38.
16. Samuel Speed, "The Legend of Duke Humphrey," *Fragmenta Carceris: or, The Kings-Bench Scuffle* (London, 1675), sig. F1.

17. Edward Sharpham, *The Discouerie of the Knights of the Poste* (London: G.S., 1597), sig. D4.
18. Gabriel Harvey, *Fovre Letters, and Certaine Sonnets* (London, 1592), 38.
19. The *Guls Horne-Booke* seems to confirm a twice-daily visit, instructing his gull to walk the main aisle from eleven until two, reappearing in new clothing after dinner for a turn or two. Those who had no money were definitely at risk of pick-pocketers; Darryll Grantley's study of London and early modern drama characterizes the middle aisle as "yet another of London's ambivalent spaces: a social place, but also a place of legal business, and of criminal risk." Grantley, *London in Early Modern English Drama: Representing the Built Environment* (New York: Palgrave Macmillan, 2008), 127.
20. The location of 1.1 of *Michaelmas Term* is not marked, but it has been identified by editors due to the mention of "bills"; the play was staged at Paul's. *Your Five Gallants* was first performed at the Blackfriars, and *Every Man out of his Humor* at the Globe.
21. Queen Elizabeth's proclamation, qtd. Milman, *Annals of St. Paul's Cathedral* (London: John Murray, 1868), 285; King Charles, *Domestic State Papers, Charles I*, ccxiv, f. 94. ccxxix f.116. Milman (a one-time dean of St. Paul's) noted that the frequent reenactment of the laws responded to their ineffectiveness. Milman, *Annals*, 285. St. Paul's was not alone in battling this sort of activity, John Lee, the prebendary of Calne, complained in 1634 that "Men, both of the better and meaner sort, mechanicks, youths and prentises do ordinarily and most unreverently walk in our church in the tyme of divine service and within hearing of the same, with their hats on their heads." "Archbishop Laud's visitation of Salisbury in 1634," qtd. John Craig, "Psalms, Groans and Dogwippers: The Soundscape of Worship in the Early Paris Church, 1547–1642," in *Sacred Space in Early Modern Europe*, ed. Will Coster and Andrew Spicer (Cambridge: Cambridge University Press, 2005), 123. For a discussion of disruptive behavior in European churches, ranging from bawdy singing to smells of rotting meat, see Sarah Hamilton and Andrew Spicer, "Defining the Holy: The Delineation of Sacred Space," in *Defining the Holy: Sacred Space in Medieval and Early Modern Europe*, ed. Andrew Spicer and Sarah Hamilton (London: Ashgate, 2005), 10–13.
22. Qtd. John Brand, *Observations on the Popular Antiquities of Great Britain*, vol. 3 (London: Bell & Daldy, 1872), 387.
23. "Death's Dance," qtd. William Sparrow Simpson, *Gleanings from Old Paul's* (London: Elliot Stock, 1889), 269.
24. Thomas Adams, "The Gallants Burdens: A Sermon Preached at Pavles Crosse" (London, 1612), 5.
25. Thomas Adams, "The Barren Tree: A Sermon Preached at *Pauls* Crosse," Appendix 4, in *Records of Early English Drama: Ecclesiastical London,* ed. Mary C. Erler (British Library, 2008), 276–77.

26. See chap. 5 in particular. Amanda Bailey, *Flaunting: Style and the Subversive Male Body in Renaissance England* (Toronto: University of Toronto Press, 2007).
27. Ibid., 116.
28. The activity in Paul's confirms Gustav Ungerer's assessment that "The sexual geography of London can…no longer be consigned to the outer borders of the civil space, the red-light districts, the suburbs, the spaces beyond, as literary representations, among them Shakespeare's plays, make us believe." For an overview of various sexual orientations from a geographical point-of-view, see *Mapping Desire: Geographies of Sexualities*, ed. David Bell and Gill Valentine (London: Routledge, 1995); Ungerer, "Prostitution in Late Elizabethan London," *Medieval and Renaissance Drama in England*, 15 (London: Associated University Presses, 2003), 141.
29. John Earle, "Portrait 61," *Microcosmography, or A Piece of the World Discovered in Essays and Characters,* ed. Harold Osborne (London: University Tutorial, 1933).
30. The same move from charges of profane behavior to charges of brothelry can be seen in a consecration sermon preached in 1625 for a new chapel at Exeter College. John Prideaux, the Rector of Exeter, focused on the "chiefest *vse*" of sacred spaces. God's House must be "peculiar" rather than "common," he argued, not "an *Ild-hall* for *playes* or *pleadings*; or a *shop* for merchandice; or a *cloyster* for idle-walkers; or a *gallery* for pleasure; or a *banqueting-house* for riot; much lesse a *brothel* for wantonnesse." John Prideaux, "A Sermon Preached on the Fifth of October 1624, at the Consecration of St. James Chappel in *Exeter Colledge*" (Oxford: John Lichfield and William Turner, 1625), sig. A2. For a discussion and list of all consecrations between 1600 and 1649, see Andrew Spicer, " 'God Will Have a House': Defining Sacred Space and Rites of Consecration in Early Seventeenth-Century England," *Defining the Holy*, 207–30.
31. Thomas Dekker, *The Guls Hornbook,* in *The Non-Dramatic Works of Thomas Dekker*, ed. Alexander B. Grosart, vol. 2 (New York: Russell & Russell, 1963), 230, 233.
32. Thomas Middleton, *Your Five Gallants*, in *Thomas Middleton: The Collected Works*, ed. Gary Taylor and John Lavagnino (Oxford: Clarendon Press, 2007), 4.4.31–33.
33. See Bailey's study of the aisle for examination of its queer resonances, the way the men effectively sold their bodies and beauties. Bailey, *Flaunting*. Thomas Middleton, *Michaelmas Term*, in *The Works of Thomas Middleton,* vol. 1, ed. A. H. Bullen, 8 vols. (Boston: Houghton Mifflin, 1885–86), 1.1.124–25, 127–29, 131–33.
34. J. H. "Characters: A Curtezan," in *The Hovse of Correction: or, Certayne Satyricall Epigrams* (London, 1619), sig. D2v.
35. Dekker, *The Dead Tearme*, in *Non-Dramatic Works of Thomas Dekker*, 51.

36. Everard Guilpin, "Satire V," "Skialetheia or A Shadowe of Truth," in *Certaine Epigrams and Satyres*, ed. D. Allen Carroll (Chapel Hill: University of North Carolina Press, 1974), 159–61.
37. Wallace Shugg points out that not only had prostitutes "invaded the sacred precincts of St. Pauls' itself," but the area around Paul's was a resort as well. The nearby Ave Maria Alley was frequented by sex workers since the first decade of the sixteenth century. "Prostitution in Shakespeare's London," *Shakespeare Studies* X (1977): 300.
38. See *The Oxford English Dictionary*, definition "copesmate" 3b; "cope," 1b, 2 (Oxford University Press, 2008).
39. Paul Griffiths, "Prostitution in Elizabethan London," *Continuity and Change* 8 (1993): 55.
40. Thomas Dekker and John Webster, *Westward Ho!*, in *The Dramatic Works of Thomas Dekker*, vol. 2, ed. Fredson Bowers (Cambridge: Cambridge University Press, 1955), 2.1.220–23.
41. Ned Ward, *The London Spy*, ed. Paul Hyland (East Lansing, MI: Colleagues Press, 1993), 86.
42. As is frequently quoted in relation to Paul's, Shakespeare's Falstaff maintains that he bought Bardolph in Paul's, with the implication that only poor servants are found there, since his comparison is finding a wife in the stews or the brothels. William Shakespeare, *2 Henry IV*, in *The Riverside Shakespeare*, 2nd edition, ed. G. Blakemore Evans (Boston and New York: Houghton Mifflin), 1.2.52. Roze Hentschell, " 'The Peruser of everie mans works': Reading the Reader in St. Paul's Precinct" (conference paper, Modern Language Association, Chicago, IL, December 2007).
43. Ben Jonson, *Every Man Out of His Humor*, ed. Helen Ostovich (Manchester: Manchester University Press, 2001) 3.1.123–26. Ostovich's notes explicate the bawdy suggestiveness of both advertisements.
44. As per Eric Partridge in *Shakespeare's Bawdy*: "use (Of a man) to copulate with, to be sexually intimate with." (London: Routledge, 1947), 274.
45. Thomas Dekker, *The Wonderfull Yeare*, 1603, vol. 1, in *The Non-Dramatic Works of Thomas Dekker*, 34.
46. *The Pilgrimage to Parnassus*, in *The Pilgrimage to Parnassus with the Two Parts of the Return from Parnassus*, ed. William Dunn Macray (Oxford: Oxford University Press, 1886), 2.1.222–24.
47. Ben Jonson, *The Alchemist*, in *Ben Jonson*, vol. 5, ed. C. H. Herford and Percy and Evelyn Simpson, 11 vols. (Oxford: Clarendon Press, 1925–63), 1.1.93.
48. Juliet Fleming, "Graffiti, Grammatology, and the Age of Shakespeare," in *Renaissance Culture and the Everyday*, ed. Patricia Fumerton and Simon Hunt (Philadelphia: University of Pennsylvania, 1992), 332.
49. Dekker, *Dead Tearme*, 58.

50. From "A Brief Relation of the Persecutions and Cruelties that have been acted upon the People called QUAKERS...," 1662, qtd. Simpson, *Gleanings from Old Paul's*, 284.
51. Richard C. McCoy, *Alterations of State: Sacred Kingship in the English Revolution* (New York: Columbia University Press, 2002), 2.
52. See Lawrence A. Sasek, introduction to *Images of English Puritanism: A Collection of Contemporary Sources, 1589–1646* (Baton Rouge: Louisiana State University Press, 1989), 13.
53. John Craig, "Psalms, Groans and Dog-wippers: The Soundscape of Worship in the Early Parish Church, 1547–1642," in Coster and Spicer, *Sacred Space in Early Modern Europe*, 104. See also Will Coster and Andrew Spicer, "Introduction: The Dimensions of Sacred Space in Reformation Europe," *Sacred Space*, 5; Paul S. Seaver, *The Puritan Lectureships: The Politics of Religious Dissent 1560–1662* (Stanford: Stanford University Press, 1970), 15–54.
54. Those referred to under the term "Puritan" were clearly a disparate group, and even early modern satirical texts, such as Oliver Ormerod's 1606 *The Picture of a Puritane*, which argues that "puritans have in sundry things joined with the *Pharisees, Apostolics, Aerians, Pepuzians, Petrobrusians, Florinians, Cerinthians, Nazarens, Beguardines, Ebionites, Catobabdites, Cathedrists, Enthusiasts, Donatist, Jovianist, Brownists* and *Papists*" highlight the difficulty of assembling those with incongruent beliefs under one label. Ormerod, *The Picture of a Puritane*, in *Images of English Puritanism*, 242.
55. Donald Lupton, *London and the Country Carbonadoed and Quartred Into Severall Characters*, 1632, qtd. William Sparrow Simpson, *Gleanings from Old Paul's*, 227.
56. Seaver, *Puritan Lectureships*, 59.
57. See Ibid., 24,60.
58. See Ibid., 83.
59. Qtd. Seaver, *The Puritan Lectureships*, 54. Seaver also quotes a Montagu description of Puritans as "riff-raff rascals" and "Allobrogical dormice," 22.
60. Published in 1607 as written by W. S., the play was erroneously attributed to Shakespeare until finally established as Thomas Middleton's work. The controversy over authorship of this play has included those who insist that Middleton could not have written the play due to his own Puritan leanings. Paul Yachnin offered a resounding riposte to this biographical arguments in "Reversal of Fortune: Shakespeare, Middleton, and the Puritans," *ELH* 70 (2003): 757–86.
61. *Michaelmas Term* is another Paul's play that includes a startling array of bawdy material.
62. Yachnin, "Reversal of Fortune," 766.
63. *The Puritan, or the Widow of Watling Street*, ed. John S. Farmer (London: Tudor Facsimile Texts, 1911), sig. A4.

64. All quotations cited under "carnal," #3 (adj), *Oxford English Dictionary.*
65. See Martin Ingram, "Puritans and the Church Courts, 1560–1640, in *The Culture of English Puritanism, 1560–1700* (New York: St. Martin's Press, 1996), 80–88.
66. A PDF of the 1559 Book of Common Prayer, or third revision for the Anglican church, can be found on the Web site of the Anglican church. The 1559 version is slightly less "Protestant" than the 1552 version (also available on the Web site), but the Nicene Creed differs only in matters of punctuation and spelling. http://justus.anglican.org/resources/bcp/1559/BCP_1559.htm
67. William Crashawe, "The Sermon Preached at the Crosse, Feb. xiiii, 1607," Appendix 4, *Records of Early English Drama: Ecclesiastical London,* ed. Mary C. Erler (London: British Library, 2008), 268.
68. Robert Bolton, "A Discovrse Abovt the State of Trve Happinesse," Appendix 4, *Records of Early English Drama: Ecclesiastical London,* ed. Mary C. Erler (London: British Library, 2008), 271.
69. See Françoise Waquet, *Latin or the Empire of a Sign: From the Sixteenth to the Twentieth Centuries*, ed. John Howe (London: Verso, 2001), 41–79; Andrew Willet, *A Catholicon* (John Legat for Simon Waterion, 1602), 133–134.
70. Prideaux, "A Sermon," sig. D1.
71. Donna B. Hamilton points out that Middleton's plot "manages, in the same actions, to satirize Puritans while also representing those Catholic practices which Protestants most abhorred." Introduction to *The Puritan*, in *Thomas Middleton: The Collected Works*, ed. Gary Taylor and John Lavagnino (Oxford: Clarendon Press, 2007), 510.
72. See Anne Dillon, "Praying by Number: The Confraternity of the Rosary and the English Catholic Community, *c.*1580–1700," *History* 88 (2003): 453–54.
73. Ibid., 471.
74. Fran Dolan, *Whores of Babylon: Catholicism, Gender, and Seventeenth-Century Print Culture* (Ithaca, NY: Cornell University Press, 1999), 26.
75. Dugdale, qtd. Edward Holdsworth Sugden, *A Topographical Dictionary to the Works of Shakespeare and His Fellow Dramatists* (Manchester: Manchester University Press, 1925), under Antony, Saint; Valerie Pearl, *London and the Outbreak of the Puritan Revolution* (Oxford: Oxford University Press, 1961), 79.
76. Crashawe, "The Sermon Preached at the Crosse," 268.
77. Ibid.
78. Pyboard rails against "Maister Pigman" and "Maister Ful-bellie," generally taken to stand for Nicholas Fenton and William Symonds, preachers at St. Antholins and St. Mary Overies. Enno Ruge has argued that the two churches were chosen not because of any radical Puritan bent, but because they were close to playhouses (St. Antholins

to Paul's and St. Mary Overies, in Southwark, to a number of public playhouses). Ruge, "Preaching and Playing at Paul's," 52–53.

79 "King James on the blazeing starr: Octo: 28: 1618," Bodleian MS Rawl. Poet. 84, fol. 72r, line 18–19. Early Stuart Libels Web site: http://www.earlystuartlibels.net/htdocs/spanish_match_section/Ni1.html.

Chapter 5

"To what bawdy house doth your Maister belong?": Barbers, Bawds, and Vice in the Early Modern London Barbershop

Mark Albert Johnston

In early modern London, barbers—who represented only a small fraction of a multifarious array of health practitioners operating in and around the city by the beginning of the seventeenth century—competed in a medical marketplace that historians have suggested was highly sensitive to patient demand.[1] Margaret Pelling has argued, moreover, that to compete in that market, English barber-surgeons were routinely engaged in considerable occupational diversity, activity we should regard "not...as an indication that there was a low level of demand for medical advice" but, on the contrary, as confirmation that there was "consistently high demand for medical services...probably at every level of society, and irrespective of the usual criteria of effectiveness."[2] By the beginning of the seventeenth century, as the number of Londoners diagnosed with venereal disease rose, unprecedented numbers of the urban sick began to demand treatments and the market, in turn, responded to meet that rising demand.[3] Offering London's male population congregation, fraternization, and fellowship, together with a variety of medical and cosmetic services and products, the early modern barber and his shop functioned as cultural palimpsests that contradictorily signaled both pleasure and pain, health and contagion, licit and illicit activity.[4]

In Philip Stubbes's *The Second Part of the Anatomy of Abuses* (London, 1583), Amphilogus catalogues the techniques London barbers were apt to employ in their efforts to increase the amount of money that their clients would be willing to part with in late sixteenth-century barbershops in Ailgna (*Anglia* spelled backward, or *England*): "they [the barbers] have invented such strange fashions and monstrous maners of cuttings, trimmings, shavings, and washings, that you would wonder to see," he marvels.[5] For, besides offering their customers "cuts innumerable" (sig. G8v) for the hair of the head and beard, barbers in Elizabethan and Jacobean London added stylistic flourishes to their bathing, shaving, and polling routines and commonly offered a wildly diverse assortment of (mostly cosmetic or curative) supplemental products and services for purchase:

> when they [i.e., the barbers] come to the cutting of the haire, what snipping & snapping of the cycers is there, what tricking, and trimming, what rubbing what scratching, what combing and clawing, what tickling & toying, and al to tawe out mony you may be sure. And when they come to washing, oh how gingerly they behave themselves therein. For then shalt your mouth be bossed [bussed, or kissed] with the lather, or fome that riseth of the balles (for they have their sweete balles wherewith they use to washe) your eyes closed must be anointed therewith also. Then snap go the fingers, ful bravely, god wot. Thus this tragedy ended comes me warme clothes to wipe and dry him withal, next the eares must be picked, and closed together againe artificially forsooth. The haire of the nostrils cut away, and every thing done in order comely to behold. The last action in this tragedie is the payment of the monie...You shall also have your orient perfumes for your nose, your fragrant waters for your face, wherewith you shall bee all to besprinkled: your musicke againe, and pleasant harmonie shall sound in your ears, and all to tickle the same with vaine delight. And in the end your cloke shall be brushed, and God be with you Gentleman....[T]hey are maisters of their science that can invent al these knacks to get money withal. But yet I must needs say (these nisities set apart) barbers are verie necessarie, for otherwise men should grow verie ougglisom and deformed, and their haire would in processe of time overgrowe their faces, rather like monsters, than comlie sober Christians. (sig. G8v–H1v)

Amphilogus's reproof rehearses only a fraction of the potential services supplementary to cutting and shaving hair that were being offered by early modern barbers—washing or bathing, ear-picking, and perfuming—which commonly also included (but were by no means limited to) coloring, curling, styling, and perfuming the hair and beard; rubbing, frication, or massage; surgical and medical procedures such as phlebotomy, dentistry, bone-setting, the removal of stones, and the treatment of wounds and sores; the sale of countless commodities such as unguents, lotions, plasters, medicinal concoctions, cosmetics, dietary (as well as alcoholic)[6] drinks, wax candles, lanterns, and other small wares.[7] Moreover, barbershops proverbially provided musical instruments or entertainment as well as diversionary displays of extraordinary or unusual curiosities to help customers pass the time while waiting for a turn in the chair.[8] Nevertheless, Amphilogus is unable to disapprove of the barber or his potentially vice-ridden and excessive goods and services entirely: without barbers, he admits, men might lose all semblance of civility, degenerate into hirsute and unrefined *barbarians* or animalistic monstrosities, and so become indistinguishable from uncultivated, uncivilized, heathen foreigners.[9] Barbers, despite their inherent cupidity and close proximity to excess and vice, are necessary to ensure what Norbert Elias has called the civilizing process.[10] Stubbes's treatise implies that what is at stake in the potential degeneration to which he alludes is nothing less than existence itself: the multiple barbering practices that occur within the space of the early modern London barbershop contradictorily seem both to constitute and threaten, regulate and unsettle, English humanity, civility, and masculinity. The barber and his shop signal myriad desirable and vicious commodities and services simultaneously; those objects, practices, and ministrations that Stubbes recognizes as potentially feminizing are also ironically necessary. For in the intimately homosocial spaces in which barbers perform their multiple services, masculinity can be either fashioned or undone as easily as the beard that ostensibly advertises it can be shaped or removed. Men, in Stubbes's rhetoric, are completely at the mercy of money-hungry barbers and their multifarious craft. What I am interested in exploring here is both what is at stake in the nexus of virtuous and vicious medical, cosmetic, economic, and erotic activity conjured by the figure of the barber in the early modern English imagination and also how we might read representations of barbers, the places in which they practice, and the bodies that enter those places in the literature and drama of the period in light of that polyvalent cluster of connotation. As Mary Bly notes of St. Paul's Cathedral, a focus on the symbolic contexts that codify spaces in light of the activities that (actually or imaginatively) occur there crucially inform our understanding of performances in which those places (and the bodies that occupy those places) are implicated.[11]

Robert Greene's *A Quip for an Upstart Courtier* offers its reader a slightly different view of the Elizabethan barber. Greene's speaker, Cloth-breeches, unlike Amphilogus, complains not about the numerous products and services that the barber provides per se but about the fact that they are proffered solely to the wealthiest customers—men like "veluet-bréeches," whose ostentatious displays of spendthriftiness afford them preferential treatment at the avaricious barber's hands. At least part of the threat posed to masculinity here (as in Stubbes's description of the barber's practice earlier) is economic: the maintenance of masculine civility has its price, and this is a system and space in which one man is afforded the opportunity to profit from the vulnerability of a homosocial collective particularly attuned to the nuances of a gendered hierarchy.

> These quaint tearmes Barber you greet maister veluet breeches withall, & at euery word a snap with your scisors, and a cring with your knée, whereas when you come to poore Clothbreeches you either cutte his beard at your owne pleasure, or else in disdaine aske him if he wil be trimd with Christs cut, round like the halfe of a holland cheese, mocking both Christ and vs.... For you maister surgeon... I seldome fall into your hands as being quiet & making no brawls to haue wounds, as swartrutting veluetbreeches dooth, neither doe I frequent whorehouses to catch the Marbles, and soe to grow your patient.[12]

Cloth-breeches' and Amphilogus' reports mutually characterize London barbers as rapacious: both speakers acknowledge that barbers' provision of supplemental services is motivated primarily by economics.[13] If Greene's report is reliable in its detail, barbers would earn only about two pence for cutting the hair and beard of the average customer but could expect to receive gratuities upward of half a crown for privately performing more exclusive medical or cosmetic functions for affluent or generous patrons (which must have made the temptation to provide as many of those services as possible irresistible).[14] In both texts, the intimate attentions barbers lavish on their wealthiest clients, which could be vilified as unnecessary or inappropriate vices and extravagances, are described as enviable luxuries regrettably extended exclusively to a fortunate few.

Cloth-breeches' nearly seamless transition between addressing first the barber and then the surgeon reflects the conjoined state of those two crafts in the period: united as one company by Act of Parliament under Henry VIII in 1540 and not separated until the mid-eighteenth century in England, the worshipful company of barber-surgeons recorded ongoing problems with keeping its barbering membership from practicing surgery despite repeated prohibitions by civic officials.[15] Cloth-breeches' insistence on differentiating barbers from "surgeans, and physicians" (sig. H2), whom he groups together, counters the more common distinction in the period between the conjoined barber-surgeons on one hand and physicians on the other.[16] The semblance of propriety that Cloth-breeches suggests his patronizing the barber rather than the surgeon-physician affords him is precisely what seems to make the barbershop an ideal front for the sort of activities that Cloth-breeches cites: frequenting brothels and (thereby) acquiring the pox.[17] Moreover, the intimate and pleasurable services that barbers provided their male clients for a price, and that both Stubbes and Greene catalogue, closely resemble—and, indeed, had strong historical ties to—those being offered by London prostitutes.

Barbers and their shops were not aggregated in specific sections of the city as most other early modern London tradesmen and shopkeepers seem to have been. According to Margaret Pelling, a survey of freeman barber-surgeons in London by 1641 suggests a "remarkably thorough distribution…over the whole City," with local concentrations particularly in areas of fashion, entertainment, and ill-repute.[18] Noting that the dispersal of prostitution from its traditional bankside location in Southwark after 1500 was encouraged by the crown's attempts to shut down the stews in the wake of the early years of the syphilis epidemic, Pelling comments that of the several areas where the prostitutes are known to have relocated, many of which are in the western suburbs, "very few…were without a resident member of the Barber-Surgeons' Company."[19] Pelling's survey concludes that "the topography…seems to suggest, firstly, that [the barber-surgeons'] services were required regularly, and secondly, that they had some degree of association with places of resort and even of vice."[20] In terms of numbers, the barbers' company seems to have had higher numbers of freemen than any other company, even before their merging with the surgeons: Young comments that in 1537, for example, "The Barbers outstripped in numbers all the [other companies]" with 185 members.[21] Judging by their relatively even distribution in and around the city, barbers would have been a visible presence in every parish, while their congregating in areas particularly notorious for prostitution and other vices suggests that some of these barbers either trafficked in or otherwise profited from illicit and immoral activities that capitalized on masculine vice. Ubiquitous and requisite, but also insidiously associated with excess and vice, the early modern London barbershop was a potentially dangerous site that simultaneously challenged and confirmed masculinity.

Henry Parrot's 150th epigram equates the pander, who grows wealthy soliciting the sexual services of diseased whores, with the tonsor or barber, who makes money "by mens losse of haire":[22]

> A Pander once appareld wondrous brave,
> Was askt why Fortune favor'd such a knave;
> Who said, by Fortunes-wheele he did not clime,
> Our riches comes (quoth he) by this bald time,
> Wherein we free our selves from paines and care,
> Living, like Barbers, by mens losse of haire.[23]

The pander's reference to balding alludes to one symptom of pox infection, but Parrot's epigram is more than simply a clever quip that compares hair loss due to venereal disease to depilation through shaving: in fact, the two processes are equated via wordplay that associates barbers, who were becoming conspicuously wealthy in early seventeenth-century London, with both panders and thieves.[24] *Shaving*, *trimming*, *polling*, and *barbering* are all depilatory acts with which the barber is routinely identified, but the terms themselves also function metaphorically to signal, via economic wordplay, *theft* and, via bawdy wordplay, *sexual acts* that could result in contraction of the pox. Like the pander (and whore), the epigram suggests, the barber acquires money by *shaving* men: removing or clipping their hair, providing them intimate (sexual) services, and taking their gold in return not for commodities but for services instead. Panders, barbers, and (implicitly) prostitutes are ironically linked in Parrot's rhetoric through their mutual economic reliance on venereal disease. In this light, Stubbes's and Greene's mutual attendance to the economic motives for the barbers' professional diversification signals an unsettling contradiction: while his services are requisite for the cultivation of civility and fashioning masculinity, the barber's invariably both literally and figuratively *shaving* his clients vexes monolithic constructions of both masculinity and civility and poses an insidious but ultimately unavoidable challenge to hegemonic male virtue and virility.

Sidney Young's *Annals of the Barber-Surgeons of London* cites the early fourteenth-century presentation and admission of the first Master of the association of London barbers, Richard la Barbour, before the Court of Aldermen in 1308. Barbour was chosen "to have supervision over the trade of the Barbers . . . and made oath that every month he would make scrutiny throughout the whole of his trade, and if he should find any among them keeping brothels, or acting unseemly in any other way, and to the scandal of the trade, he was to distrain upon them, and cause the distress to be taken into the Chamber &c."[25] Although the record indicates that similar inspections were regularly undertaken with varying degrees of vigor by subsequent masters of the guild, Young curiously never produces a single company court record in which a barber is explicitly charged with keeping a brothel. Since what seems to be at stake in the oath is the possibility that scandal might cast an unfavorable light on the company and its membership, it may be that occurrences of barbers keeping brothels were simply not reported or left unrecorded by the company court. Surely a number of barbershops must have been operating as brothels, or a number of barbers were allowing prostitutes to conduct business on their premises, in order for inspections to have become and remained necessary. Henry VIII's own household records reflect barbers being perceived as likely sources of contamination due to the company they commonly keep.[26] The barbershop's imagined potential as a source of pollution stems, no doubt, at least in part from the barber's regularly handling bodily waste (including hair) and his close proximity to disease but also carries moral and sexual charges.[27]

In the literature and drama of the period, the early modern barbershop and its appurtenances function (often proverbially) as metaphors for prostitution: the barber's glass or mirror, chair, cittern or lute (or any other musical instrument kept in the shop), because *common to all men*, are comparable to whores. The barber's warming pan or chafing dish could function as metaphors for female pudenda; and, as the title of the anonymous ballad "The buxom wife that went a maying with a brisk barber for his long pole" suggests, the barber's pole or razor could also operate figuratively and explain the barber's imagined proclivity for turning the women associated with him or his shop into masculine, diseased, and /or lascivious whores. John Flint South and D'Arcy Power, in the *Memorials of the Craft of Surgery*, suggest that the verity of the imputation that barbers were operating brothels is "the less unlikely, if it be borne in mind that in addition to their occupation of shavers and hair and beard trimmers, they were also professional bathers."[28] Since antiquity, baths had been associated with brothels, and both sites—the areas in which they were located and the bodies made available in them—were commonly referred to as *stewes*.[29]

It is reasonable to assume that a number of medical practitioners in London—particularly those who, like barber-surgeons, routinely treated the symptoms of venereal disease—would have frequented sites where such baths were made available, situated their businesses near those sites, or have themselves maintained hothouses, medicinal baths, or stews: spaces wherein a man could simultaneously procure a thermal or medicinal bath and sexual companionship.[30] Thomas Langley's 1546 English translation of Polydore Vergil includes a section entitled "Who instituted stewes, diyng [*sic*] of heare, barbours, with other thingis," which suggests that colored hair, barbers, and prostitutes share common origins.[31] Vergil's precedent for prostitution is in "the rites of Bacchus sacrifices, wherein men used to c[om] pany dissolutely with women in the night," a reference that Langley equates with "our shewes or daunces called maskes in Englande" (sig. L1v–L2). Vergil's associating prostitutes and barbers apparently reminds Langley of the type of illicit revelry and entertainments reserved for either festive occasions or liminal spaces like the stews on London's south bank, where brothels and barbershops, bathhouses and alehouses, bear-gardens and theaters stood side by side and offered London's male population (and those hoping to *shave* them) a veritable pageant of riotous activity.[32]

The fourteenth epigram of Samuel Rowlands's *Humors Ordinarie* recounts another story about a visit to the barber's shop:

> Fine *Phillip* comes unto the Barbers shop,
> Where's nitty locks must suffer reformation:
> The chaire and cushion entertaine his slop:
> The Barber craves to know his worships fashion:
> His will is, shaven, for his beard is thin,
> It was so lately banish'd from his chin.
> But shaving oft will helpe it, he doth hope,
> And therefore for the smooth-face cut he calles:
> Then fie, these cloathes are washt with common sope,
> Why dost thou use such ordinary balles?
> I scorne this common trimming like a Boore:
> Yet with his heart he loves a common whoore.[33]

The barber's trade in Rowlands's epigram carries significant sexual freight: Phillip's hair loss due to venereal disease; bawdy wordplay on the barber's chair and cushion entertaining Phillip's *slop*;[34] Phillip's *will* to be shaven;[35] allusions to the removal and washing of Phillip's clothes (and Phillip?); the barber's using "ordinary balles" to wash with; and the final lines, which ironically juxtapose Phillip's scorn at receiving common services with his desire for a "common whoore." Rowland's epigram implies that Philip has both acquired and sought treatment for his venereal disease in the barber's shop. Henry Parrot's epigram "Juvenus Tonsus" from *Cures for the Itch* employs similar rhetoric as it recounts how young Petrus has acquired the disease that rendered him bald:

> That Petrus proves so bald, and yet so yong,
> What one who sees him may but wonder at it,
> Knowing how late his haire was thick and long:
> Tut, come, 'tis quickly question'd whence he got it,
> Not by the Barber's rasor, nor his knife,
> But very neere, t'was by the Barber's wife.[36]

The barbershop in this Parrot epigram is a site at which men lose their hair due not only to literal shaving and polling but also as a result of sexual shaving. The wordplay in this case implicates not (only) the barber, however, but (also) the barber's wife who, due to her close proximity to the barber, his shop, and his trade, is assumed to be both sexually available and disease-ridden, much like the prostitutes barbers were commonly suspected of trafficking in.[37] John Florio's early modern Italian and English dictionary, *A Worlde of Wordes*, defines *Barbiere* as " a barber," *Barberia* as "a barber's shop," and *Barbiera* as "a sheebarber. Also a common harlot" (38), which suggests that female barbers or women associated with the barbershop are tantamount to whores.[38]

A somewhat later seventeenth-century ballad, "The Crafty Barber of Debtford," is worth noting for the familiar metaphors that it invokes in recounting a barber's seduction of two women, one of whom is a "long-back'd Nurse" who resides in a "bawdy-house:"[39]

> A very gentile Dame was she,
> and wore her clouded stockings;
> But some there are do think that she
> got such fine things by knockings. (37–40)

The implication is that the "Nurse," like a prostitute, trades sexual favors ("knockings") for "fine things," and the woodcut at the top of the broadside ballad depicting her smiling with her breasts bared, nursing a swaddled infant, does nothing to dispel this notion of easy availability.[40] The second woman,

> The fidlers wife was fine and neat,
> and decently attired;

And she full well could do the feat
the Barber oft desired:
He oft embrac'd her in his Arms,
and catch'd her by the thing too;
So that she won him by her charms,
and he touch'd the Fidlers strings too. (45–48)

Note how the fiddler's "strings," operate as a metaphor for the fiddler's wife's *reins* or *loins* (*OED* 2): the "Fidlers strings" here, like those on the cittern in the barbershop, can be played upon or "touch'd," by any man who so desires. As the ballad continues, bawdy wordplay sexualizes both the acts performed by and tools associated with the barber:

While he did please his ladies fair
and trimm'd them both so neatly,
That she [the hostess, who is now drunk on brandy] did wish to have a share,
he did it so completely....
And when she drinks a Glass of Wine,
the Barber he doth shave her;
And up and down where e're he goes,
he mightily doth praise her;
A gentle hand he hath she knows,
And well she likes his Razor.
And now good people to conclude, mythinks it is a pitty
The Barber should these two delude that are so neat and pretty
Then women all pray have a care,
for Barbers' minds are waving;
And now methinks he's had his share,
he may leave off his shaving. (53–56; 67–80)

The rather obvious sexual innuendoes informing the wordplay on *shaving*, *trimming*, and the barber's *razor* signal the barber's notoriety for making the women he encounters whores, a sentiment that is confirmed in the ballad when the speaker warns "women all" to "have a care" to avoid his company: "Think it not strange what now you hear, / for if you will believe it, / The barber loves the sport so dear, / I doubt he ne'r will leave it" (59–60).

The wordplay on *shaving* and *trimming* as euphemisms for sex acts also obtains in John Weever's seventh epigram in "The fourth weeke" of his *Epigrammes*:

A shave-beard Barber Bunna chanc'd to meete,
As she was going all along the streete;

The Barber sweares hee's glad they met so right,
She should barb him, or he barb her that night:
What was the reason of this their debate?
Or what's the cause why Barbers Bunna hate?
Bunna, she barbs too cheap, and barbs by 'th score
And whom she barbes they ne're neede barbing more.[41]

Since Bunna will give the men she "barbs" venereal disease, Bunna's "barbing" puts the barber out of business in Weever's clever epigram since the pox-infested clients will no longer have hair or beards for him to cut. But Thomas Freeman's seventeenth epigram, "On Hersilium," from his *Rubbe and a Great Cast* seems to answer Weever's epigram by relating a similar tale about the barber Hersilius and the prostitute Lucy:

Hersilius the Barber-Surgeon
Hates Lucy cause shee barbeth many one
And them so artificially doth trimme
That they need nevermore be shav'd by him:
This is the cause Hersilius doth hate her
But would the foolish man well weigh the matter
How tis his profite that shee plaies the Barber
His heart gainst her would no such hatred harbor:
What though she makes him loose a lowsy science,
Shee fits his Surgery with fatter Clients.[42]

The "fatter" clients whom Lucy produces are better sources of income (*OED* 9b) for the barber as surgeon because they are diseased; although Hersilius will lose the business of tending Lucy's clients' hair and beards, he will gain the more lucrative job of treating the symptoms of the venereal disease that they contract as a result of her *barbing*, *trimming*, and *shaving* them. Considering the several directions in which these verbal metaphors gesture (depilatory, economic, sexual), Lucy and Hersilius both figuratively *shave* the same customers in multiple ways.[43]

Finally, I would like to gesture briefly toward how the early modern suspicion that barbers may be panders and barbershops bawdy houses can inform our reading of early modern drama in which barbers and their shops are featured or alluded to. How, for example, might the knowledge that many barbershops and their immediate environs functioned as *stews* influence our reading of Ben Jonson's *Epicoene, or the Silent Woman*, wherein the gentlemen's son who plays the part of Epicoene, and is maintained by Dauphine Eugenie, is reported to be "lodged i' the next street to him [i.e., Cutbeard the barber]" (1.2.27–28) and to lie "right over against the barber's" (1.2.57)?[44] Might we be meant to read the boy-actor playing Epicoene as a male prostitute, the equivalent of Clerimont's ingle, who appears in the first scene of the play? How ludicrously funny would it have been for an early modern audience that the old patriarch Morose naively petitions his barber, of all people, to find him an honest, subservient, and silent bride?

In the second scene of the first Act of John Marston's *The Dutch Courtesan*, Cocledemoy calls Mary the bawd a "pretious pandres supportres of *Barbar Surgeons* and inhauntres [or frequent consumer] of *lotiums* and dyet drinke," charges that allude to Mary's frequenting of barbershops and financially supporting barber-surgeons.[45] In the second act of the play, Cocledemoy purchases the wares of a young barber's boy calling himself Holifernes Rains-cure, a surname that alludes to the pox since it connotes *one who cures the groin*. When the boy first enters the scene, Cocledemoy asks him whether he is a barber-surgeon, and Holifernes says, "Yes sir an apprentise to surgery." Cocledemoy replies, "Ti's [tell us] my fine boy, to what bawdy house doth your Maister belong?" (sig. C1v). Upon the boy's telling Cocledemoy his name, Cocledemoy comments, "*Rainscure*? good M. *Holifernes* I desire your further acquaintance, nay pray yee bee covered my fine boy, kill thy itch and heale thy scabes, is thy Maister rotten?" (sig. C2). Evidently, Cocledemoy not only associates barbershops with bawdy houses or brothels, but he also assumes that both barbers and their boys share the venereal diseases that they ostensibly propagate and treat.

In 2.2 of Shakespeare's *King Lear*, Kent accuses Goneril's servant Oswald of being "one that wouldst be a bawd in way of good service" and a "whoreson cullionly barber-monger."[46] While editors tend to gloss this last epithet as a reference to Oswald's foppishness, the implication seems to be not only that Oswald regularly visits the barber but also that he conducts disreputable business with him.[47] The term *barber-monger*, which Shakespeare apparently coins here, could also function as a pseudonym for *whoremonger*, so the charge may imply either that Oswald has contracted venereal disease and so regularly needs the barber's services or that his association with prostitutes occurs at the barber's shop.[48] In any case, Kent clearly implicates the barber in the vitriolic invective associating Oswald with bawds and whores, and there is more at stake in his accusation than mere foppishness alone.

Barbershops provided Renaissance London's male population the potential for camaraderie, homosocial interdependence, physical and psychic intimacy, entertaining music and mirth, *esprit du corps*, and a range of cosmetic and medical services intended to care for and maintain the health, appearance, and humoral balance of the civilized male body, but a citizen could also place himself in considerable mortal, moral, and social peril by venturing inside the wrong barber's shop.[49] Concomitant to the ostensibly laudable and necessary cosmetic and surgical services provided by the early modern London barber were a number of more dubious, immoral, and illicit ministrations that some barbers reputedly offered, the associations with which indubitably cast aspersions on the entire trade. Stubbes's and Greene's texts ironically allude to the likelihood of financial diminution at the barber's hand but simultaneously downplay any suggestion that there may be a corollary loss of reputation in a man's being associated with the multiple connotations that *shaving* imply. Although the barber may be viciously rapacious, Stubbes concedes, he is a necessary evil, and his services are requisite for the maintenance of early modern English civility and masculinity.

So, while early modern London's reputable male citizen would to some extent have had to be cautious about which barber he visited, the precise nature of that particular barber's occupational diversification, and the location of the shop in question, the figurative construction of the London barber that resulted from occupational diversification and routine company inspections would have made any visit to a barbershop potentially hazardous to the male reputation. Even though clearly not all barbershops *were* operating as brothels in sixteenth and seventeenth-century London, their concentration in notoriously vice-ridden districts of the city, the multivalent wordplay invested in descriptions of them, their tools, their activities, and the spaces in which they plied their craft, and the frequency with which morally dubious women accompany or are associated with them in the drama and literature of the period all anxiously acknowledge the perception that they *could* be. So, despite the hazards—the potential loss of reputation, virility, money, and health that accompanied and inflected depilation at the hands of the barber—the barbershop constituted an indispensable and quotidian site of civil male self-fashioning in the urban and cultural geography of early modern London.

NOTES

For their generous comments on past drafts of this chapter, I would like to thank Paul Werstine, Elizabeth Harvey, Bruce Smith, Patricia Parker, Natasha Korda, Roze Hentschell, and Amanda Bailey. Thanks also to attendees at the 50th Anniversary RCSC and the Fourth Annual Blackfriars Conference. I am very grateful to the Social Sciences and Humanities Research Council of Canada for postdoctoral research funding.

1. See for example Harold J. Cook, *The Decline of the Old Medical Regime in Stuart London* (Ithaca, NY and London: Cornell University Press, 1986), esp. pp. 28–69.
2. Margaret Pelling, *The Common Lot: Sickness, Medical Occupations and the Urban Poor in Early Modern England* (London and New York: Longman, 1998), 203. See esp. 203–29. Pelling goes on to say that "Barbers were particularly prone to diversification in their careers, and they were notorious for diversifying in the direction of physic as well as surgery" (209).
3. See Siena's Introduction to *Sins of the Flesh: Responding to Sexual Disease in Early Modern Europe*, ed. Kevin Siena (Toronto: CRRS, 2005), 7–29, in which he argues that "healers of all stripes scrambled to offer treatment. The medical division of labour, which was supposed to see different forms of healing restricted to particular kinds of healers…was in practise difficult to enforce and compromised at the best of times. When it came to the pox with so much market share at stake, monopolies were ignored as all manner of practitioners flooded the market peddling their 'cures'" (23, n.51). See also Siena's "The 'Foul Disease' and Privacy: The Effects of Venereal Disease and Patient Demand on the Medical Marketplace in Early Modern London," *Bulletin of the History of Medicine* 75.2 (2001): 199–224.
4. Jonathan Gil-Harris reads early modern syphilis itself as a palimpsest with "polyvalent signifying power" (113). See "(Po)X Marks the Spot: How to 'Read' 'Early Modern' 'Syphilis' in *The Three Ladies of London*" in *Sins of the Flesh*, 109–32.
5. Philip Stubbes, *The Second Part of the Anatomy of Abuses* (London, 1583), sig. G8 and cited hereafter in text by signature page.
6. Pelling, *Common Lot*, 220. Siena ("Foul Disease," 212) notes that seventeenth-century advertisements confirm the availability of pox medicine in alehouses.
7. For an example of the ways we might read barbers' wares in light of the barbers' own vicious potential, see Natasha Korda's "Vicious Objects: Staging False Wares" in this volume.
8. Also see Pelling, *Common Lot*, 223–24.
9. Despite etymological distinctions between the Latin-derived English terms *barber* and *barbarian*, early modern wordplay registers an

association between the two that is persistent but inconsistent. For a sustained reading of the nexus of associations among barbers, barbarians, and Barbary, see Patricia Parker's "Barbers and Barbary: Early Modern Cultural Semantics," *Renaissance Drama* 33 (2004): 201–44.

10. Norbert Elias, *The Civilizing Process* (New York: Urizen, 1978).
11. See Mary Bly's "Carnal Geographies: Mocking and Mapping the Religious Body" in this volume.
12. Robert Greene, *A Quip for an Upstart Courtier* (London, 1592), sig. C4 and cited hereafter in text by signature number.
13. Pelling (*Common Lot*, 204) suggests that Barbers capitalized particularly on a public desire to appear physically/morally healthy, for "the clean, straight, unmarked body which the searchers were seemingly to have in mind during witchcraft trials." Barbers, then, stood to profit from both causing and disguising venereal infection.
14. See Greene, *Quip*, sig. C3v: "Mary (q[uo]d Cloth-bréeches) first to the barber[:] he cannot be but a partiall man on veluet-bréeches side, sith he gets more by one time dressinge of him, than by ten times dressing of me."
15. Barbers had practiced surgery (including dentistry and phlebotomy) from about the twelfth century in England. On July 18, 1583, "the Lord Mayor and Court of Aldermen [of the city of London] having recommended that persons using Barbery should not practise Surgery, the Masters and Governors" of the company vowed to "compel all their free Barbers to enter into bonds not to 'medle or deale wth any sick of the plauge [*sic*] or infected cum morbo gallico'" (320), but ongoing complaints suggest that many barbers never stopped the practice. Prosecutions persisted throughout the history of the company. Sidney Young, *Annals of the Barber-Surgeons of London* (London: Blades, 1890), esp. pp. 23, 223–320, 349–52.
16. Greene's reference to "Marbles" may be a corruption of the French *morbilles* or "the small pockes" (*OED* 6a.). The ostensible boundary between barber-surgery and physic was supposed to replicate that between the exterior and the interior of the body. As Pelling explains, that division grew into a tripartite one among "physicians, surgeons or barber-surgeons, and apothecaries" but those divisions "existed more as a weapon in conflicts between practitioners than as an agreed framework" (32). After addressing the barber and surgeon / physician, Cloth-breeches turns to the "Apoticarie" (sig. C4), whose shop he also denies visiting.
17. Siena identifies a "powerful stigma attached to sexually transmitted diseases" in the period and argues that, as a result, "assurances of [patient] privacy were crucial" ("Foul Disease," 206–7). Barbershops in particular would have allowed men to obtain consultations and treatments without arousing suspicion.

18. Margaret Pelling, "Appearance and Reality: Barber-Surgeons, the Body, and Disease" in *London 1500–1700: The Making of a Metropolis*, ed. A. L. Beier and Roger Finlay (London and New York: Longman, 1986), 85.
19. Ibid., 88. For the dispersal of the bawds and their lodgings within the liberties outside the city walls after 1500 as well as the locations of the Southwark brothels, see E. J. Burford, *Bawds and Lodgings: A History of the London Bankside Brothels c. 100–1675* (London: Peter Owen, 1976).
20. Pelling, "Appearance and Reality," 87.
21. Young, *Annals*, 94. For the ratio of practitioners to population in Norwich, see Pelling, *Common Lot*, 86.
22. Henry Parrot, *Laquei ridiculosi: or Springes for Woodcocks* (London, 1613), 6.
23. Ibid., sig. F6.
24. I have attempted to avoid retrospective diagnoses and anachronistic terminology in my references to *the pox* rather than to *syphilis* (also commonly referred to in the period as *morbus gallicus*; the French, foul, venereal, or Neapolitan disease; *lues venerea*; or the Marbles), a sexually transmitted disease that causes blistering pustules (or pocks) to appear in its early stages and corrupts the organs, bones, flesh (including the scalp), and brain in its late stages. As Siena points out, "patients suffering from what we term syphilis and what we term gonorrhea received the same diagnosis, as did a wide range of patients likely suffering from other genito-urinary or skin conditions that we would diagnose entirely differently" (*Sins*, 12). Hair loss or balding was one of a number of early and visible symptoms and signals of pox contamination. Siena notes how patients, "disfigured by ulcers, baldness, and collapsed noses characteristic of infection, bore not just symptoms, but symbols" of the disease (Ibid., 7).
25. Young, *Annals*, 24.
26. Young's transcription of Harley MS 642 contains a stipulation "that the Kings Barbor...take a speciall regarde to the pure and cleane keepinge of his owne person and apparrell useinge himselfe allwayes honestlye in his conversationne withoute resortinge to the Companye of vile personnes or of misguided woemen" (*Annals*, 90). In part, this order reflects anxiety about the proverbial garrulousness of the barber, but the stipulation also assumes both the probable uncleanness of the barber and his being prone to association with depraved characters who might pollute the barber who might in turn infect the king.
27. Since barbers routinely let excess blood and bodily fluids, surgically removed corrupted flesh, shaved and cut (excremental) hair, and sweated out toxins from disease, the barber's shop was always a potential source of pollution and contamination. Robert Copeland's 1541 translation of Guy de Chauliac's *Chirurgia magna* entitled

Questyonary (London, 1542) provides an illustration of hair's association with excremental bodily waste through purgation in its claim that the purpose of hair is "to encrease beaute and to purge" (sig. D3). The early fourteenth-century city ordinance against blood remaining on display in barbershops needed repeating in 1566 and again in 1606 (Young, *Annals*, 23, 119, 181). For blood as "a contradictory site of multiple, competing, even self-contradictory discourses" (Paster, 90), see Gail Kern Paster's *The Body Embarrassed: Drama and the Disciplines of Shame in Early Modern England* (Ithaca, NY: Cornell University Press, 1993), esp. pp. 64–112.

28. John Flint South, *Memorials of the Craft of Surgery*, ed. D'Arcy Power with intr. by Sir James Paget (London: Cassell, 1886), 14. Kathy Stuart notes in *Defiled Trades and Social Outcasts: Honor and Ritual Pollution in Early Modern Germany* (Cambridge: Cambridge University Press, 1999) that in Germany, the bathmasters "joined with the barbers to form one guild" during the Caroline reform (106).

> The crafts of the bathmasters and barbers were almost identical, with the one defining difference that bathmasters operated public baths while the barbers did not. Both shaved and cut hair, though the barbers were limited to "dry-cutting"(*truckhen scheeren*), which simply meant that the haircuts and shaves did not include a bath. Both cured syphilis and did surgery, let blood, set broken bones, and amputated limbs... Economic competition and incessant conflict over what constituted the correct division of labor between the two trades led bathmasters and barbers to split up and form separate guilds in 1638. (106–107)

Although there were no official public baths in London, barbers commonly administered private baths. Public baths outside London and abroad were widely reputed to be notorious sites of sexual debauchery. Poggio Bracciolini observed of the bath at Baden in 1416, "they are all lovers, all suitors, all men for whom life is based on fun, who come together here so that they may enjoy the things for which they hunger; many pretend to have bodily ills" (29). See *Two Renaissance Book Hunters: The Letters of Poggius Bracciolini to Nicholaus de Niccolis*, ed. and trans. Phyllis Gordan (New York: Columbia University Press, 1974). I owe this reference to Charles R. Mack's "The Wanton Habits of Venus: Pleasure and Pain at the Renaissance Spa" in *Explorations in Renaissance Culture* 26 (2000): 257–76. Mack notes that the medical or thermal bath was "more to be endured than enjoyed," however. "Long exposure to the almost scalding temperatures produced a general softening of the skin and a consequent eruption of the surface. This painful condition was not to be feared, however, but rather was awaited as a sign that the offending humors and impurities within the body could escape" (263). Like the barbershop, then, the *bagnio* was evidently a site at which men could procure both sexual titillation and the painful medicinal treatments for consequent infections.

29. The *OED* asserts that the association arose from the frequent use of baths for immoral purposes (*OED* 4) and that the word functions metonymically to connote a prostitute or prostitutes (*OED* 4d). In 4.2 of Philip Massinger's *The Picture* (London,1630), Ubaldo tells Sophia when she inquires whether Ubaldo's rival courtier Ricardo is "holsome" or not,

    Holsome? I'll tell you for your good, he is
    A spittle of diseases and indeed
    More lothsome and infectious, the tubbe is
    His weekely bath; He hath not dranke this seauen yeare
    Before he came to your house, but compositions
    Of Sassafras, and Guacum, and drie mutton
    His daily portion; name what scratch soever
    Can be got by women and the Surgeons will resolve you
    At this time or at that *Ricardo* had it. (sig. K3)

    Ricardo's diet, "compositions," or drinks, and "tubbe" are all treatments commonly prescribed by early modern barber-surgeons for patients suffering from the pox. As Timon advises Timandra, mistress to Alcibiades, in Shakespeare's *Timon of Athens*,

    Be a whore still; they love thee not that use thee;
    Give them diseases, leaving with thee their lust.
    Make use of thy salt hours; season the slaves
    For tubs and baths, bring down rose-cheeked youth
    To the tub-fast and the diet.

    William Shakespeare, *Timon of Athens*, in *The Riverside Shakespeare: The Complete Works*, 2nd edition, ed. G. Blakemore Evans (Boston and New York: Houghton Mifflin, 1997), 4.3.83–88. John Jowett notes in his edition of the play (Oxford: Oxford University Press, 2004) that *lust* here can be read here as "expended and deposited in the whore's body, like semen (and the trade-off for her giving them diseases)" (272 n. 84). Both whore and client, then, "pollute" one another in the sexual exchange and, afterward, both have need of the tubs, baths, prescriptive diets, and drinks that barbers trade in.

30. Contemporary medical manuals and translations of classical models, like Anglicus Bartholomaeus' thirteenth-century text translated as *Batman vppon Bartholome his booke* (London,1582), commend stews and baths for their purgatory properties and recommend them for a host of ailments, including the "drie scabbe and itch" (112), "the morphew" (115), "consumynge membres" (Hieronymus Brunschwig's *The noble experyence of the vertuous handy warke of surgeri* [London, 1525], sig. R2v), and "fractures and dyssolucyons or dislocations of bones or ioyntes" (Guy de Chauliac's *The questyonary*

of cyrurgyens [London, 1542], sig. X3v), to name just a few. In Shakespeare's *Measure for Measure*, Mistress Overdone reportedly "professes a hothouse, which is a very ill house too" after her brothel in the suburbs is pulled down. While it is unclear who runs this establishment, Elbow calls it "a naughty house" and admits that his own wife's resorting there exposes her to accusations of "fornication, adultery, and all uncleanliness." Moreover, Elbow accuses Pompey of serving Overdone as a "tapster" there: in light of Pelling's associating barbershops with the food and drink trade (*Common Lot*, 205), it is feasible that the "hothouse" Overdone professes is maintained by a barber. William Shakespeare, *Measure for Measure*, in Evans, *The Riverside Shakespeare*, 2.1.65–67, 77, 81, 63.

31. *An abridgement of the notable woorke of Polidore Vergile* (London : Richard Grafton, 1546), sig. L1 and hereafter cited in text by signature page.
32. For further reading on the significance of the early modern beard's removal to (economic and sexual) emasculation, see my "Playing with the Beard: Courtly and Commercial Economies in Richard Edwards's *Damon and Pithias* and John Lyly's *Midas*," *ELH* 72 (2005): 79–103 and "Prosthetic Absence in Ben Jonson's *Epicoene*, *The Alchemist*, and *Bartholmew Fair*," *ELR* 37.3 (2007): 401–28.
33. Samuel Rowlands, *Humors Ordinarie* (London, 1603?), sig. B3v–B4.
34. Frankie Rubenstein glosses *cushion* as deriving from the French and Latin words for *thigh*: "it means the fleshy part of the rump" (67). Rubenstein defines *slop(s)* as "Liquid refuse . . . full baggy breeches" (246) and notes that the term is commonly associated with excrement. See *A Dictionary of Shakespeare's Sexual Puns and Their Significance*, 2nd edition (New York: St. Martin's, 1995).
35. Eric Partridge glosses *will* as "a passionate, or a powerful, sexual desire" (284). See *Shakespeare's Bawdy*, 3rd edition (London and New York, Routledge, 1968).
36. Henry Parrot, *Cures for the Itch* (London, 1626), sig. G4.
37. Siena notes that patients suffering from venereal diseases were likely to demand same-sex practitioners and that of the extant seventeenth-century promotional advertisements by venereologists he considers, many utilize female assistants (usually wives) to attract female clientele ("Foul Disease," 200; 220–23). In this light, infected men seeking treatment may have been drawn to the homosocial atmosphere provided by the London barber and his shop, while barbers' wives or widows, daughters, and female apprentices may have played active roles in attracting and treating female clients.
38. I owe this reference to Parker, "Barbers," 202.
39. Anon., "The Crafty Barber of Debtford" (London, c. 1637–1686), 29 and hereafter cited in text by line number.

40. William Clowes, in the 1585 edition of *A Briefe and necesarie Treatise* also makes a point of alerting his readers to the danger posed by "leude and filthie" and "wicked and filthy Nurses" (sig. A3).
41. John Weever, *Epigrammes* (London, 1599), sig. E1v.
42. Thomas Freeman, *Rubbe and a Great Cast* (London, 1614), sig. B3v–B4.
43. Philip Massinger's *The City Madam* (1658) names its central bawd "Shavem," evidently in order to play with the notion that *shaving* can infer literal or economically/sexually metaphoric processes, all of which are believed to feminize men by removing the signifiers of masculinity (procreative seed/money/beard). Although limitations restrict my discussion here to the associations among barbers, barbershops, and female prostitution, the pervasive economic and bawdy wordplay that both eroticizes the homosocial intimacy of the barbershop and also associates shaving with sex acts exposes not only the heteroerotic but also the homoerotic implications of depilation. For a more sustained homoerotic reading of barbers and their shops, see my forthcoming essay in *Thunder at a Playhouse: Essays on Shakespeare and the Early Modern Stage,* ed. Peter Kanelos and Matt Kozusko (Susquehanna University Press).
44. My references to act, scene, and line numbers of *Epicoene* correspond to the New Mermaids edition edited by R. V. Holdsworth (New York and London: Norton and A.C. Black, 1990).
45. John Marston, *The Dutch Courtesan* (London, 1605), sig. B1v and hereafter cited in text by signature page.
46. William Shakespeare, *King Lear*, in Evans, *The Riverside Shakespeare*, 2.2.20, 33.
47. See *OED*, *monger* (1; 1b).
48. Ibid. In Shakespeare's *Much Ado About Nothing*, by comparison, Benedick's friends tease him about the possibility that he is in love: Don Pedro asks whether "any man [hath] seen [Benedick] at the barber's," and Claudio replies, "No, but the barber's man hath been seen with him, and the old ornament of his cheek hath already stuffed tennis balls." The castrative image of beard hair—a sign of male virility—stuffing tennis balls feminizes Benedick, as do the accusations that he "rubs himself with civet," "[washes] his face," and "[paints] himself," all of which activities were associated not only with emasculation but also with barbers. William Shakespeare, *Much Ado About Nothing*, in Evans, *The Riverside Shakespeare*, 3.2.43–47, 50, 56–57. See note 30, above.
49. As Cassio reminds us in Shakespeare's *Othello*, a man's reputation was "the immortal part of [himself], and what remains is bestial." Interestingly, in the same scene of that play, Othello, disrupted while

consummating his marriage to Desdemona by the drunken Cassio's injuring Montano, tells Desdemona, "Come away to bed" in the same breath that he uses to advise Montano, "Sir, for your hurts, / Myself will be your surgeon." William Shakespeare, *Othello*, in Evans, *The Riverside Shakespeare*, 2.3.263–64, 253–54.

Part III

Remapping Misconduct: Sewers, Shops, and Streets

Chapter 6

Coriolanus and the "rank-scented meinie": Smelling Rank in Early Modern London

Holly Dugan

In "Dreaming of Infrastructures," her introduction to the *PMLA*'s 2007 special issue on cities, Patricia Yaeger argues that it is time to redraw Raymond Williams's influential map of urban and literary histories and to reexamine the ways in which labor relationships create "forms of living" and "structures of feeling."[1] New global crises of post- and over-industrialization in cities such as Baghdad, Harare, Aceh, Detroit, and New Orleans challenge Williams's argument. Exponential and unpredictable population growth has made traditional, planned infrastructures impossible. How can literature provide a metaphorical structure through which to process the tension between economic conditions and individual experiences of them if new urban realities are defined by a profound lack of material infrastructure? Waste, rather than structure, overwhelms these landscapes. Reading the nameless, postindustrial metropolis in José Saramago's *Blindness* as representative of such trends, Yaeger argues that the novel depicts "yet another city where it is impossible to move without bumping into other people's bodily wastes."[2]

Such tactile and olfactory proximity to waste represents the limits of Williams's structure of feeling. The problem is metaphoric sanitation: how can one represent the experience of the city if it is defined by proximity to waste? As Barthes famously noted, written shit does not stink.[3] Nor do modern cities, at least in modern literary imagination. Yet, sewage crises are not new: unlike their modern counterparts, early modern cities are often imagined as pungent places. Early modern London's nascent sewer system, for example, traversed the city's boundaries and bifurcated its center. One could not move without fording rivers of waste.[4] Such proximity was not a mark of failure or excess but rather urbanity: the sewers connected and defined the metropolis, demarcating its borders.[5]

Early modern London's sewers remind us that urbanity and deodorization were not always historically linked; rather they emerged through a politics of waste management that linked olfactory hazards with other urban dangers. As the city expanded in the late sixteenth and early seventeenth century, early modern London experienced a sewage crisis. London's exponential population growth fueled such fears; as Ian Munro has recently argued, early modern London was a space defined by "the visible and tangible presence of more and more bodies."[6] Phenomenological experiences of such rapid population growth were not only visible and tangible, but they were also olfactory. Shakespeare's *Coriolanus*, a play that dramatizes both a city (and a sewage system) in crisis, provides one way of sensing the implicit link between olfaction and metaphoric threats of city life. The stench of the masses, I argue, represents the threat posed by urban rioters. In the play, Coriolanus, a paragon of Roman masculine *virtus,* identifies the rank-scented meinie of Rome as his fluid antithesis: whereas he believes he singularly embodies Rome, they collectively represent anonymous and pervasive urban waste. He cannot "nose" their offense. His confrontation with the rioters turns on who will "run reeking" over the other, demonstrating the politics of rank embedded within discourses of rankness.

"The State is the Sewer": Rome's *Cloacæ* and London's Common Shores

As many critics have noted, *Coriolanus* is a play that imagines not a crumbling Roman empire but an aspirational one. Its Rome is a city in transition, a Republic emerging from the monarchial tyranny of the Tarquins, who used slave labor to construct its vast public spaces, including the *Cloaca Maxima.*[7] For Livy, Plutarch, and Shakespeare (among others), urban class strife defined this transition, as the multitudes began to participate in civic life. Dramatizing the tragic history of Gaius Marcius, Shakespeare's play is one in a long line of conflicted literary portraits of the powerful general and weak governor known as Coriolanus.[8] Yet his alone portrays class strife between patricians and plebeians as a tragedy of one noble man's battle against the olfactory rankness of urban life. Shakespeare distills the anti-usury riots of 494 BCE and the famine revolts of 491 BCE into a singular event: the conflict between Coriolanus and the reeking multitudes. Their riots lead to threats of invasion.[9]

For Renaissance men and women, Rome was a paragon of civilization and urban infrastructure: its colossal sewer in particular was a testament to its advancement. Rome's sewage system was one of the earliest and largest examples of an ancient, urban sewer. Built between the seventh and sixth centuries BCE under Tarquinius Priscus's supervision, Rome's sewage system consisted of a series of seven sewers, or *cloacæ*, which drained the marshlands between the Capitoline and Palatine hills. This valley eventually became the civic center of Rome.[10] The minor sewers connected underneath the Roman Forum, forming the *Cloaca Maxima*, four meters (fourteen feet) wide and three meters (eleven feet) high, which emptied into the Tiber. The current was so strong that, at times, it shook the walls of the buildings located above it.[11] At the height of use, more than 100,000 pounds of waste flowed through it daily.[12] Rome's subterranean sewers were foundational to its public life, first draining the valley, and later, forming its spatial and social topography. Earthquakes underneath it, the movement of massive stones above it, even Rome's swift sewage within it could not weaken the structure.[13] Through its imperial influence, Rome's waste management system was imported to other urban spaces as a template of urban life.[14] As Victor Hugo concludes in *Les Miserable,* the sewer of Rome swallowed the world: "Eternal city, unfathomable sewer."[15]

Like Hugo, Renaissance writers marveled at its power and early modern English translators of classical descriptions often drew parallels between Rome's sewers and London's. For example, in his translation of John Bartholomew Marlianus's "Topography of Rome in Ancient Time," appended to his translation of Livy's *Romaine History,* Philemon Holland calls it "the great sink, or town ditch," a label that could easily describe London's Townditch, located east of its walls and north of its tower. Marlianus's topography draws direct parallels between Rome's imperial heights and its massive sewer: during Rome's epoch, the "sweet clear water" of Lake Curtius ran underneath the Forum's many vaults and chambers for public use. But when Rome falls, the sewers suffer from disastrous privatization:

> [b]ut after the citie was woon by the Gaules & burnt, whiles every man made hast to rebuild his house, where hee could meet first with a convenient place; they tooke no heed to the streets as they were before: so as neither the citie was devided as aforetime into quarters, nor yet the sinkes which in times past went under the streets, were marked where they lay: but afterwards were conveighed under private mens houses, whereby it came to passe, that each house almost at this day hath a sinke or privie belonging to it.[16]

Though Marlianus bemoans the fact that he must describe the city "as it standeth," that is, as a city that had no regulated, public sewage system but rather allowed each building to empty its filth into the streets, he emphasizes that Rome's "sinkes" used to be "common," with "appointed publicke overseers to looke unto them."[17] Marlianus's nostalgia is for regulated infrastructure. Haphazard building above ground ignored the city's original layout, resulting in overextended sewer lines, blockages, backups, and an abundance of private sinks and privies, making Rome sound very much like early modern London.[18]

Structurally weakened, the *Cloaca Maxima* became a tourist destination, a monument to the city's former greatness. Seventeenth-century English travel guides to Italy also emphasized the *Cloaca Maxima*'s role in ancient Rome's magnificence. One argues that although it "were but a *Sinke,* yet it deserues to be mentioned among the rare magnificencies of ancient *Rome*" for "this sink was one of the evident tokens of the greatness and magnificence of *Rome* anciently."[19] For early modern tourists, ancient Rome's waste management system seemed an urban paradox: its civic magnitude was girded by subterranean labyrinths of waste.

Rome's triumph of waste management contrasted strongly with early modern London's. London became a modern metropolis only when its sewers were covered and its shores embanked in the nineteenth century. Before that, the city's sewage system resembled that of medieval London. Geographers note that the city's modern sewage system follows the ancient tributaries of the Thames, forming a palimpsest of its premodern counterparts.[20] The largest of these were the Walbrook, the Tynburn, and the Fleet. As the city expanded in the sixteenth century, these tributaries intersected with a growing network of common shores, through which waste and rainwater flowed, delimiting urban space. Premodern sewers were designed to drain rainwater rather than sluice waste. As a result, industrial and household waste traversed the city, moving from private cesspits through local sinks and kennels on major roadways into the stagnant common shores.

The Walbrook, for example, ran underneath London's ancient Roman wall into the heart of the early modern city, connecting Townditch, an open sewer that ran parallel to the wall, to the Thames. The area known as Houndsditch, between Bishopsgate and Moregate, was particularly offensive, clogged with dead dogs and other carrion. Bayswater brook became Ranelagh sewer. Finally, the Fleet river traversed the western border of the city, flowing (when it was not stagnant from refuse) from Holborn toward Brideswell and Blackfriars, where it deposited into the Thames, bifurcating London and Westminster. High traffic made it, and its stench, an integral part of London's social map. Just as prevailing winds shaped the acoustic environment of London (blowing from west to east), so too did London's ditches shape its olfactory environment (flowing both around and through its center).[21] All of these tributaries were used as sewers as early as the thirteenth century; by the late fifteenth century, a number of public privies were housed on bridges above them.[22]

Royal commissions of sewers existed in England as early as the fourteenth century, but these commissions mainly regulated ditches that drained marshlands and formed seawalls.[23] London's commission was formed in 1531 under the statute of sewers, which provided chiefly for the drainage of London's surface waters into existing tributaries or common shores.[24] It consolidated power over the city's medieval sewage system, connecting the cleansing of London's ditches to Royal commissions monitoring its borders. The statute expressly prohibited drainage of private privies or cesspools into public streets or shores. Such drainage, it alleged, was considered a privilege and was subject to regulation, restriction, and, most importantly, fines.[25] The statue was expanded greatly during James I's reign, enabling large-scale projects such as the draining of Morefield, the diversion of New River, and the paving of many thoroughfares. In 1622, the commission levied fines to fund further changes. In 1637, it funded bridging over parts of the polluted Fleet river. After the great fire of 1666, Charles II passed a reform bill, which sought to widen streets in order to provide greater "liberty of air."[26] By the end of the seventeenth century, the concept of liberty had expanded to include not only individual rights and urban enclaves but also air-quality and health. The first attempt at sanitary reform was the Sewage and Paving Act of 1671, which sought to remove waste channels from the center of major thoroughfares to side gutters.

Such regulations underscore that London's population explosion in the late sixteenth and early seventeenth century required new strategies of dealing with urban waste.[27] Large-scale, public initiatives, however, resulted in class struggles such as those dramatized in Shakespeare's play. Consider, for example, the controversial draining of Morefield in 1607. Located beyond the city's wall to the north were marshlands, open fields, fens and moors, where Londoners dumped private wastes into brick-lined cesspits or into the fields directly. In the early fifteenth century, when Moregate was added to the city's ancient wall, this boggy realm was drained in order to cleanse a number of nearby ditches, including Shoreditch, Deepditch, and Moreditch. It was cleansed and drained again in 1512. In 1515, nearby landowners had "so inclosed the common fields with hedges and ditches that neither the young men of the city might shoot nor the ancient persons walk for those pleasures."[28] As result, "a great number of the city" assembled to remove the hedges and tear down the early sluices: "within a short space all the hedges about the city were cast down, and the ditches filled up, and everything made plain."[29] Despite such protests, Morefield was drained and cleansed again in 1527; ditches connected it to Townditch, the Walbrook, and the Thames. By the early seventeenth century, it had become "a most noisome and offensive place . . . a generall laystall, a rotten morish ground."[30]

A contemporary account, Edward Howe's *Annals,* emphasized Morefield's olfactory menace: it was "enuironed, and crossed with deep stinking ditches, and noysome common sewers . . . loathsome both to sight and sent."[31] In 1607, London merchant and mayor, Sir Leonard Holliday, and merchant adventurer, Nicholas Leate, spent £5,000 of the city's funds on the draining and planting of "royal walks."[32] The citizens of London greatly protested such expenditures; however, rather than rioting, they verbally expressed their discontent, speaking "very bitterly, and rudelie, against those two worthy men."[33] Like the foul-breathed masses in *Coriolanus*, the commoners are represented as fickle: "when the multitude saw this worke brought unto desired effect, then their unconstant mindes changed: unto this worke there were diuers Cittizens desirious to put to their helping hands."[34] The mutable, rank-scented mienie of London, at least in Howe's *Annals*, were easily swayed, rerouted through the construction of new sewage channels. History would prove otherwise: in 1647, apprentices of London rioted once again in Morefield, a "confluence" of rioters attacking its walls.[35]

Urban rioting was a consistent threat to civic order. Riots broke out in London thirty-five times between 1581 and 1602; in 1595, twelve separate instances occurred within three weeks of one another.[36] As Ian Munro has argued, the urban aspect of these riots, "the circulatory anonymity" of city life, made prevention almost impossible; crowds could quickly disperse and regroup, stronger than before.[37] Though there is evidence to suggest London crowds, like their rural counterparts, understood rioting to be an effective—and legal—form of petitioning, London authorities did not.[38] City bans on assemblies targeted "loose" or "base" peoples, while searches and interrogations sought to impose visible control over the city and its inhabitants.[39]

The draining of fields and the cleansing of sewers were part of these attempts to control civic space. In 1615, along with the creation of a stock to house the city's "great encrease of Roagues and Vagabonds," London paved Smithfield, formerly a grazing pasture and open field, transforming it into a formal market: "And this Sommer 1615, the Citty of London reduced the rude vast place of Smith field into a faire and comely order, which formerly was neuer held possible to be done, and paued it all ouer, and made diuers shewers to onnay the water, from the new Channels which were made by reason of the new pauement."[40] This nascent act of "zoning" produced results that were formerly impossible: paving and sewers create "faire and comely order." Such descriptions emphasize that noisome hazards can—and should—be purged from city limits.

The definition of "noisome" threats widened greatly in this period as certain industries and workers were coded as dangerous and forcibly relocated to the suburbs, further reinforcing boundaries between intra- and extramural spaces.[41] For example, Towerditch was originally designed to sluice waters from the Thames into its moat, though this operation was never quite successful. Rather, it served as a muddy pasture and meeting space. Although Tower Hill served as a lofty space of civic entertainment, particularly of sonic displays of artillery, the ditch fulfilled more lowly spatial needs, as a covert space where pawnbrokers, sellers of "disconsolate cast-off apparel," prostitutes, and usurers congregated.[42] Such spatial boundaries defined London's intra- and extramural neighborhoods through proximity to what was increasingly classified as the city's noxious waste.

The most noisome industries were proximate to water sources, located on the banks of the Thames, near Southwark, along the Fleet dyke, and near Tower-, Town-, and Hounds-ditch. Butchers, for example, clustered along the Fleet ditch, especially near Fleet prison;

so, too, did tanners and chandlers, with the refuse from such industries draining into the dyke.[43] By the late fourteenth century, this produced a sickening stench so vile that parliament complained to the mayor and aldermen.[44] A number of scalding houses also emptied directly into Houndsditch and the Walbrook, depositing blood, hair, and animal refuse into nearby gardens.[45] Within geographies of the city, these trades were inextricably linked to such pollution.

Attempts to cleanse the ditches and to regulate the dumping of odiferous refuse continued throughout the fourteenth and fifteenth centuries; London's population explosion in the late sixteenth century produced renewed efforts to minimize offal and waste in the common shores. In 1589, Queen Elizabeth collected almost £1,000 to reroute the Fleet's tributaries in Hampstead Heath into one riverhead in an attempt to "scourge" Fleet ditch. In 1603, John Stow describes it as clogged with refuse and offal; in 1606 James I commissioned a series of dams to stop its flow; in 1652 Cromwell ordered it cleansed. None of these civic undertakings worked. It was finally paved over during the Great Stink of 1858, forming part of the city's underground sewer.[46]

The stench of the Fleet formed an integral part of London's literary landscape.[47] Ben Jonson's "Famous Voyage" catalogued it in great (and gross) detail, chronicling the adventures of two aristocrats, Shelton and Heydon, and their crew, up the polluted ditch. Its dock was an "ugly monster yclepéd Mud," which, when stirred by their oars, "[b]elched forth an air as hot as at the muster," like carts discharging a "merde-urinous load" in the city's many sinks.[48] In Jonson's poem, the link between rank and rankness compels the crew to participate in their own "beshiting."[49] The aristocratic travelers journey to brothels near Holborn, an area known for its prostitution. Eager to arrive, they compel their crew of "stinkards," "slaves," and "rogues" to row ever closer to the ditch's shit-stained walls. The crew's protests are ignored, since they are already "stinkards," a pejorative term, signaling vile excrement.[50] Almost a century later, Jonathan Swift also described the Fleet's swelling kennels, overflowing with "[s]weepings from Butchers Stalls, Dung, Guts, and Blood, / Drown'd Puppies, sinking Sprats, all drench'd in Mud, / Dead Cats and Turnip-Tops."[51] The stench provides an urban map: the "[f]ilths and all Hues and Odours seem to tell / What street they sail'd from by the Sight and Smell."[52] These metaphoric studies of the city's waste underscore that stench was an important part of London's landscape.

In other accounts of London's stinking ditches, waste is trenchant and pervasive. For example, in 1603, Garvin Smith, a Scottish engineer, offered his services to the aldermen of London to orchestrate a "cleansing" of London's muddy ditches. His proposal targeted the "noisome, thick, filthy, grosse and corrupt" street sewers of Townditch. To clean these ditches, Smith proposed not only unclogging the many dams, which had become stopped by all kinds of rotting flesh (including dead dogs and cats, carrion, oxen, and needles), but also carting the mud itself far from the city's borders.[53] Similarly, in a letter to James I, dated December 12, 1624, an anonymous inhabitant of London complained about the city's noisome and foul stench, noting that it was so strong that even "strangers" take notice of it; he warned that it will only get worse, given that a hot summer was predicted.[54]

Shakespeare's *Coriolanus* hints at London's sewage crises by dramatizing Rome's urban revolts. Many critics have argued that the play's focus on plebeian revolt cites the Midlands revolt of 1607, in which starving farmers protested enclosure acts and the hoarding of grain by wealthy landowners, one of the largest of whom was Shakespeare himself.[55] Peasant men, women, and children systematically destroyed the earthwork mounds and ditches that demarcated private enclosures.[56] Although these riots were quickly suppressed, reports of the damage quickly spread to London.[57] Riots in rural ditches would have triggered fears about the potential for riots in London's ditches, particularly if they targeted recently drained fields. Urban rioters posed a bigger threat to early modern civic order; unlike their rural counterparts who were known within their respective communities, urban rioters were, in some ways, "ungraspable" because of the size of the city.[58] As Ian Munro argues, their "evanescence" made them difficult to prosecute, yet their status as citizens afforded them intimate knowledge of city space.[59] The play's staging of urban revolt inside a city would have exploited such fears.

It also offers clues to its performance history. One of the implications of my argument is that the play's poetics of waste would have resonated strongly if staged indoors at Blackfriars, which Shakespeare's company, the King's Men, acquired in 1608 and produced plays in as early as 1609.[60] Like other internal London liberties, Blackfriars was both a distinctive enclave and an imaginative space.[61] London's internal liberties, Mary Bly argues, bred "their own distinct brew of disorder," self-regulating much of city life, including traffic and garbage disposal.[62] Many feared that the internal liberties weakened the city, generating noisome hazards within the city itself. Sir Stephen Soame, lord mayor of London and a prominent member of the Grocer's guild, linked the hazards of internal liberties to the sewers, describing the internal liberty of St. Katherine's, near Tower Ditch, as a "very sink of Sin" and of "lewd People" and "rogues, theeves, and Beggars."[63] Although prominent foreigners, Puritans, and city elites lived in this wealthy neighborhood, Blackfriars liberty abutted Fleetditch and its noisome hazards. Blackfriars's unique juxtaposition of rank and rankness would have been an ideal setting against which to stage the play's osmologies of rank.[64]

Recent criticism has interpreted the play's urbanity as part of a broader fable about early modern Republicanism, about cross-identified sexual identities, and about the point of violence in the era of emerging civility.[65] Likewise, its long and varied critical reception makes clear that its politics are open to multiple interpretations. As one critic concluded, any political meaning of the play seems to reflect only the sympathies of the reader.[66] Nor does the play reveal a new way of understanding Shakespeare's political leanings. There are strong readings of the play that suggest he was sympathetic to the urban rioters, just as there are strong readings that argue the opposite.[67] Rather, as Stanley Clavell argues, one must risk "one's critical balance" in order to "traverse" the play's "assessments of the balance civilization exacts."[68] As I argue below, the play's assessment of such balance is best understood not through modern definitions of "civilization," in which waste is always imaginatively purged from urban space. Rather, Shakespeare's *Coriolanus* defines the city as a space marked by its people and their airborne and waterborne waste. To "traverse" such assessments, one must deal with the multisensorial urban landscape against which the play's politics unfold. The material history of London's sewers, along with its stench, is embedded within the play's dramatization of urban revolt.

"The People are the City": Smelling Rank in Rome

Coriolanus begins with a riot: "mutinous Citizens" take up arms, vowing rather to die than to famish. Denied "superfluous" grain by the city's patricians, the plebeians vow revenge.[69] As they mobilize, one patrician is singled out as a "very dog to the commonality": Caius Martius. Though his military service to his country is commendable, the plebeians focus on his motivation: pride. Whereas the people are collectively defined, Martius's pride defines him as singular. As one rioter concludes, "what he hath done famously, he did it to that end... he did to please his mother and to be partly proud, even to the altitude of his virtue" (1.1.38–39). Another rioter counters: "what he cannot help in his nature, you account a vice in him" (1.1.40). The play thus begins with two nameless rioters debating whether Caius Martius is a vice or a virtue to Rome.

He is, of course, both. But *Coriolanus* begins with such a question to examine the relationship between the "commonality" of the urban rioters and the city itself: are they an integral part of Rome? If they are not, then their collectivity engenders a real threat. If they are, then Martius's pride is a dangerous catalyst of urban sedition. Put another way, which poses more danger: airborne stench, metaphorically represented as plebeians' political "voices," or waterborne waste that, like the plebeians' riots, threatens to overwhelm Roman civic structure? For Martius, there is no distinction: the plebeians embody both. Included in the civic structure of Rome, their voice pollutes the air. Ignored, their riots threaten to overwhelm the city's infrastructure, like polluted, overflowing city fens.

When read against the material history of Rome's cloacæ and London's sewers, the spatial politics of the play emphasize this point. At the start of the play, a riot unfolds at the outskirts of a walled city, a space defined by city fens in both ancient Rome and sixteenth-century London. The play's famous fable of the belly hints at the olfactory dimensions of such an imagined space. There, Menenius attempts to draw the angry crowd into the civic structure of Rome. Addressing them as "masters, my good friends, my neighbors" and my "countrymen," Menenius draws on rhetorical bonds of work, kinship, city, and nation. The rioters resist, using patrician derision of their pungent breath to define themselves as separate. Denied a voice in Rome, and a legitimate form of political protest, they turn to crowd-based violence: "They say poor suitors have strong breaths: they shall know we have strong arms too" (1.1.50–51). They imagine their power as a distinctive olfactory menace—airborne, stinking breath—that leads to violence.

Such a metaphor, however, is quickly converted into bodily waste by Menenius and his famous fable of the belly. Countering their metaphor of bodily power with bodily politics, he posits digestion as a model of civic order. The rioters' "arms" are like mutinous members of a body, railing against its belly. They need the senate, which is a "storehouse, the shop of the body" to "digest things rightly" (1.1.121). The rioters answer his metaphor by extending it: what if the belly fails to digest properly? What should the arm do if the cormorant belly is a "sink o' the body?" Rejecting Menenius's model of digestion, and perhaps fueled by the stench of nearby fens, the rioters query: who is the butt of this political joke? Menenius's and the rioters' debate turns on the definition of urban waste: do the patrician storehouses of grain represent Roman superfluity or waste? Are the citizens who are "wasting" away dispensable within the political structures of Rome? As the first citizen miserably concludes, "we are accounted poor citizens; the patricians good" (1.1.15). Menenius implicitly corroborates this point: as the riot intensifies, he abandons his hopes for inclusion, dismally concluding that Rome and "her rats" will battle (1.1.151).

If the rioters are rats, then Martius is Rome. It is at this moment in act one that Martius enters the play. Denouncing the mutability of the crowd and mocking their inability to judge virtue—"your virtue is / to make him worthy whose offence subdues him / and curst that justice did it"—Martius answers their collective power with his own: "Would the nobility lay aside their ruth, / And let me use my sword, I'd make a quarry / with thousands of these quarter'd slaves, as high as I could pick my lance" (1.1.200–204). Martius's desire to "make a quarry" hints at his desire to rebuild Rome by purging it of such "slaves": the term "quarry" connotes both a heap of corpses as well as an architectural foundation, excavated from stone.[70] Only the news of the Volscian army interrupts the threat of civil strife in Rome: Martius "vents" his "musty superfluity" on the battlefield rather than in the city. Martius's desire to singularly do battle with thousands of enemies comes to fruition in Corioles rather than in Rome. There, "he is himself alone, to answer all the city" (1.4.51–52).

Coriolanus thus dramatizes a link between the threats of urban riots and fears of material rankness, notably diverging from its source material to do so. Plutarch's account chronicles peasant complaints about urban stench, rather than patrician ones. The patricians believe that, although it may "disburden Rome of a great number of cittizens," war with the Volsces will unite the classes.[71] Sicinius and Brutus, as representatives of the people, however, oppose a war that would send "their poore cittizens into a sore infected cittie and pestilent ayer, full of dead bodies unburied."[72] They advocate plebeian sedition on behalf of public health: foul air and pestilence stem from an unnecessary war and a volatile colonization plan rather than Rome's multitudes and civic structure.[73] The hazards of war produce airborne pestilence, displaced in foreign, "infected" cities. Rome's sewage system is mentioned only as a means of subduing the people: Plutarch chronicles that Martius tamed early rebellions by cutting off Rome's aqueducts and sewers.[74] In Plutarch's account, the people are rioting to prevent exposure to a noxious airborne stench of death produced from an unnecessary war. For Shakespeare's Coriolanus, they comprise an excremental waste, imaginatively quarried by his lance.

Martius is a paragon of military power, embodying the Roman quality of *virtus*.[75] Yet, as the name Coriolanus emphasizes, his place is on the battlefield. An inverse of the fussy Lord of *I Henry IV*, who disdains the stench of battle, Martius cannot brook the stench of urban life.[76] When he returns to Rome, his *virtus* becomes a vice. Meninius warns that when Martius "speaks not like a citizen," the people "find him like a soldier" (3.3.55–56). As a soldier, he is a "thing of blood," who runs "reeking o'er the lives of men, as if / 'Twere a perpetual spoil" (2.2.109, 119–20). As such, he is a threat to urban peace, offering his own excremental threat to Rome.[77]

The play's second confrontation between Martius and the plebeians occurs inside the city's walls, emphasizing and intensifying the political divisions established in act one. As Martius struggles with presenting himself to the "fusty plebeians" and their "dull tribunes" in the senate, Aufidius and the Volscian army camps outside Corioles's borders, in the "cypress groves," located just "south" of the city mills, mills that would have resonated with London's corn mills, built near the bridge and the location of Shakespeare's Globe (1.10.30–31).[78] If staged in Blackfriars, such a clue would intensify the play's dramatization of an external threat of invasion and an internal threat of revolt through an audience's intimate knowledge of London's landscape.

The play's politics of space work centripetally. Martius's "deed-achieving" honor inspires a spectacle that rivals the scope of the earlier riot. His valor, which was previously dismissed as an attempt to please his mother, now inspires the "veil'd" women of Rome to expose themselves to the sun's "wanton spoil." The "prattling" nurses, in a "rapture," ignore their babies' cries; kitchen "malkens" clamber "the walls to eye him"; and shopping comes to a halt, for the "stalls, bulks, windows" of the city's shops "are smothered up" to see him (2.1.204–9). The tribunes, witnessing such display, exploit both Coriolanus's pride and the plebeians they represent: knowing that he vowed never to "show his wounds to th'people, begging their stinking breaths," they reorganize the play's earlier failed confrontation between Martius and the plebeians so that it occurs in the heart of the city: the marketplace (2.1.230–33).

Their plan works. Martius hates the stench of the crowd and their mouthpiece, Brutus: they are a many-headed "Hydra," "measles which we disdain," "the cockle of rebellion, insolence, sedition," and "barbarians . . . though in Rome littered" (3.1.236–37).

Brutus is the "horn and noise o'the monster," who can turn the "current in a ditch" and "make your channel his" (3.1.95–96).[79] For Coriolanus, patrician power is threatened by the civic inclusion of so many into the structures of Rome, for, as Annabel Patterson has argued, "what has many heads can have no single agenda."[80] Whereas Patterson focuses on Jacobean politics of voice embedded within the play, I argue that these dynamics of voice also intersect with London's politics of waste management. The stinking breath of the people is conflated with waterborne channels of power. Their inclusion changes the political (and urban) landscape of Rome. Rather than sluice noxious waste away from the city, the many-headed hydra diverts it to its heart: the marketplace. Cominius concludes that Martius's "manhood" is "foolery" when facing such a crowd, "whose rage does rend / Like interrupted waters, and o'erbear / What they are us'd to bear" (3.1.246–48). Military defiance will only exacerbate the problem, causing their filth to overflow and release greater havoc in Rome.

The play's key rebellion scene thus queries who will "run reeking" o'er the other: Coriolanus, a thing of blood, or the noisome plebeians? Linking the stinking breath of the people to steaming vapors from city fens, Martius curses the "mutable, rank-scented meinie" of Rome (3.1.65). Rejecting their "voice" in the senate, he refuses their banishment of him from Rome:

> You common cry of curs, whose breath I hate
> As reek o'th rotten fens, whose loves I prize
> As the dead carcasses of unburied men
> That do corrupt my air: I banish you! (3.3.120–23)

His similes emphasize that the crowd's stench is both airborne and waterborne and much greater than the sum of their individual parts. It is as vile as the rotten city fens and as dangerous as dead carcasses.[81] Martius's syntax mimics the dramatic turn, collapsing his hatred of the people into the smell of the city itself: "Despising/ for you the city, thus I turn my back. / There is a world elsewhere!" (3.3.133–35). As such, it registers a different threat of enclosure: the breath of the people intensifies as it traverses city space, mingling with urban sewage and culminating in its markets, not its pastures. And when Coriolanus smells it, he smells only a unified rankness that defines the whole city. Like the rioters, he vows revenge on Rome (4.5.90).

CONCLUSION

In September 1666, the Great Fire of London burned through the city's industrial and residential enclaves alike, providing a reason and opportunity for the city to develop new infrastructures. As the city coordinated a large-scale response to the destruction, it sought to codify links between public health and regulation of the city's insalubrious spaces. When parliament passed its rebuilding act, it dissolved the city's previous Commission of Sewers, reincorporating it and greatly expanding its purview to include all aspects of the city's sewage, lighting, paving, and cleaning. Christopher Wren's plans for the new city included widened thoroughfares, covered sewers, and embankments to increase air circulation. Though they were not fully implemented, they reveal how fears of urban rankness began to reshape London's spatial—and social—boundaries.

Ironically, Shakespeare's play anticipates such topographical shifts. At the end of the play, Martius vows to scourge Rome's pestilence through fire. Cominius, sent to beg Coriolanus to spare the city on account of his loved ones, reports of a stoic refusal:

> His answer to me was
> He could not stay to pick them in a pile
> Of noisome, musty chaff. He said 'twas folly,
> For one poor grain or two, to leave unburnt
> And still to nose th'offence. (5.1.24–28)

Rome would not be razed; it must be burnt, in order to purge the "offense."

Reimagining revolt over enclosure acts in the country in an urban olfactory environment, *Coriolanus* emphasizes particular fears about proximity to urban stench. Noisome olfactory hazards of urban life shape the play's social topography. The stench of sewers becomes a contested synecdoche in the early seventeenth century for other intangible threats of urban life, particularly aristocratic fears about fluidity of rank and the potential for the outbreak of riots. But what is perhaps most fascinating about Coriolanus and the "rank-scented" meinie of Rome is that the play posits a vision of a past urban experience that is more advanced than its present: it offers a prescient vision of a renaissance of sewage rather than the total annihilation of the city, in which noisome fluids and airs are purged through fire. In the end, only Coriolanus tragically falls. Rome survives as a republic, continuing to nose its offense. *Coriolanus* thus reminds us that a teleological progression of premodern, modern, and postmodern urban space exists only in imaginative space, where the stench of urban life is safely contained. If the people are the city, then olfaction and waste are, too.

NOTES

I would like to thank Amanda Bailey, Elizabeth Blake, Roze Hentschell, Gayle Wald, Kelly Williams, and the University of Maryland's Renaissance Reckonings' seminar participants, particularly Theresa Coletti, Jane Donawerth, Jasmine Lellock, Maynard Mack, and Gerard Passannante, for their helpful comments on earlier drafts of this chapter. I would also like to thank an anonymous reviewer for her or his incisive comments and critiques of this chapter.

1. Raymond Williams, *The Country and The City* (New York: Oxford University Press, 1973), 27 and *Marxism and Literature* (New York: Oxford University Press, 1977), 132.
2. Patricia Yaeger, "Introduction: Dreaming of Infrastructure," *PMLA* 122.1 (2007): 16.
3. Roland Barthes, *Sade, Fourier, Loyola* (Berkeley: University of California Press, 1989), 140. On the sanitation of the English language, see Dominick LaPorte's *History of Shit* (Cambridge, MA: MIT Press, 2002), 57.
4. Laura Brown, *Fables of Modernity: Literature and Culture in the English Eighteenth Century* (Ithaca, NY: Cornell University Press, 1991), 25.
5. Ibid.
6. Ian Munro, *The Figure of the Crowd in Early Modern London: The City and Its Double* (New York: Palgrave Macmillan, 2005), 5.
7. Catherine Edwards, *Writing Rome: Textual Approaches to the City* (New York: Cambridge University Press, 1996), 107.
8. Cicero, Ampelius, and Eutropius condemned him as a traitor, whereas Dionysius and Livy argue for his tragic greatness. Livy celebrates Coriolanus's military might, but chronicles his disastrous tenure as governor. See Philip Brockbank, introduction to *Coriolanus,* by William Shakespeare (London: Methuen, 1976), 29–35.
9. Robert S. Miola, *Shakespeare's Rome* (New York: Cambridge University Press, 2004), 203.
10. Robert Fowler Leighton, *A History of Rome* (New York: Clark & Maynard, 1878), 17.
11. Pliny expressed wonder at the structure's durability. See John Dennie, *Rome of To-Day and Yesterday: The Pagan City* (New York: G.P. Putnam's sons, 1896), 47.
12. Emily Gowers, "The Anatomy of Rome from Capital to *Cloaca,*" *Journal of Roman Studies* 85 (1995): 23–32, 25.

13. Pliny's *Natural History*, xxxvi 24.105, cited in Gowers, "Anatomy of Rome," 25.
14. Medieval descriptions of cities emphasized their concordance with scriptural descriptions of Jerusalem. See Karen Newman, "Toward a Topographic Imaginary: Early Modern Paris," in *Historicism, Psychoanalysis, and Early Modern Culture*, ed. Carla Mazzio and Douglas Trevor (New York: Routledge, 2000), 62. The aphorism, "Rome is the epitome of the civilized world," was in use as early as the first century CE; likewise, Freud argued that Rome was an analogy for "consciousness itself." See Gowers, "Anatomy of Rome," 23.
15. Hugo writes, "The cloacæ of Rome...absorbed all the well-being of the Roman peasant. When the Campagna of Rome was ruined by the Roman sewer, Rome exhausted Italy, and when she had put Italy in her *cloaca*, she poured Sicily in, then Sardinia, then Africa. The sewer of Rome engulfed the world. This *cloaca* offered its maw to the city and to the globe. *Urbi et orbi.* Eternal city, unfathomable sewer." See Victor Hugo, *Les Miserables,* trans. Chas. B. Wilbour, book five, "Jean Valjean" (New York: Carleton Publisher, 1887), 55.
16. See "A Summarie collected by Iohn Bartholomew Marlianvs, a gentleman of Millaine, Tovching the Topographie of Rome in Ancient Time," in *The Romane Historie by T. Livivs of Padva, translated out of Latine into English by Philemon Holland, Doctor in Physicke* (London, 1600), sig. Zzzzziiij.
17. So common was this practice that an ordinance was passed to protect pedestrians. See John Joseph Cosgrove, *History of Sanitation* (Pittsburgh: Standard Sanitary Mfg, 1909), 35.
18. H. Baue, "Die *Cloaca* Maxima in Rom," *Mitteilungen des Leichtweiss-Institutes für Wasserbau der Technischen Universität Braunschweig* 103 (1989), 45–67, cited in Gowers, "Anatomy of Rome," 25, n. 16.
19. Richard Lassels, *The Voyage of Italy, or, A Compleat Journey Through Italy in Two Parts* (Paris and to be sold in London by John Starkey, 1670), 83.
20. Brown, *Fables of Modernity,* 24.
21. On London's acoustic environments, see Bruce Smith, *The Acoustic World of Early Modern England* (Chicago: University of Chicago Press, 1999), 58.
22. Ernest L. Sabine, "Latrines and Cesspools of Mediaeval London," *Speculum* 9 (1934): 313–15.
23. The Sewers Act of 1427 sought to regulate the draining of fens due to damage from flooding. See Joseph Fletcher, "History and Statistics of the Present System of Sewerage in the Metropolis," *Journal of the Statistical Society of London* 7.2 (1844): 145.
24. 23 Henry VIII, c 5.

25. See Bruce Boehrer, *The Fury of Men's Gullets: Ben Jonson and the Digestive Canal* (Philadelphia: University of Pennsylvania Press, 1997), 157.
26. Act 19 Charles II., c. 2, section 24.
27. See Boehrer, *Fury of Men's Gullets,* 159.
28. See Stowe, *A Survey of London* (New York: Routledge, 1890), 389.
29. Ibid.
30. Ibid.
31. See Howes, *Annales*, sig. Kkkk4, 1021.
32. Ibid.
33. Ibid.
34. See Howes, *Annales*, sig. Kkkk4, 1021.
35. See Anon., *A briefe and true relation of the great disorders and riot attempted and committed upon the house of Thomas Hubbert Esquire*...(London, 1647), 3.
36. See Brian Manning, *Village Revolts: Social Protest and Popular Disturbances in England, 1509–1640* (New York: Oxford University Press, 1988), 187.
37. See Munro, *The Figure of the Crowd,* 35–40, 38.
38. The Norfolk enclosure riots of 1549, in which protestors saw their riots as an extension of their legal right to "organize, agitate, and petition," heavily influenced both the agrarian riots of 1607 and the London's apprentice riots of 1596 and 1607. See Barrett L. Beer, *Rebellion and Riot: Popular Disorder in England during the Reign of Edward VI* (Kent, OH: Kent State University Press, 1982, 2005), xxi and "London and the Rebellions of 1548–1549," *Journal of British Studies* 12.1 (1972): 15–38. See also Andy Wood, *The 1549 Rebellions and the Making of Early Modern England* (New York: Cambridge University Press, 2007), 53. The agrarian rioters of 1607, for example, emphasized their loyalty to the King. However, the King's decision to prominently punish a few of the rioters by hanging in order to impose fear on the many emphasized that rioting was not akin to petitioning. Royal proclamations clarified that it was not "a legal course for subjects to remedy their grievances by force, but that they should petition the king to be relieved according to justice." See H. S. Scott, ed., *Journal for Sir Roger Wilbraham* (*Camden Miscellany* 10, Camden Society, 4, 1902), 91–94.
39. In response to the food riots of June 1595, public whipping soon gave way to what Ian Archer calls "martial law," which specifically targeted vagrants in the city and the suburbs. Five apprentices were accused of levying war on the crown and were sentenced to be hanged, drawn, and quartered. See Ian Archer, *The Pursuit of Stability: Social Relations in Elizabethan London* (New York: Cambridge University Press, 2003), 1–3; see also Munro, *The Figure of the Crowd,* 38. In the seventeenth century, constables of the watch patrolled the suburbs for signs of large crowds and violence. See K. J. Lindley, "Riot

Prevention and Control in Early Stuart London," *Transactions of the Royal Historical Society,* 5th series, 33 (1983): 119.

40. See Howes, *Annales*, sig. Llll, 1023.
41. In 1623, the court of aldermen of London tried to eject felt-makers from inhabiting the city because "their trade (in regard of the unsavory things which belong thereto) being noisome to their neighbors." See Mary Bly, "Playing the Tourist in Early Modern London: Selling the Liberties Onstage," *PMLA* 122.1 (2007): 69.
42. George Walter Thornbury, *Old and New London* (London: Cassell, Petter, Galpin & Co., 1881), 163.
43. E. L. Sabine, "Butchering in Medieval London," *Speculum* 8 (1933): 343.
44. Ibid, 345–46.
45. Ibid, 340.
46. David S. Barnes, "Confronting Sensory Crisis in the Great Stinks of London and Paris," *Filth: Dirt, Disgust, and Modern Life* (Minneapolis, University of Minnesota Press, 2005), 103.
47. For more on this literary history, see Brown, *Fables*, chap. 1 and Andrew McRae, "'On the Famous Voyage': Ben Jonson and Civic Space," in *Literature, Mapping, and the Politics of Space in Early Modern Britain,* ed. Andrew Gordon and Bernhard Klein (New York: Cambridge University Press, 2001), 181–203.
48. All quotes are from Ben Jonson, "On the Famous Voyage," in *Ben Jonson and the Cavalier Poets,* ed. Hugh Maclean (New York: W.W. Norton, 1974), 14–20, l. 63–65.
49. Ibid., 90.
50. The term also had an audible dimension. Valerie Allen argues that the "[t]he -ard ending, according to the *Oxford English Dictionary*, denotes 'one who does to excess.' Of great popularity in the sixteenth century, the suffix was just the ticket to describe this noisy explosive. The pet-ard meant something like 'Old Fart Butt,' and carried the same derogatory innuendo as did 'dotard,' 'drunkard,' 'coward,' 'laggard,' 'stinkard,' 'wizard,' and, worst of all, 'Spaniard.'" See Valerie J. Allen, "Broken Air," *Exemplaria* 16.2 (2004): 314.
51. Jonathan Swift, "A Description of a City Shower," in *Swift: Poetical Works,* ed. Herbert Davis (London: Oxford: Clarendon Press, 1948), 60–63.
52. Ibid, 54–56.
53. British Library MS. Add 12503, f. 213–215, Titus B.V., f. 273, 269.
54. British Library MS Royal 17 A XVIII, f. 259.
55. See Bryan Reynolds, "'What is the City but the People?': Transversal Performance and Radical Politics in Shakespeare's *Coriolanus* and Brecht's *Coriolan*," in *Performing Transversally: Reimagining Shakespeare and the Critical Future*, ed. Bryan Reynolds (New York: Palgrave Macmillan, 2003), 85–111; Nate Eastman, "The Rumbling Belly Politic: Metaphorical Location and Metaphorical Government

in *Coriolanus*," *Early Modern Literary Studies* 13.1 (2007): 2.1–39; Arthur Riss, "The Belly Politic: *Coriolanus* and the Revolt of Language," *English Literary History* 59.1 (1992): 53–75. On the Midlands Riots, see Edwin Francis Gay, "The Midland Revolt and the Inquisitions of Depopulation of 1607," *Transactions of the Royal Historical Society,"* n.s., 18 (1904): 217.

56. Gay, "The Midland Revolt," 217.
57. Richard Henry Tawney, *The Agrarian Problem in the Sixteenth Century* (New York: Longmans, Green, 1912), 320.
58. Munro, *Figure of the Crowd,* 38.
59. Ibid., 35–36.
60. Andrew Gurr, "London's Blackfriars Playhouse and the Chamberlain's Men," in *Inside Shakespeare: Essays on the Blackfriars Stage,* ed. Paul Menzer (Selinsgrove: Susquehanna University Press, 2006), 29.
61. Leah Marcus, *Puzzling Shakespeare: Local Readings and Its Discontents* (Berkeley: University of California Press, 1990), 208–9; Bly, "Playing the Tourist," 62.
62. Bly, "Playing the Tourist," 62.
63. Ibid., 63.
64. See *The Shakespeare Company, 1594–1642* (Cambridge: Cambridge University Press, 2004), 37.
65. See James Kuzner, "Unbuilding the City: *Coriolanus* and the Birth of Republican Rome," *Shakespeare Quarterly* 58.2 (2007): 174–199; Madhavi Menon, "Coriolanus and I," in *Queer Times, Queer Becomings*, ed. E.L. McCallum and Mikko Tukhanen, forthcoming; Jonathan Goldberg, "The Anus in *Coriolanus*," in *Historicism, Psychoanalysis, and Early Modern Culture*, ed. Carla Mazzio and Douglas Trevor (New York: Routledge, 2000), 260–271, and Nate Eastman, "The Rumbling Belly Politic," 2.1–39. See also Cathy Shrank, "The City and Civility in *Coriolanus*," *Shakespeare Quarterly* 54.4 (2003): 406–23, and Munro, *The Figure of the Crowd*.
66. Stanley Cavell argued, "A political reading is apt to become fairly predictable once you know whose side the reader is taking, that of the patricians or that of the plebeians." See "Who Does the Wolf Love? Reading *Coriolanus*," in *Shakespeare and the Question of Theory,* ed. Patricia Parker and Geoffrey Hartman (New York: Taylor & Francis, 1985), 247. See also Reynolds, "What is the City but the people?" 89.
67. See, for example, Annabel Patterson, *Shakespeare and the Popular Voice* (Cambridge: Blackwell, 1989) and Reynolds, "What is the City but the people?"
68. Stanley Cavell, *Disowning Knowledge in Seven Plays of Shakespeare* (New York: Cambridge University Press, 2003), 175.
69. All quotations from *Coriolanus* are from the Arden Edition, ed. Philip Brockbank (London: Metheuen, 1976). Act 1.1.21–22, and hereafter cited parenthetically in the text.

70. See the Oxford English Dictionary's entry for "quarry," n1 and n2.
71. Plutarch writes, "when the poore with the riche, and the mean sorte with the nobilitie, should by this deuise be abroad in the warres, & in one campe, and in one seruice, and in one like daunger: that then they would be more quiet and louing together." See *The Lives of Noble Grecians and Romanes...*, trans. Thomas North (Imprinted at London: By Thomas Vautroullier and Iohn VVight, 1579), sig. Xij, 243.
72. Ibid.
73. Ian Munro argues that such a shift is part of the "hidden" plagues of *Coriolanus,* reading this episode against the Colony of Virginia's invitation to Londoners to send vagrants to the new world to ease overcrowding. See *The Figure of the Crowd,* 194.
74. Plutarch, *Lives,* sig. RR, 469. See also Brockbank, "Introduction," 25.
75. When Cominius catalogs Coriolanus's military exploits, he asserts that if "valour is the chiefest virture and / Most dignifies the haver," then Coriolanus "cannot in the world / Be singly counter-pois'd," 2.2.84–85.
76. Hotspur resents the aristocratic lord's presence on the battlefield, who was "neat, trimly dressed, / fresh as a bridegroom ... [and] perfumed like a milliner," *1 Henry IV.*
77. Within Galenic systems, blood was believed to be excrement. See Gail Paster Kern, *The Body Embarrassed* (Ithaca, NY: Cornell University Press, 1993), 69–70.
78. See also Brockbank's editorial note, 150, n.31.
79. For an analysis of Coriolanus's fear of the plebeians' mouth, see Janet Adelman, *Suffocating Mothers: Fantasies of Maternal Origin in Shakespeare's Plays, Hamlet to the Tempest* (New York: Routledge, 1992), 152.
80. See Patterson, *Shakespeare and the Popular Voice,* 130.
81. The Oxford English Dictionary defines the parasynthetic phrase "rank-scented" as imbued with "rank," a term that connotes both a foul scent and a rebellious temperament. Scented can be transitive or intransitive, emphasizing that the meinie both emit and are imbued with rank.

Chapter 7

Vicious Objects: Staging False Wares

Natasha Korda

Although we tend to think of virtue and vice as attributes of subjects, rather than objects, in the context of early modern market regulation it was often things that were deemed virtuous or branded—and punished—as vicious. Market regulation was viewed not simply as an economic, but as a moral imperative. The term virtue, from the Latin *virtus* (manliness, valor, worth) and *vir* (man), was associated with the masculine vigor and worth of "honest" work. As applied to objects, it conveyed the superiority, excellence, and potency of goods produced by such work.[1] Vice, from the Latin *vitium* (fault, defect, failing), was conversely associated with unmanliness, imperfection, and impotency. Vicious objects were impaired or spoiled by some fault, flaw, blemish, or impurity. Evil was similarly used in the regulation of markets to stigmatize commodities produced by noncitizen laborers. Evil objects were purportedly unwholesome, inferior in quality and generally unsatisfactory and defective; used as an adverb, the term meant not only wickedly, but also badly, defectively, imperfectly, or unskillfully, as in the phrase "evil made." Goods produced outside the masculine fellowship of the urban guilds by foreigners, aliens, and women were thus by definition not good in a moral as well as an economic sense and were variously branded as "evil," "unworkmanly," "unwholesome," and "false and deceitful."[2] They were also, as we shall see, frequently associated with the "faults" of womankind.

When vicious objects were discovered in workshops or for sale in London's markets, they were destroyed with a degree of ceremonial display worthy of critical scrutiny. The ritual destruction of false wares was a routine aspect of civic and guild regulation of economic production. The "powers of search," as they were called, were carried out at regular intervals throughout the year by civic and livery company officials, dressed in official regalia and carrying official insignia, who inspected workshops, warehouses, fairs, and markets. A variety of sanctions were exacted against offenders, including not only the levying of fines and various forms of punishment (public shaming, stocking, imprisonment), but also the seizure and destruction of goods deemed "false" on account of their unlawful manufacture.[3] In one common form of punishment, the producer was made to wear the offending object around his or her neck as a form of public humiliation. Thus, for example, bakers accused of using "evill and unholsome paste" or of using short measures were bound and drawn on a hurdle from the Guildhall to their own houses through the streets with the vicious loaves hung around their necks.[4] Sometimes these processions through the streets and markets resorted to more elaborate forms of pageantry and "rough music": one baker accused of eking out his flour with sand was born to the pillory "with one of the obnoxious loaves carried behind him on the point of a lance," while another whose bread was short of weight was carried through the streets on a hurdle while a minstrel played on a tabor behind him.[5]

Borrowing elements of public shaming rituals used to humiliate men who were beaten, scolded, or cuckolded by their wives, the punishment of noncitizen laborers and ritual destruction of their wares likewise took on gendered overtones. Male artisans and tradesmen who had not completed a seven-year apprenticeship and were accused of producing or selling wares that were adulterated (and therefore not fully potent), short of measure, or faulty were punished for their lack of masculine virtue in the practice of their crafts and trades in the same manner as men whose wives were deemed emasculating. The form of their punishment implied that their masculinity was itself faulty, adulterated, or short of measure. If masculine virtue was at stake when male artisans and tradesmen were accused of producing false wares, female virtue was likewise at stake when crafts- and tradeswomen were accused of market abuses; yet their punishment took a different form and carried a very different set of cultural associations.

Since female virtue was associated with chastity or sexual purity, women accused of manufacturing impure, adulterated, or defective wares were stigmatized as sexually unchaste or impure (or as aggressive usurpers of male authority) and were disciplined with the same forms of punishment used for prostitutes, adulteresses, and scolds. Records of women dating back to the thirteenth century specify an apparatus known as the "thew" as the punishment set aside for women who committed market infractions.[6] The term appears to have referred to a variety of devices, including the bridle or *collistrigium* (an iron collar or cage worn about the head and neck, sometimes with a tongue depressor to prevent speech, also used to punish scolds and shrews), the cart (used to punish prostitutes and adulteresses), and the ducking- or cucking-stool (a chair or close-stool used to dunk disorderly women in a pond or river). The word "thew" derived from the Old English *théaw*, meaning "virtue," both in the sense of a "good quality or habit" and of the "bodily powers or forces of a man." To be "thewful" was to be "characterized by good qualities; good, virtuous, moral," while to be "thewless" was to be "vicious, immoral." The thew thus not only doled out corporal punishment for women's informal marketing activities, but defined such women as thewless or lacking in the masculine virtue associated with "honest" work.

We might pause here to ponder the cultural significance of the ritualized punishment not only of subjects who produced "evil" wares, but also of the offending objects themselves. The aim of removing such wares from the marketplace or of protecting consumers from unwholesome or defective goods does not sufficiently explain the necessity of their ritualized, and often quite dramatic, destruction. While such rituals might seem to have had the effect of obliterating what Peter Stallybrass and Ann Rosalind Jones have termed "material memory"—that is, the cultural memory that inheres in material objects, in this case, the memory of an object's maker[7]—this explanation evades a crucial aspect of this cultural practice, namely, the way in which the obliteration of false wares was publicly staged. On account of such stagings, and in the accounts through which they were memorialized for posterity in livery company records, the obliteration of material memory in a crucial sense fails. Staging the eradication of vicious objects was clearly as (if not more) important than their eradication itself, I would suggest, because the "evil" character of the things destroyed was the effect rather than the cause of their ritualized destruction. The very necessity of such rituals points to the temporary and provisional nature of the cultural meaning of things; it is precisely because the meaning and value of objects are never fixed that such meanings must be continually, and sometimes violently, staged.

The ritual destruction of false wares was part of an ongoing contest over the cultural meaning and value of early modern London's consumer goods and over who was entitled to produce and profit from them. The exponential population growth of London during late sixteenth and early seventeenth centuries made civic and guild control of informal commercial activity extremely difficult. Increasing numbers of migrants took up occupations outside of guild control, swelling the ranks of noncitizen laborers. The effective enforcement of existing regulations was further hampered by the absence of a professional police force. The searching out of market abuses was left to civic and livery company officials, whose numbers were unequal to the task, and to an unpaid and overworked constabulary. City and guild officials were forced to rely on private informers called "promoters" to search out offenders.[8] Economic offenses "were those most zealously pursued" by promoters because they were the most lucrative: the informer was entitled to a share (usually half) of the penalty, which was set in proportion to the value of the confiscated property. During the period when promoters were most active, from 1550 to 1624, they functioned as "a chief instrument for the enforcement of economic legislation."[9] Yet the legions of promoters who sought to earn a living or to supplement their incomes by informing on marketing offenses were themselves prone to "chickanery and blackmail."[10] The expense of going to trial led most defendants, whether guilty or not, to negotiate out of court settlements or "compositions" (in cash or goods) with promoters, which amounted to a kind of informal tax, and sometimes to outright blackmail.[11] Unlike civic and livery company officials, private promoters thus benefited from the continuance, rather than the cessation, of illicit commerce. The corruption of promoters consequently became a frequent subject of complaint and satire during the period leading up to the legislative reforms of 1624, which greatly reduced the numbers of private informers. Informations against marketing offenses brought by promoters rose by 80 percent between 1609 and 1613, reaching their peak in 1616, when serious reforms began.[12] It was during this period, when the activity of private informers reached its apex and effective governmental reforms had yet to be enacted, that the drama of contestation over the parameters of legitimate trade and the policing of "false" wares became a popular topic on the public stage.

Yet this drama had quite different cultural implications when performed onstage by professional players than by civic officials in

London's streets, markets, and fairs. For in the eyes of London's civic and religious authorities, the profession of playing was itself the very antithesis of virtuous, civic masculinity: it was "a softe, a silken... kind of life, fitter for women than for men."[13] Like other occupations in the informal sector, playing was relegated to the status of mere idleness, and was thus considered, by definition, not-work.[14] Idleness, the "Mother of vice," purportedly rendered the players effeminate or "unfit for manly discipline."[15] Playing in turn rendered spectators idle and effeminate by luring them away from "honest" trades.[16] City authorities repeatedly complained to the Privy Council that the players and playhouses "maintaine idlenes in such persons as have no vocation & draw apprentices and other servantes from theire ordinary workes... to the great hinderance of traides."[17] John Stephens's collection of *Essayes and Characters* (1615) describes the common player as "A daily Counterfeit," claiming, "there is no truth in him: for his best action is but an imitation of truth... he is but a shifting companion; for hee lives effectually by putting on, and putting off. If his profession were single, hee would think himselfe a simple fellow, as hee doth all professions besides his owne."[18] By "putting on" other occupations, the players figured the flexibility of those who labored in the informal economy; for they likewise arrogated to themselves trades to which they were not entitled.

The charge that players counterfeited legitimate trades often centered on their own trafficking in "evil" wares. Stage-properties were viewed by antitheatrical writers as inherently "false" both because of their fictive status and because they were often actual counterfeits. The players could rarely afford the "real" thing in their manufactures, and therefore relied on the same techniques (e.g. gilding, the use of cheap or defective materials, etc.) purportedly used by deceitful crafts- and tradesmen. Antitheatrical polemics often focused their invectives on the falseness of the props and costumes staged in the public playhouses. Stephen Gosson derides the "waste of expences in these spectacles that scarce last like shooes of browne paper, the pulling on."[19] Gosson here refers to the players' practice of making properties out of brown paper and paste, likening their insubstantial wares to those of a cobbler who produces flimsy or defective shoes. He further describes theaters as "markets of bawdry, where choise without shame hath bene as free as it is for your money in the royall exchaung to take a short stocke, or a longe, a falling band, or a french ruffe," cataloguing the expensive yet insubstantial wares on offer in the theaters to suggest that the "soule of... playes is... meere trifles."[20] The players' use of copper-lace instead of gold-lace to adorn costumes was likewise cited as evidence of their status as counterfeits. Henry Crosse, in his *Vertues Common-wealth* of 1603, derides players as "copper-lace gentlemen" who "growe rich" and "purchase lands by adulterous Playes."[21] Although Crosse is undoubtedly referring to the "adulterous" plots of many plays, his reference to copper-lace also suggests that the players grow rich by attracting crowds with their display of falsely gilded and adulterated costumes and properties. In response to such attacks on the legitimacy of playing as a profession, the anonymous author (possibly John Webster) of the character of "An Excellent Actor," written in response to that of the "common Player" cited earlier, claims "I valew a worthy Actor by the corruption of some few of the quality, as I would doe gold in the oare; I should not mind the drosse, but the purity of the metall."[22] While it may be true, he acknowledges, that the common player is mere dross, the value of a "worthy Actor" is pure gold; playing is indeed a "quality" or legitimate calling, he insists, involving skills that must be perfected as in any other trade. For their own part, the players defended the status and reputation of their craft as a legitimate calling. Professional playing, in the words of actor Nathan Field, was a trade just like that of "the mercer, draper, goldsmith, or a hundred trades and mysteries that at this day are lawful."[23] Against this backdrop, it becomes clear that the staging of false wares in the commercial playhouses had implications that bore on the legitimacy of playing itself as a profession. In order to bolster their own claim to virtuous, civic masculinity, the players had to distinguish their trade from other forms of informal commerce that were branded as idle and effeminate. In doing so, however, they also sought to distinguish themselves from hypocritical promoters and Puritan preachers who purported to "discover" market abuses while profiting from them themselves.

In the remainder of this chapter, I explore how this rather complex agenda is negotiated in two city comedies whose ostensible aim is the satirical discovery of such abuses. Both were written not only at the height of the controversy surrounding how informal commerce ought to be policed, but also at a particularly tense moment in the ongoing debate over the legitimacy of playing as a profession. Thomas Middleton's *A Chaste Maid in Cheapside* (1613) and Ben Jonson's *Bartholomew Fair* (1614) appeared just after the publication of Thomas Heywood's *Apology for Actors* (1612), which sought to defend the "ancient Dignity" of the profession, and just before the publication of I. G.'s response to Heywood, *A Refutation of the Apology for Actors* (1615), reasserting the argument that players are "Idle, for they…know not how to worke, nor in any lawfull calling to get their living," but rather "avoid labour and worke" by taking money from "every one that comes to see them loyter and play. Hence it is that they are Vicious; for idlenesse is the mother of vice."[24] Recent scholarship on city comedy has contributed a great deal to our understanding of the genre's participation in the construction of new forms of urban masculinity attendant upon London's growth as a commercial center. The genre, Jean Howard argues, staged "complex narratives about the pressures on masculinity in the urban context and the struggle between old and new ways of achieving and displaying masculine privilege."[25] One such pressure, I argue, arose from the expansion of informal commerce in the city's markets and its growing population of noncitizen laborers, including market women, who threatened the ideal of virtuous, civic masculinity fostered by the urban guilds. If city comedies represented the expanding metropolis as a crucible where gender identities were constantly being renegotiated and differentially defined, I want to suggest, these identities were materially crafted through the staging of virtuous and vicious objects as well as subjects. In staging the contestation over the manufacture and sale of false wares, Jonson and Middleton sought to forge a new definition of civic masculinity to which the professional players themselves might lay claim.

* * *

Although first performed in the suburbs of the city at the Swan Theatre on the bankside just after Lent in 1613, *A Chaste Maid in Cheapside* takes as its subject and location the walled city's commercial center: the Cheapside market district located in "the heart of the city of London."[26] In so doing, the play reveals that the effeminating vices of the marketplace are not confined to the "skirts" of the city where the public theaters were located, but run rampant at its core, in what purports to be a bastion of virtuous, civic masculinity and honest trade. Middleton no doubt chooses Cheapside from among the city's many official markets not only because of its exemplarity (Stow describes Goldsmith's Row at its center as harboring "the most beautiful frame of fayre houses and shoppes, that bee within the Walles of London"),[27] but because of its peculiar architecture as well: the physical contours of Cheapside market were delimited by three conduits—the Little or "Pissing" Conduit at its western end, the Standard at its center, and the Great Conduit at its eastern end—which in the play stand as emblems of its commercial incontinence, its inability to contain or regulate market abuses. Although in other respects the geography of Cheapside suggested an orderly, bounded structure, with side streets named after discrete trades such as Milk Street, Bread Street, Ironmonger's Lane, and Goldsmith's Row, by the late sixteenth century this structure had begun to give way to a disorderly influx of immigrant and itinerant traders. In 1588 the city attempted to improve the market's organization by assigning itinerant traders to discrete locations within the market, but with little success.[28] By the second decade of the seventeenth century, Goldsmith's Row (the pride of Cheapside) was in decay, signaling "the [Goldsmith's] Company's loss of control over the sale of jewels, gold and silver plate within the city due to competition from strangers."[29]

A Chaste Maid in Cheapside opens in a shop on Goldsmith's row, where Maudlin, the wife of Yellowhammer the goldsmith, is chastising their daughter Moll for her shortcomings in terms that might be borrowed from the Goldsmith's Company's ordinances proscribing the manufacture of false wares. Boasting that she herself was "lightsome, and quick, two years before [she] was married" (1.1.8), Maudlin reproves Moll for being "dull" and "drossy spirited" (10). Although ostensibly bragging about her own light-hearted, cheerful, and animated disposition in her youth, Maudlin's revelation that she was "lightsome" and "quick" well before she married further intimates that she was sexually active, if not actually pregnant, before her espousal. Insofar as the terms "lightsome" and "quick" were also used to describe the vivid, bright, dazzling luminosity of gold, Maudlin's betrayal of her sexual lightness reminds the audience that the luster of gold is never a guarantee of its purity. The Goldsmith's Company ordinances are replete with references to deceptive practices used to counterfeit pure gold or gems. The "Oath of the New Men" of the Company dictated "you shall work and cause to be worked good and true gold and silver without any deceit; and you shall not set glass or counterfeit stones in gold," while another ordinance stipulated "no member of the Company shall set a deceptive color upon gilt wares, such as layting up in helle." The phrase "lighting up in hell" (from the Middle High German *hellen*, to make bright) referred to a method of gilding wares to make them appear brighter (while also suggesting the infernal destination of those who engaged in such practices).[30] Although a citizen's wife, Maudlin betrays that she is herself "lit up in hell," that she is not what she seems, so that when she describes her daughter as "drossy" we suspect the veracity of her appraisal. Her use of the term "drossy" likewise reveals her familiarity with deceitful market practices; for gold that was "drossy" was mixed with impure, worthless matter. Although in Maudlin's estimation, lightness is better than heaviness, market regulation dictated otherwise: "light" gold was gold that, due to adulteration, was below the standard or legal weight.

When Yellowhammer enters, Maudlin informs her husband that she has been telling their daughter "of her errors" (22), to which he replies,

> "Errors," nay the city cannot hold you wife, but you must needs fetch your words from Westminster; I ha' done i' faith. Has no attorney's clerk been here alate and changed his half-crown-piece his mother sent him, or rather cozened you with a gilded twopence, to bring the word in fashion for her faults or cracks in duty and obedience, term 'em e'en so, sweet wife? As there is no woman made without a flaw, your purest lawns have frays, and cambricks bracks. (23–30)

Yellowhammer's assertion that "there is no woman made without a flaw" gives voice to Maudlin's implicit equation of women with false wares, while diverting attention from the "faults or cracks" of goldsmiths' wares to those of clothmakers. His speech simultaneously acknowledges the ubiquity of "light" wares and coins in the city, while deflecting criticism from such "cracks" in the formal economy by insisting that even the "purest" wares (and women) have flaws. Priding himself on being "of the freedom" (126–27), that is, on his status as a citizen-tradesman, he chides his wife for her linguistic/commercial (and, we surmise, sexual) incontinence, linking her use of the latinate term "errors," instead of such "plain, sufficient subsidy words" (128–29) as "frays" and "bracks," to the permeable boundaries of the city's walls and wives. Maudlin's response once again associates "evil" wares with the "fault" of female sexuality: "But 'tis a husband solders up all cracks" (31), she teases, implying that her own "cracked" sexual purity has been soldered up by her marriage to him.

The incontinency of Cheapside's cracked wives is compared throughout the play to the defects of the wares on offer in its shops: simply put, they are, to borrow Gail Kern Paster's apt phrase, "leaky vessels."[31] Female incontinence within the play comes to figure the porous boundaries of the formal economy and the false wares or leaky vessels that breach these boundaries. The faults or cracks of Cheapside's wives are revealed at the christening of the bastard child of Allwit, whose wife is pregnant by Sir Walter Whorehound. The scene's satire of female incontinence is aimed in particular at the Puritan wives, who commend the event for being "Without idolatry or superstition" (3.2.4), while proceeding to gorge themselves gluttonously on comfits and wine until they hiccup and wet themselves. Their incontinency becomes a subject of conversation as one of the gossips tells another that she cannot marry her nineteen-year-old daughter because she has "a secret fault . . . she's too free . . . she cannot lie dry in her bed" (3.2.107, 111, 113). The scene ends when the wives all run off to see a show performed "by the Pissing-conduit" (205), and Allwit discovers puddles of liquid under their stools and surmises they have "drunk so hard" (201) that they could not contain their urine. The vulgarity evidenced in their conduct at the christening is likewise reflected in their lowly theatrical tastes: Allwit gets them to leave his house by telling them that "two brave drums and a standard bearer" (206) are playing "yonder," to which they eagerly cry "Where? Where sir? . . . O brave" as they rush out the door (204, 207).

Despite his name, Allwit is hardly a paragon of wit, nor for that matter of virtuous, civic masculinity. Rather, he epitomizes the vice of idleness so abhorred by city and guild officials. He professes himself to live in the "happiest state that ever man was born to" (1.2.22), namely, that of a wittol, or a willing, complacent cuckold. Allwit gladly hands over his wife to Sir Walter because the latter is willing to pay all his family's expenses, allowing him to eschew any and all productive work: "the knight / Hath took that labour all out of my hands; / I may sit still and play . . . / . . . I live at ease; / He has both the cost and torment; when the strings / Of his heart frets, I feed, laugh, or sing, / La dildo, dildo la dildo, la dildo dildo de dildo" (1.2.51–57). Although a common refrain used in ballads, the term "dildo" also referred to a substitute or counterfeit phallus, and thus to a particular variety of false wares. The suggestion here is that Allwit's failure to produce legitimate wares or children causes his wife to resort to a substitute phallus and thereby produce illegitimate or adulterated offspring herself. When one of his servants enters to find Allwit singing this refrain, the servant comments: "Now's out of work he falls to making dildoes" (1.2.59). Allwit makes dildoes, he intimates, because he shuns honest work. When used to describe a man, the term dildo suggested effeminacy, cowardice, and a lack of manly virtue, as in the phrase "a milk-livered dildoe."[32] When Allwit's servant refers to Sir Walter as his master, Allwit asks "Pray am not I your master?" to which a second servant replies, "O you are but our mistress's husband" (1.2.64–65). Allwit's idleness, his making of dildoes, is represented as a threat to honest trade and the virtuous, civic masculinity associated with it. The dildo stands as an apt emblem of the sex/gender trouble associated in the play with Cheapside's incontinent, unruly marketplace; for it simultaneously suggests male impotence, female usurpation of masculine "tools" and prerogatives, and the counterfeit or adulterated goods that result from such commercial disorder. Throughout the play, Allwit brags of his state of unconstrained idleness, boasting, "That's all the work I'll do, nor need I stir, / But that it is my pleasure . . . / . . . I am tied to nothing / . . . what I do is merely recreation, / Not constraint" (2.2.2–6). The only work Allwit is willing to perform is aimed at trying to maintain his state of idleness by ensuring that Sir Walter never marries (1.2.115).

Middleton's play is focused on the unconstrained reproduction, rather than destruction, of illicit commerce, associated in the play with the rampant reproduction of illegitimate children. Cheapside is replete with bastards, the products of its many adulterous liaisons, who are likened to its false, hastily manufactured wares, insofar as they too are "Put to making in minutes" (2.1.37–38). We see four onstage, but many more are referred to. Touchwood Sr. alone admits to having gotten no fewer than seven illegitimate children (62). When one of the wenches he has impregnated confronts him, she demands "Do you see your workmanship?" (65), implying that it is faulty indeed. His apology does not refute her analogy: "Do but in courtesy faith wench excuse me / Of this half yard of flesh, in which I think it wants / A nail or two" (82–84). His analogy references clothworkers who sell by short measure (a "nail" was a measure of cloth, one-sixteenth of a yard), as well as the offspring of syphilitics, who were sometimes born without fingernails. It thus builds on the play's continual conflation of sexual and commercial reproduction, as does Touchwood Sr.'s offer of money to the wench, which likens his illegitimate offspring to faulty shop-wares that must be sold as quickly as they were "put to making": "Here's all I have, i'faith, take purse and all, / And would I were rid of all the ware i' the shop so" (98–99).

Set during Lent, the play foregrounds the problematic of market regulation and the vice it breeds, rather than prevents, by centering this problematic around the "flesh" trade—evoking the illicit trade both in contraband meat (prohibited during Lent) and in human flesh (prostitution). When the wench accepts Touchwood Sr.'s offer of cash and exits with his purse, he wonders "What shift she'll make now with this piece of flesh / In this strict time of Lent . . . / Flesh dare not peep abroad now" (106–8). The play's conflation of illicit sex and commerce comes to a head in a scene that brings to light what Allwit refers to disparagingly as the "corruption of promoters, / And other poisonous officers that infect / And with a venomous breath taint every goodness" (112–14). Shortly after Touchwood Sr.'s encounter with the wench, two promoters enter searching for infractions of the prohibition against eating or selling flesh during Lent. Allwit, who espies them, brings to light their corruption, revealing that they are involved in the "flesh" trade in more ways than one:

> This Lent will fat the whoresons up with sweetbreads
> And lard their whores with lamb-stones; what their golls
> Can clutch goes presently to their Molls and Dolls.
> The bawds will be so fat with what they earn
> Their chins will hang like udders by Easter eve. (2.2.68–72)

The promoters, he claims, take compositions in kind, confiscating the flesh of those against whom they inform for themselves or to fatten the prostitutes they keep on the side.

We witness the corruption of the promoters in action, in the form of their abetting, rather than averting, illicit commerce in "flesh," when a man enters with a basket of contraband meat. Discovering and confiscating the meat, they regret that it is "all veal," as they had promised "a fat quarter of lamb to a kind gentlewoman in Turnbull street that longs" (123–26)—Turnbull street being a notorious prostitution district. City commerce in Middleton's play is represented as a vicious, endless, cycle of trade in "flesh": the wares of unlicensed butchers are confiscated by promoters, who fatten pregnant prostitutes, who in turn produce bastards, populating the city with noncitizens, who grow up to be unlicensed butchers, and so on. In the end, the promoters get their comeuppance when the final patron of the illicit flesh-market whom they apprehend turns out to be Touchwood Sr.'s wench with her bastard child hidden in a basket "under a loin of mutton" (145 s.d.). Seeing them, she confides in an aside, "Women had need of wit, if they'll shift here, / And she that hath wit may shift anywhere" (148–49). She leaves the rump of mutton uncovered to bait the promoters, and when they threaten to confiscate it, pretends to be the servant of a wealthy but ill gentlewoman whose doctor has prescribed mutton as physic. They insist that she leave her basket with them, and she makes them swear to keep it until she returns. Searching through the basket, they wager as to whether it conceals "a quarter of lamb" or a "shoulder of mutton," and as they grope, the promoter who wagered on lamb is gleeful when he feels what he takes to be "a lamb's head" (180–81, 187). Eventually he discovers that the head belongs to the foundling infant, and curses, "Life had she none to gull but poor promoters / That watch hard for a living?" (197–98). They resolve to "go to the Checker [Inn] at Queen-hive and roast the loin of mutton, till young flood; then send the child to Brainford" to be brought up in a bawdy-house (213–15). And so the cycle of illicit commerce continues.

Although Middleton's city-comedy satirically lays bare the "shifts" of wit that characterize early modern London's feminized, informal economy, *A Chaste Maid* can hardly be said to contain a moral lesson, as vice goes unpunished. Indeed, the wench, who in the play stands in for the multitudes of migrant women who brought their wares in baskets to sell in Cheapside market, gets the better of the corrupt promoters. While the flexibility and ingenuity of women's informal commerce are referenced by her motto ("she that hath wit may shift anywhere"), it is simultaneously effaced, insofar as she trades in bastards, not beef. Middleton's emphasis is on the reproduction of illegitimate children, rather than on the destruction of illegitimate commodities: Cheapside's informal economy is characterized by a hyperproductivity/fertility that cannot be staved. In the end, all are invited by Yellowhammer to dine at Goldsmith's Hall, suggesting that Cheapside commerce will continue to accommodate the incontinent commercial practices the play has revealed. Nor does Middleton work terribly hard to distinguish the "idle occupation" of the professional players from the other forms of contested commerce his play uncovers. The distinction remains implicit in the difference between the mode of entertainment enjoyed by the incontinent women of Cheapside (two brave drums and a standard-bearer at the Pissing Conduit) and his own play's discovery of the incontinent vices of the city. Middleton's play thus raises a question at the center of the controversy surrounding professional playing: is the representation or discovery of vice in and of itself a virtuous activity and honest trade, or do those who earn their living in this way, whether they be promoters or professional players, participate in and profit from the very vices they purport to put down? Left unresolved in *A Chaste Maid in Cheapside*, this question is addressed directly in *Bartholomew Fair*.

* * *

First performed a year after *A Chaste Maid* at the newly built Hope Theatre on the bankside (and soon after at Court), Jonson's *Bartholomew Fair* likewise takes as its subject the discovery of market abuses, here located in one of London's renowned market-fairs, which took place in and around suburban Smithfield for three days every August. Yet Jonson's play explores in far-greater depth the status of playing and play-making in relation to the "idle occupations" of the suburbs, highlighting the similarities as well as the differences between the false wares of the theater and those of the fair. Like Middleton, Jonson foregrounds the corruption and hypocrisy of the agents of civic enforcement charged with reforming market abuses. Yet Jonson is engaged in his own project of theatrical reform, aiming to enlighten the reformers themselves as to the higher purpose of playing, and thereby to defend its status and legitimacy. Consequently, Jonson's Justice Overdo, unlike Middleton's promoters, undergoes his own reformation; whereas the latter clearly intend to continue their corrupt practices after the play ends, having learned nothing from the trick played on them by the wench, Justice Overdo ultimately recognizes that correcting the vices of the market (and the theater) is not best accomplished through outright destruction—that it is better to build up or edify, than to tear down: "*ad correctionem, non ad destructionem; ad aedificandum, non ad diruendum*."[33] Yet Jonson's attitude toward the false wares associated with theatrical spectacle is not simply one of loathing, but rather is characterized, as Jonas Barish famously argued, by an "unsettling ambivalence."[34] His comedies, and *Bartholomew Fair* in particular, manifest an undeniably virtuosic showmanship that places his condemnation of antitheatricalism in tension with the performative effects his plays enact. In *Bartholomew Fair* this tension or ambivalence manifests itself in Jonson's staging of the spectacle, as well as the destruction, of false wares, and in particular those manufactured and sold by market women.

Jonson's play even more than Middleton's brings to the fore the problematic status of stage-properties as false wares through its lavish staging of the trumpery on offer at the fair. His reproduction of the fair's market-stalls and merchandise onstage highlights the status of the commercial theaters as showplaces of eye-catching costumes and properties, drawing customers in through their display of insubstantial, yet dazzling, wares. By staging his drama at a seasonal fair, rather than one of London's permanent markets, Jonson underscores the ephemeral aspect of stage spectacle, while also distinguishing the temporary "standings" of the fair from the new permanence of London's purpose-built theaters, thereby implicitly conferring a legitimacy on the professional players that is lacking in the informal and itinerant tradespeople they portray. This distancing of actor and role does not, however, prevent Jonson from staging the paraphernalia of the fair to full dramatic effect, deploying a wide range of stage-properties to recreate the fair's wonder-inducing merchandise.

Like Middleton, Jonson sexualizes market women who trade in "flesh." "Here you may ha' your punk [i.e. whore] and your pig in state, sir, both piping hot" (2.5.38–39), Ursula the pig-woman advertises. Unlike Middleton's city wives, however, the independent, unmarried market women of Bartholomew Fair reproduce false wares instead of bastards: Ursula is described as the "mother o' the pigs" (2.5.68; see also 2.3.2), and Joan Trash's wares are called her "gingerbread-progeny" (2.2.1). Jonson's suburban market women are not "daughters of the freedom" like Middleton's city wives, but independent commercial agents who seek to earn their living beyond the purview of guild and city control. The strong female presence at the fair includes not only the memorable Joan Trash and monumental Ursula the pig-woman, but also an offstage population signaled by passing references to market women who populate the suburbs, such as the "blue-starch woman" (1.3.129) or the "Catherine-pear-woman" (1.5.109). This presence is likewise foregrounded by the striking embodiment of the play's female vendors, whose market abuses are literally made flesh: Joan Trash's body is as crooked as her commercial practices, while Ursula's "enormities" (Justice Overdo's term for market infractions) are materialized in her prodigious corpulence. She is called the "Body o' the Fair" (2.5.67) because she not only practices, but herself embodies, its myriad vices. Justice Overdo describes her booth as "the very womb and bed of enormity, gross as herself!" (2.2.102–3). Ursula's incontinence, like that of Middleton's city dames, figures that of the market itself, its breaching of all boundaries and structures of stability.

Jonson mines market women's commercial activities for their theatrical potential, while at the same time seeking to distinguish his own theatrical progeny from their faulty products. In giving Joan the surname "Trash," he references the devaluation of market women's wares as defective, adulterated rubbish. Both Joan Trash and Ursula are mercilessly taunted for the purportedly inferior quality of their merchandise. Quarlous teases Ursula that she should be publicly punished for her market abuses: "Do you think there may be a fine new cucking-stool i' the Fair to be purchased? One large enough, I mean. I know there is a pond of capacity for her" (2.5.106–8). Leatherhead, the hobby-horse seller, likewise threatens Joan: "Do you hear, Sister Trash, Lady o' the Basket? Sit farther with your gingerbread-progeny there, and hinder not the prospect of my shop, or I'll ha' it proclaimed i' the Fair what stuff they are made on" (2.2.2–5). Leatherhead condescends to Joan because she is an itinerant vendor who sells out of a basket, rather than from a stall, and implies that her gingerbread is made from cheap or unwholesome ingredients. Joan does not allow his aspersion of her wares to go uncontested, however, replying,

"Why, what stuff are they made on, Brother Leatherhead? Nothing but what's wholesome, I assure you" (6–7). Leatherhead persists, making his accusation explicit ("Yes, stale bread, rotten eggs, musty ginger, and dead honey, you know" [8–9]), and threatening, "I shall mar your market, old Joan" (11). She responds in kind, calling him a "too-proud pedlar" and taunting, "Are you puffed up with the pride of your wares? Your arsedine?" (12, 17–18).

In claiming that Leatherhead's wares are gilded with arsedine or orsedue, an alloy made of copper and zinc used to imitate gold leaf, Joan suggests that his wares are not what they seem. The reference to arsedine likewise underscores the theatrical status of the false wares staged in *Bartholomew Fair* as stage-properties; for arsedine was commonly used to gild the props used in plays, pageants, and masques.[35] At the end of the play, the status of Leatherhead's false wares as props is actualized when Bartholomew Cokes learns that Leatherhead sidelines as a puppet-master and all-around theatrical impresario. Cokes ends the competitive quarrelling between Leatherhead and Joan by offering to buy the entire contents of his stall and her basket. At this point, the two end their competition and begin to collude together to increase their profits. Joan advertises Leatherhead's "qualities" as a theatrical jack-of-all-trades, known for his puppet-shows, trials of wit, parodies of contemporary players, and mock bear-baiting contests (114–23). Thrilled at the prospect of such spectacles, Cokes asks whether Leatherhead can "set out a masque," to which Joan replies, "O Lord, master! Sought to, far and near, for his inventions" (124–25). Their gambit pays off, as the delighted Cokes orders Leatherhead to "shut up shop," promising that his wares "shall furnish out the masque" (133) for Cokes's own wedding, and that Joan's gingerbread will provide the wedding banquet (148–50). Far from denying the status of stage-properties as false wares, Jonson highlights it; he does so, however, as we shall see, in service to his project of theatrical reform.

Certainly, Coke's belief that such lowly spectacles performed at his wedding will bring him "credit" (135) is being mocked. Throughout the play, he stands as an emblem of mindless consumerism (he sacrifices all he has for toys and trifles) and of mindless spectatorship (he gawks at the spectacles of fair and puppet-show, like the uncouth "stare-abouts" who frequent plays, we are told, only to have their purses cut [3.5.121]). Cokes gains nothing through his vulgar consumption of false wares; indeed, he loses himself and everything he owns at the fair. Yet Jonson does not simply renounce the theater's reliance upon false wares through his satire of Cokes; for he equally derides those who favor the outright destruction of false wares through his satire of Zeal-of-the-Land Busy, the Puritan preacher. Drunk on Ursula's ale, Busy focuses his wrath with greatest venom on Joan Trash's wares, crying, "Hence with thy basket of popery, thy nest of images, and whole legend of ginger-work" (3.6.68–69). Decrying her "idolatrous grove of images" (90), he "Overthrows the gingerbread [basket]" (s.d.), destroying her merchandize. Leatherhead threatens him with arrest "for disturbing the Fair" (3.6.71). Jonson thereby reverses the typical outcome of market justice: here it is the Puritan preacher (Busy) and civic magistrate (Overdo), who are arrested and thrown in the stocks, rather than the vendors of such wares.

Jonson does not simply renounce the dependence of dramatic illusion on "trash"; rather, he draws our attention to this reliance from the start, before the play proper even begins. For the play is famously introduced to the theater audience by the Stage-Keeper, who is busy sweeping up the "trash" left on the stage—including Joan's broken ginger-bread—from the previous day's performance. When the Book-Holder or prompter enters, he chides the Stage-Keeper for offering his uncouth judgment of the play to the audience: "Your judgement, rascal? For what? Sweeping the stage? Or gathering up the broken apples for the bears within? Away, rogue, it's come to a fine degree in these spectacles when such a youth as you pretend to a judgement" (Ind., 49–52). Among the detritus that litters the stage and the pit, he observes, are the remnants of apples (sold by apple-wives during the performance of plays).[36] The Stage-Keeper thus sets the stage for the destruction of market women's wares within the play, by sweeping the remnants of such female "trash" from the stage. In so doing, however, he does not simply erase the material memory of market women's wares, but rather calls attention to the "stuff" of the stage as an integral aspect of the performance to follow.

By dividing the initial action of the play between the Stage-Keeper and Book-Keeper, Jonson personifies the distinction between the play-as-spectacle and the play-as-text. The Stage-Keeper's focus is entirely on the (often faulty) "stuff" of theatrical staging; he informs us that one of the actors has "a stitch new fallen in his black silk stocking" (Ind., 3–5), which is being mended backstage, and he complains that the play does not contain enough "fine sights" (19) for his liking. As we have seen, Jonson does stage many of the "fine sights" of the fair, including its "birds o' the booths" (2.2.35), drunken brawls, bawdy ballads, and puppet-show. Yet in making his own representation of the spectacles of the fair a subject of explicit controversy, he opens to critical scrutiny the antitheatrical claim that the commercial theaters were mere "markets of bawdry" or purveyors of unwholesome, light or counterfeit wares. Jonson's counterattack against this claim is predicted by the Scrivener, the third character of the Induction, whose interest is neither in play-spectacle nor play-text per se, but rather in the business of show—the theater as a commercial institution. He famously draws up "Articles of Agreement" between author and audience (62–65), which position the audience as consumers who may judge the playwright's wares only to the extent of the fee each has paid to see the play. Yet he warns that none should expect "better ware than a Fair will afford" (111). To the extent that the audience comes to inspect and judge the "wares" of Bartholomew Fair, they are positioned as surveyors of the market the play represents, who stand ready to decry its abuses. The Scrivener warns, however, that the playwright likewise stands ready to inform against any corrupt or hypocritical promoters in the audience. The author, he advises, "prays you to believe his ware is still the same, else you will make him justly suspect that he that is so loth to look on a baby or an hobby-horse here, would be glad to take up a commodity of them, at any laughter or loss, in another place" (155–59). It is the hypocrisy of those who profit from or take pleasure in the very faults or vices they decry, whether they be promoters or Puritans, playgoers or playwrights, that the ensuing play will discover.

This discovery perhaps most memorably targets Puritan diatribes against the professional players as idle, effeminate drones who eschew virtuous, masculine trades to flaunt their vicious, idolatrous wares onstage.[37] Jonson's counterattack cleverly redeploys the term "hypocrite," commonly used in Puritan attacks against the players, repeatedly using it to describe the Puritans themselves, who frequent Bartholomew Fair while simultaneously decrying it.[38] The hypocrisy of city magistrates who police market abuses, while ignoring their own "faults," likewise comes under attack in the play. Setting out to rectify the abuses of both market vendors and idle officers (foolish constables and lazy watchmen), Overdo ends up revealing his own faults as an informant: he believes everything he sees and hears and fails utterly in the exercise of his critical faculties. He constantly misapprehends what he observes, as when he mistakes the identity of Edgworth the cutpurse because Mooncalf (ironically) calls him a "civil young gentleman" who "has ever money in his purse" (2.4.22–24; see also 2.3.31–32). Rather than simply watching the fair from afar, he tries to "wind out wonders of enormity" (2.2.10–11) by participating in its activities. As a result of this participation, he is himself is accused of being a cutpurse or "lewd and pernicious enormity" (3.5.203–4) and is put in the stocks, becoming in the end the very thing he seeks to detect.

When the action of the play moves from fair to puppet-show, the opposing extremes established between mindless consumerism and overzealous, hypocritical market justice are seamlessly aligned with mindless theatrical spectatorship and overzealous, hypocritical antitheatricalism, respectively. The puppet-show staged by Leatherhead is performed by the very toys and trifles found in his "shop of relics" (3.6.88), and thus functions as an arena in which the theater's staging of false wares may be brought center stage, and the arguments for and against it rehearsed. Yet the puppet-show not only serves as a metaphor for the theater, but also allows Jonson to distinguish between its staging of mere "trash" and the greater aspirations of the play proper. The puppet-show effectively reduces theater to false wares or the "stuff" of spectacle; for the puppets are themselves false wares, which are brought onstage in a basket reminiscent of that from which Joan sells her "trash." Littlewit compares the puppets to Joan's ginger-bread men, joking that one might "eat 'em all, too, an they were in cake-bread" (5.3.71). When Cokes exclaims, "What, do they live in baskets?" Leatherhead replies, "They do lie in a basket, sir, they are o' the small players" (5.3.64–65). The description of the puppets as "small players" or "players minors" simultaneously sets up an analogy to the professional players, while also signaling that the puppets' minor form of entertainment, which reduces theater to mere stuff, is to be distinguished from the larger ambitions of the "players major."

Identifying himself as a rabid opponent of the theater, Busy seeks nothing less than its outright destruction. Addressing the Puppet Dionysius as though he were a player, Busy's first line of attack is to rehearse the familiar charge that playing is not an honest trade or legitimate occupation: "thou hast no calling...I mean no vocation, idol, no present lawful calling...I say, his calling, his profession is profane; it is profane, idol" (45, 49, 58–60). He further argues that theater is "the waiting-woman of Vanity" (73), suggesting that their rejection of legitimate trades for the trumpery of the stage effeminizes them and puffs them up with pride. The puppet derides the hypocrisy of this line of attack, pointing out that the Puritans are themselves known "tire-women" (74) or manufacturers of luxury attires, such as "perukes...puffs [soft protuberant masses of fabric on a dress]...fans...[and] huffs [paddings used to raise the shoulders of a dress]" (77–78). The puppet thereby reveals that the Puritans themselves produce false wares designed to puff up and trick the eye with deceitful show. "Is a bugle [or bead]-maker a lawful calling? Or the confect-maker's?" (81–83), he chides.

When Busy confesses defeat, Justice Overdo reveals himself and forbids the continuance of the puppet-show, claiming, "It is time to take enormity by the forehead, and brand it; for I have discovered enough" (114–15). Reprimanding both Busy and Leatherhead for representing two extremes of enormity, the former as a "superlunatical hypocrite" and the latter as a "profane professor of puppetry, little better than poetry" (38–40), Overdo nonetheless betrays his own faults in ranking puppetry above poetry. There are inklings throughout the play of the cracks in Justice Overdo's status as "Mirrour of Magistrates," and that through these cracks he is beginning to glimpse the error of his ways. When he sees that he has driven Trouble-all mad with his overzealous policing of the market, he resolves to make amends to him. His recompense takes the form of a blank check or "warrant," which he gives to Quarlous (disguised as Trouble-all) to ease his own conscience, believing that the madman will not take advantage of his generosity (5.2.121–24). When the inebriated Mistress Overdo reveals herself by suddenly waking up and vomiting in a basin, however, Overdo is humiliated into silence. Quarlous then takes over his project of discovery, revealing to Overdo the enormities he himself has committed (5.6.71–79) and counseling, "remember you are but Adam, flesh and blood! You have your frailty. Forget your other name of Overdo, and invite us all to supper" (92–95). Overdo consents, avowing, "This pleasant conceited gentleman hath wrought upon my judgement, and prevailed...I invite you home with me to my house, to supper. I will have none fear to go along, for my intents are *ad correctionem, non ad destructionem; ad aedificandum, non ad diruendum* [To correct, not destroy; to build up, not to tear down]" (107–8). Cokes agrees and invites the "actors" to perform "the rest o' the play at home" (110–11).

Far more than Middleton's play, Jonson's aims to edify its audience as to the purpose and legitimacy of playing as a profession. This purpose rejects the mindless consumerism and spectatorship of Cokes, the reduction of playing to the stuff of mere spectacle, while rejecting the hypocritical disavowal or destruction of such stuff by Puritan reformers and overzealous magistrates. In foregrounding the theater's reliance on false wares while deriding mere spectacle, Jonson suggests that although such wares are necessary to theatrical spectacle, they are not sufficient to convey the greater purpose of playing. Although this paradigm reinscribes the gendered division of theatrical labor by subordinating, or literally sweeping away, the feminized "trash" of suburban market women to make way for the virtuous, civic masculinity of the professional players, it nonetheless acknowledges the theater's dependence on such wares, which litter the stage after each performance. Bearing silent testimony to their own staged destruction, they function as material mementoes of women's work outside the formal economy and are thereby recollected from oblivion.

NOTES

1. All definitions of early modern terms and their usages in this chapter are from the *Oxford English Dictionary Online* (Oxford: Oxford University Press, 2008).
2. On market regulation and efforts to control informal commerce, see Michael Berlin, "'Broken All in Pieces': Artisans and the Regulation of Workmanship in Early Modern London," in *The Artisan and the European Town, 1500–1900*, ed. Geoffrey Crossick (Aldershot: Ashgate, 1997), 75–91; J. R. Kellet, "The Breakdown of Gild and Corporation Control Over the Handicraft and Retail Trade in London," *The Economic History Review,* 2nd series 10.3 (1958), 381–94; Ian Archer, *The Pursuit of Stability: Social Relations in Elizabethan London* (Cambridge: Cambridge University Press, 1991), 124–31; Steve Rappaport, *Worlds within Worlds: Structures of Life in Sixteenth-Century London* (Cambridge: Cambridge University Press, 1989), 45–46, 111–17, 187–88, 225. On the moral ethos of the craft guilds see Anthony Black, *Guilds and Civil Society in European Political Thought from the Twelfth Century to the Present* (Ithaca, NY: Cornell University Press, 1984), 26–27.
3. Berlin, "'Broken All in Pieces'," 79–82; Archer, *The Pursuit of Stability*, 127.
4. Silvia Thrupp, *A Short History of the Worshipful Company of Bakers of London* (Croydon: Galleon Press, 1933), 42–43, 58.
5. Ibid., 43.
6. See *OED*, thew, n.2 and Ibid., 44.
7. Ann Rosalind Jones and Peter Stallybrass, *Renaissance Clothing and the Materials of Memory* (Cambridge: Cambridge University Press, 2000).
8. See G. R. Elton, "Informing for Profit: A Sidelight on Tudor Methods of Law-Enforcement," *Cambridge Historical Journal* 11.2 (1954): 149–67; Margaret Gay Davies, *The Enforcement of English Apprenticeship: A Study in Applied Mercantilism, 1563–1642* (Cambridge, MA: Harvard University Press, 1956); M. W. Beresford, "The Common Informer, The Penal Statutes and Economic Regulation," *The Economic History Review,* n.s. 10. 2 (1957): 221–38; John L. McMullan, "Criminal Organization in Sixteenth

and Seventeenth Century London," *Social Problems* 29.3 (1982): 311–23.

9. Beresford, "Common Informer," 221, 225, 230; Elton, "Informing for Profit," 151.
10. Elton, "Informing for Profit," 150.
11. One promoter collected fees at the rate of 20 shillings for each promise not to inform. Beresford, "Common Informer," 229; Davies, *The Enforcement of English Apprenticeship*, 58–60.
12. Beresford, "Common Informer," 226, 228.
13. Stephen Gosson, *Plays Confuted in Five Actions* (London, 1582), sig. E2.
14. Ibid., sig. B3.
15. Ibid., sig. E2. The notion that "ydlenes is the Mother of vice" was commonly held by Puritan writers of the period. See Philip Stubbes, *The Anatomy of Abuses* (London, 1583), sig. L8. Antitheatrical writers argued that playing effeminated both actors and spectators.
16. According to Gosson, "these outward spectacles effeminate, & soften the heartes of men." Gosson, *Plays Confuted in Five Actions*, sig. G4. Thomas Beard similarly maintained that playing makes "people idle, effeminate, and voluptuous." Thomas Beard, *The Theater of Gods Judgements* (London, 1597), 374.
17. Petition concerning "The inconveniences that grow by Stage playes abowt the Citie of London" sent by the Lord Mayor and Aldermen to the Privy Council in July 1597. E. K. Chambers, *The Elizabethan Stage*, 4 vols. (Oxford: Clarendon, 1923), 4: 322.
18. Ibid., 4: 255, 257.
19. Gosson, *Plays Confuted in Five Actions*, sig. E7v.
20. Ibid., sig. C6, G5v.
21. Henry Crosse, *Vertues Common-wealth: or the High-way to Honour* (London, 1603), sig. Q1.
22. Chambers, *The Elizabethan Stage*, 4: 258.
23. Letter from Nathan Field to Revd. Mr. Sutton of 1616. Reproduced in Tanya Pollard, ed., *Shakspeare's Theater: A Sourcebook* (Oxford: Blackwell, 2004), 277.
24. Thomas Heywood, *Apology for Actors* (London, 1612), sig. A2v; I. G., *A Refutation of the Apology for Actors* (London, 1615), 55.
25. Jean E. Howard, *Theater of a City: The Places of London Comedy, 1598–1642* (Philadelphia: University of Pennsylvania Press, 2007), 27–28. On the emergence of new forms of masculinity in early modern England, see Alexandra Shepard, *Meanings of Manhood in Early Modern England* (Oxford: Oxford University Press, 2003).
26. Thomas Middleton, *A Chaste Maid in Cheapside*, 1613, ed. Alan Brissenden, The New Mermaids (New York: W. W. Norton, 1994), 1.1.92–93 and hereafter cited in text parenthetically.
27. John Stow, *A Survey of London*, 1603, ed. Charles Lethbridge Kingford (Oxford: Clarendon Press, 1908), 345.

28. Ian Archer, Caroline Barron, and Vanessa Harding, eds., *Hugh Alley's Caveat: The Markets of London in 1598* (London: London Topographical Society, 1988), 90.
29. Howard, *Theater of a City*, 137. See also Paul Griffiths, "Politics Made Visible: Order, Residence and Uniformity in Cheapside, 1600–45," in *Londinopolis: Essays in the Cultural and Social History of Early Modern London*, ed. Paul Griffiths and Mark S. R. Jenner (Manchester: Manchester University Press, 2000), 176–96.
30. T. F. Reddaway, *The Early History of the Goldsmiths Company, 1327–1509* (London: Edward Arnold, 1975), 212, 249.
31. Gail Kern Paster, "Leaky Vessels: The Incontinent Women of City Comedy," *Renaissance Drama* 18 (1987): 43–65. Although Paster centers her analysis of incontinent women in city comedy on *A Chaste Maid in Cheapside* and *Bartholomew Fair*, she does not, despite her title, draw the connection between female incontinence and false or "leaky" female wares that is the subject of this chapter.
32. *OED*, citing Ford 1638 *Fancies*, IV, i.
33. Ben Jonson, *Bartholomew Fair*, 1614, ed. G. R. Hibbard, *The New Mermaids* (London: A.C. Black, 1994), 5.6.107–8 and hereafter cited in text parenthetically.
34. Jonas Barish, *The Antitheatrical Prejudice* (Berkeley: University of California Press, 1981), 132.
35. In his dedicatory poem to his friend Christopher Brooke's book on Richard III, George Chapman refers to "Pageant Orsadine / That goes for gold." Christopher Brooke, *The Ghost of Richard the Third... Containing More of Him Then Hath Been Heretofore Shewed, Either in Chronicles, Playes, or Poems* (London, 1614), sig. A2. As we have seen, the professional players were notorious for their gilded wares more generally, including copper-lace.
36. For references to apple-wives in playhouses, see Gerald Eades Bentley, *The Jacobean and Caroline Stage*, 7 vols. (Oxford: Oxford University Press, 1941–68), 1: 315, 6: 42.
37. In 1661, Pepys described the play as being "so satyricall against Puritanism" that it had not been performed "these forty years." Cited in Jonson, *Bartholomew Fair*, ed. Hibbard, *The New Mermaids*, xv.
38. See, for example, Gosson, *Plays Confuted in Five Actions*, sig. E8; Stubbes, *The Anatomy of Abuses*, sig. L5v.

Chapter 8

City of Angels: Theatrical Vice and *The Devil is an Ass*

Ian Munro

Vice in all its forms dominates Ben Jonson's late comedy, *The Devil is an Ass.* The play opens with a minor devil, Pug, begging Satan for permission to travel to London with the morality Vice Iniquity, whom Satan quickly dismisses as unfit for the times. Fifty years ago, Satan allows, "When every great man had his Vice stand by him / In his long coat, shaking his wooden dagger" (1.1.84–85), this might have worked.[1] But today a theatrical Vice of this sort will no longer serve the metropolitan taste:

> This is not that will do; they are other things
> That are received now upon earth for Vices,
> Stranger, and newer: and changed every hour.
> They ride 'em like their horses off their legs,
> And here they come to Hell, whole legions of 'em,
> Every week, tired. We still strive to breed
> And rear 'em up new ones; but they do not stand
> When they come there: they turn 'em on our hands.
> And it is feared they have a stud o' their own
> Will put down ours. Both our breed and trade
> Will suddenly decay, if we prevent not. (100–10)

London has outstripped Hell's ability to corrupt it: not only does the urban world continually renovate and transform vice, but it has started to breed its own, without the help of Hell. Indeed, Satan ends up sending Pug to London as a kind of industrial spy, hoping to discover how the city has managed to be so viciously productive. In what might be termed the play's central conceit, Pug in London is less a tempter than a shocked bystander, repeatedly aghast at the depravity he witnesses.

The play's vicious focus lead ultimately to a *coup de théâtre* in which vice literally takes center stage. Convinced that he must appear demonically possessed to regain the estate he has unwittingly signed away to an ally of his estranged wife, the hapless country squire Fitzdottrel performs an extended, scatological, insane tirade—particularly directed at his wife, but encompassing many targets—that culminates in glossolalic ravings in Greek, Spanish, and French:

> Gi'me some garlic, garlic, garlic, garlic…
> My wife is a whore, I'll kiss her no more, and why?
> Mayst not thou be a cuckold as well as I?
> Ha, ha, ha, ha, ha, ha, ha, ha, ha, &c….
> Buzz, buzz, buzz, buzz….
> She comes with a needle, and thrusts it in,
> She pulls out that, and she puts in a pin,
> And now, and now, I do not know how, nor where,
> But she pricks me here, and she pricks me there!….
> O, they whisper, whisper, whisper,
> We shall have more, of devils a score,
> To come to dinner in me the sinner…
> Provide me to eat, three or four dishes o' good meat,
> I'll feast 'em, and their trains, a Justice head and brains
> Shall be the first….
> A spare-rib o' my wife,
> And a whore's purtenance! A Gilthead whole….
> Yes, wis, knight, shite, Paul, jowl, owl, foul, trull, bowl….
> Οιμοι κακοδαιμων,
> Και τρισκακοδαιμων, και τετρακισ, και πεντακισ
> Και δωδεκακισ, και μυριακισ….
> Quebremos el ojo de burlas….
> Di grátia, Signòr mio se haúete denári fataméne parte….
> Oui, monsieur, un pauvre diable! Diabletin! (5.8.24–120)[2]

This astonishing breakdown of social and theatrical decorum particularly figures a crisis in masculinity: freed from the dictates of conventional behavior, Fitzdottrel abandons masculine identity and sexual propriety. Consumed with vice, Fitzdottrel becomes a theatrical Vice—a modern day Iniquity—ranting and speaking ambidextrously.

The trajectory of the play changes abruptly in its final moments, however. On hearing proof of Satan's visit to London to collect Pug, "Fitzdottrel leaves counterfeiting," as the stage direction has it, and declares: "I am not bewitched, nor have a devil, / No more than you" (5.8.136–38). Masculinity is also restored to its true form, via a character actually *named* Manly, the holder of Fitzdottrel's feoffment. When Fitzdottrel renounces his double-dealing and theatrical excesses, Manly returns his estate and reassures him of Mrs. Fitzdottrel's true chastity; to close the play, he offers a homily on repentance, orthodox behavior, and the value of shame in maintaining social decorum.

This "eruption of moral absolutes," as Lawrence Manley wryly calls it, has received mixed critical evaluations.[3] In his introduction to the Revels edition of the play, Peter Happé evaluates the ending in positive terms, as part of Jonson's evolution past the cynical pessimism of his earlier work.[4] A more typical verdict is Stephen Greenblatt's, delivered as a by-blow in a profound meditation on theater and exorcism: "The problem in this late play is that the antitheatrical Jonson has all too clearly won the war; in consequence, the exorcised theatrical performance seems dead."[5] Although they disagree on the theatrical value of the play's conclusion, both viewpoints accept the abrupt turnaround from counterfeiting to reality it proposes. From the point of view of this chapter, however, what is most striking about this conclusion is how unpersuasive it is, and how poorly it resolves the broader concerns of the play. In particular, it seems to offer nothing to alleviate the state of urban anxiety—the specific context of the proliferation of vice—with which the play begins. At the encouragement of this demonic induction, I want to explore the play's construction of masculine vice in relation to its model of urban epistemology, the problematic of urban knowledge and learning. In this context, I will argue, the conclusion is less absolute, and less efficacious, than is typically supposed.

As the title of this chapter suggests, I particularly want to argue that the epistemological failures of *The Devil is an Ass* are best understood in a context that may seem irredeemably anachronistic: the urban protocols of *film noir*. Certainly the play's terrain of scams, sleaze, vicious women, official corruption, and dark obsessions fits well into the generic expectations of *film noir*, and the play clearly proposes a kind of *noir* moral progression: Fitzdottrel's fatal attraction to the social performances of the theater leads him further and further into a world of financial "projects" and phantasms that threatens to destroy him. More specifically, *film noir* is imbricated with an anxious masculinity seeking reassurance and stabilization, often coupled (as in *The Devil is an Ass*) with an abiding anxiety about the changing space of the city.[6] Even more relevant than such thematic connections, however, is the structural analysis put forward by Slavoj Žižek, who suggests that *noir* is less a genre than "a kind of anamorphotic distortion affecting different genres," or even "a kind of logical operator introducing the same anamorphotic distortion in every genre it is applied to."[7] Most basically, *noir* produces a problem of knowledge by allowing a virtualization of reality, through which "reality itself is posited as a semblance of itself, as a pure symbolic edifice."[8]

If detective fiction forms the dominant raw material of cinematic *noir*, for *The Devil is an Ass* the genre that undergoes "anamorphotic distortion" is clearly city comedy, particularly in terms of its typical claims to urban knowledge.[9] Like the coney-catching pamphlets that influenced its development, city comedy typically trades on its urban competence: it knows all, and will provide privileged access to the world of the city. In his opening address Iniquity boasts to Pug of his knowledge of the length and breadth of London, his ability to peer into the secrets of the metropolis:

> I will fetch thee a leap
> From the top of Paul's steeple to the Standard in Cheap:
> And lead thee a dance through the streets without fail,
> Like a needle of Spain, with a thread at my tail.
> We will survey the suburbs, and make forth our sallies
> Down Petticoat Lane, and up the Smock Alleys,
> To Shoreditch, Whitechapel, and so to Saint Katherine's
> To drink with the Dutch there, and take forth their patterns.
> From thence we will put in at Custom House Quay there,
> And see how the factors and prentices play there
> False with their masters: and geld many a full pack,
> To spend it in pies at the Dagger, and the Woolsack. (1.1.55–66)[10]

Despite being one of the most famous speeches in the play, this inaugural panorama is a kind of bait-and-switch: "Peace, dotard" (76), Satan replies, rejecting not just Iniquity but his vision of the city. Noting that here Jonson "evokes London in more detail than in most of his other plays," Happé asserts that Iniquity's imaginary journey has "great thematic importance.... the effect of these initial tours is to bring into theatrical reality a spiritual world underlying and commenting upon all the wickedness of contemporary London."[11] This seems exactly wrong to me: rather, the sort of urban knowledge that Iniquity professes is as out-of-date as the jogging doggerel in which he delivers it. In its relentlessly innovative viciousness, London no longer has such a straightforward moral geography. It cannot even be classified as a diabolical city, as in the tradition of civic complaint; the net effect of Pug's urban expedition, as Satan bemoans when he comes to fetch him at the end of the play, is to increase London's emancipation from the authority of Hell. Rather than being subtended by a "spiritual world," London has divested itself of all supernatural apparatus: the only angels in this city are coins.

On one level Satan's dismissal of Iniquity signals a repudiation of theatrical tradition, a tactic intended (as in many of Jonson's plays) to establish the novelty and modernity of what will follow. If the old theatrical model of Vice will not serve, it is because the traditional theater is no longer capable of comprehending what London has become; the personification of vice as Vice will no longer serve to frame moral questions in the metropolis.[12] At the same time, the ability of a new type of theater to rectify this situation is severely compromised by the play's explicit inclusion of itself within its satirical frame: Fitzdottrel, an inveterate theatergoer, is absolutely desperate to see *The Devil is an Ass.* If, as Greenblatt implies, the root urban vice is the permeating of the theatrical into all aspects of life, the theater lacks the distance necessary to anatomize the city.

The remainder of the chapter divides into three interlinked discussions. The next section will explore the play's complex articulation of vice in relation to theatricality, masculinity, and signification, particularly via a focus on Fitzdottrel, the only character to participate in all of the tangled plotlines of *The Devil is an Ass.* In giving center stage to a character that would once have been only a gullible foil to the witty protagonists, Jonson overhauls his comic apparatus, and it is through the descent of Fitzdottrel that the play's *noir* aspect is most clearly established. The following section will turn to the broader context of the city and urban epistemology in relation to issues of vice and masculinity. The final section will return to the problematic of the theater's relationship to its urban representations, reengaging with Žižek's model of *noir* in an attempt to articulate the play's complex investment in its redemptive conclusion.

* * *

The theater's permeation of all aspects of urban life is shown most vividly in the possession scene, which appears to put theatricality itself on trial. We first meet Fitzdottrel as he "expresses a longing to see the Devil" (1.2.32), as the unusually elaborate stage directions of the play put it, calling on him like a modern-day Doctor Faustus: "Pray thee, come, / I long for thee.... Come yet, / Good Beelzebub" (30–33). But Satan has no direct involvement in the act of possession at the climax of the play. In fact, in preparing for his performance Fitzdottrel rejects the aid of Pug, who is posing as his servant, in favor of the corrupt promoter Merecraft, who declares that his knowledge of the theatrical tricks of possession is so complete that "if [Pug] *were* the Devil, we sha' not need him" (5.8.38). The dramatic coaching of Merecraft and Everill, his partner in crime, continues throughout the possession scene: "You do not tumble enough...Wallow! Gnash!"; "Speak, sir, some Greek if you can"; "Your Spanish that I taught you" (5.8.67, 111, 115). "How the Devil can act!" exclaims the merchant Gilthead; "He is the master of players!" responds the presiding Justice, Sir Paul Eitherside (77–78).

This possession of Fitzdottrel by theatrical imposture is prefigured by the profound dispossession of Fitzdottrel's masculinity and masculine persona. Like many a country squire drawn to London, Fitzdottrel is in a protracted process of converting his landed patrimony into urban insubstantials, locked into a pattern of self-consuming behavior. Fitzdottrel's particular addiction is to clothing—or to costume, to put a finer point on it, as clothing serves merely to support his theatrical habits. "He dares not miss a new play, or a feast," his nemesis Wittipol scornfully comments, "What rate soever clothes be at" (1.4.22–24). As he cannot afford enough new clothing to keep up with London's busy entertainment scene, Fitzdottrel supplements his wardrobe via the clothing-broker Engine, hiring aristocratic cast-offs on a weekly basis and then reselling them once they have been publicly viewed. As he explains to Mrs. Fitzdottrel, one goes to the theater specifically to perform masculine prowess before an adoring audience:

> Here is a cloak cost fifty pound, wife,
> Which I can sell for thirty, when I ha' seen
> All London in't, and London has seen me.
> Today I go to the Blackfriars Playhouse,
> Sit i' the view, salute all my acquaintance,
> Rise up between the acts, let fall my cloak,
> Publish a handsome man, and a rich suit,
> As that's a special end why we go thither,
> All that pretend to stand for't o'the stage.
> The ladies ask who's that, for they do come
> To see us, love, as we do to see them. (1.6.28–38)

In this case, however, to "publish a handsome man" in the theater means to abnegate his masculine prerogatives at home. To acquire this expensive cloak, Fitzdottrel agrees to let Wittipol speak at length to Mrs. Fitzdottrel of his passion for her; despite taking place in Fitzdottrel's presence, this attempted seduction does succeed in winning the unhappy wife's affections, and the association between Wittipol and Mrs. Fitzdottrel will eventually lead to the downfall of all of Fitzdottrel's plans.

Fitzdottrel's clothing compulsion also leads to his ensnarement by Merecraft and Everill, as they are led to this easy mark by Engine (in many ways the lynchpin character of the play) in exchange for a portion of the takings. First-rate grifters, Merecraft and Everill run short and long cons on Fitzdottrel, bilking him out of jewelry and ready money while preparing to acquire his entire fortune. The opening gambit is a proposal to make Fitzdottrel the "Duke of Drowned-land" (2.4.22) as part of an alleged scheme to pump out the fenlands; appropriately, the pursuit of this ambition steadily drains Fitzdottrel's financial reserves. As the two work on him, however, a surer option presents itself. Everill poses as the "Master of the Dependances" (3.3.62), a new government office with the mission of regulating public dueling:

> For since there will be differences daily
> 'Twixt gentlemen, and that the roaring manner
> Is grown offensive, that those few, we call
> The civil men o' the sword, abhor the vapours,
> They shall refer now, hither, for their process:
> And such as trespass 'gainst the rule of the court
> Are to be fined. (3.3.68–74)

Fitzdottrel is determined to inaugurate the Office of Dependancy through a challenge to Wittipol, whom he had recently discovered in intimate contact with Mrs. Fitzdottrel. Seizing on the opportunity, Everill informs him that petitioners must first settle their estate on another, in case of death. Taken together, the two scams neatly complement the business with the cloak. Just as a performance of masculinity threatens to make Fitzdottrel an emasculated cuckold, so two performances of aristocratic privilege threaten to lose him his wealth and social status.[13] In the penultimate movement of this prodigal journey, Fitzdottrel falls madly in love with a Spanish Lady, whom he has hired to teach his wife the manners of a Duchess—not realizing that she is Wittipol in disguise, hired to the part by Merecraft. Enraptured by her aristocratic grace and bearing, Fitzdottrel asks the Spanish Lady to decide who will be his feoffee. The deed secured, Wittipol reveals himself and, confounding both Fitzdottrel and the con men, declares that the estate will be given over into the keeping of Mrs. Fitzdottrel.

The playing of possession is thus the last in a chain of denials of masculinity through theatrical artifice. Having become "a cuckold, and an ass, and my wife's ward" through his fantastic impostures (4.7.78), Fitzdottrel draws the wrong lesson, and determines to throw away his identity and even his immortal soul in a last-ditch attempt to make theatricality work to his benefit. The association of theater and vice is ancient, of course; Plato asserts in *The Republic* that "the mimetic poet sets up in each individual soul a vicious constitution by fashioning phantoms far removed from reality."[14] However, Jonson's mimetic conception of vice, as Victoria Silver has persuasively demonstrated, is ill suited to a simple opposition between "phantoms" and "reality." As "dress, speech, gesture, property... supply the singular indices of a person's moral nature," Silver argues, Jonsonian vice is "not so much pretending to be something ontologically false, as it is the wholesale jeopardizing of this social symbology in which moral order and identity consist."[15] The normative, appropriate employment of social signification is itself necessarily gendered masculine: "Jonson's hypocrites are also effeminate, and by their very sexuality disturb just those legible distinctions of gender on which every patriarchal economy depends."[16] Put another way, "masculinity" means not only a required set of behaviors, attitudes, and qualities—sexual moderation, moral rectitude, financial probity, emotional temperance, stable patrimony, and so on—but also a principle of knowledge, the means whereby sign connects with referent.[17]

If we focus on the greed and vanity of individual characters such as Fitzdottrel, "vice" in *The Devil is an Ass* is thus located through the triangular relation between social theatricality, patriarchal abdication, and a destabilized symbology. But we can also see vice in this play through the urban environment inhabited by the individual character. Within this context, the specific elements that have undone Fitzdottrel—financial fictions and theatrical posturing—appear less as discrete practices or moral choices than as aspects of a larger system of vicious consumption.

It is the city, of course, that has led Fitzdottrel to dispossess himself, by providing both the lure of luxury and the sort of permanent floating stage where luxurious consumption can be shown to the world. Fitzdottrel is hardly the only character thus ensnared by urban pleasures; Merecraft upbraids the perpetually broke Everill for "eating / Pheasant, and godwit, here in London! Haunting / The Globes and Mermaids!" (3.3.24–26). But Fitzdottrel appears to act as under a special compulsion to urban publicity: as Wittipol puts it, his wit "ravishes him forth, / Whither it please, to any assembly'or place, / And would conclude him ruined, should he scape / One public meeting" (1.4.31–34). The theatrical act of Fitzdottrel's possession also takes place within a network of urban relations. In orchestrating the event, Merecraft declares,

> I'll to Justice Eitherside,
> And possess him with all, Trains shall seek out Engine,
> And they two fill the town with't; every cable
> Is to be veered. We must employ out all
> Our emissaries now. (5.5.43–47)

Fitzdottrel's possession thus becomes a kind of theatrical commodity, spread throughout the city via Merecraft's network of disseminating agents. As this acting of possession involves a kind of psychological and physiological disintegration, the scene carries overtones of Ovidian *sparagmos* that might connect it to the climatic dismemberment of Sejanus at the hands of the Roman populace: as Fitzdottrel comes apart, he is distributed piecemeal into the urban environment. Supporting such an association is a language of money that circulates around Fitzdottrel. Wittipol remarks that the scam artists who deceive Fitzdottrel "are the race may [who] may coin him" (1.5.21), and Merecraft instructs his servant to "cry up" Fitzdottrel to the goldsmith Gilthead: "Double his price, make him a man of metal" (2.8.105); in response, Gilthead declares, "his name is current" (3.1.12). A circulating token in a city of money, Fitzdottrel transforms into currency.

* * *

By foregrounding this consuming aspect of the urban world, the play offers a rebalancing of the usual representational terms of Jonsonian city comedy, which predominantly imagines urban space as legible and rational, a matrix of lucid social positions and character types—albeit one whose coherence is always under threat from social posturing, as Silver indicates.[18] Despite this tendency, another imagining of urban space threatens to break through at various points in various plays: an opaque, anonymous, and irrational city that eludes comprehension because of its excessive complexity and relentless change. *Bartholomew Fair*, which immediately preceded *The Devil is an Ass*, shows the opposition clearly: although the urban fair is mostly a busy yet comprehensible space of knowledge—one where all participants are known by name or profession, and where the competent Winwife and Quarlous can interpret everything to their pleasure—it also includes the vapors scene, an incomprehensible space of antilinguistic chaos.[19] While the rational city supports the dramaturgy of social identity by providing an appropriate stage and audience—think, for example, of the panoptic theatricality of *Epicoene*, which supports the public performances of wit and fool alike—the irrational city undermines social identity, consuming the individual subject into an excessive, plastic, and unbordered theatricality.

The most compact and extensive literary expression of such a city is found in early modern verse satire, which repeatedly uses a peripatetic journey through the streets of London to limn the dimensions of urban depravity. In the seventh satire of John Marston's *The Scourge of Villanie*, the cynic searches the city for a true man, but finds only "Apparitions, Ignes fatui, Glowormes, Fictions, / Meteors, Ratts of Nilus, Fantasies, / Colloses, Pictures, Shades, Resemblances."[20] Like Fitzdottrel, these resemblances of men have been consumed with vice; the satirist remarks that one is "an incarnate deuill / That struts in vice" (lines 26–27), and declares of another: "Infeebling ryot, all vices confluence, / Hath eaten out that sacred influence / Which made him man" (lines 121–23). Manley has insightfully analyzed early modern satire in Baudrillardian terms, suggesting that it charts a movement from "a semiotics of representation to a semiotics of simulation . . . . a mode of signification governed not by underlying truth but by relationships among signs themselves."[21] In such a system, as Manley further explains, "The social practices, manners, and codes which in a semiotics of representation are oriented, as means to ends, to the order of values they signify, become oriented instead, as products to process, to the potential they contain for recombination and mutation."[22] Although the satirist begins with the intent of rectifying social performance so that it matches reality, the self-referential quality of these performances makes that impossible. Instead, as the earlier quotations suggest, something like the reverse happens: caught within the network of signs, the satirist moves toward the unpleasant conclusion that the world is nothing but interlocking regimes of signification, a simulated hyperreality. And given Silver's emphasis on the gendering of social meaning, it is entirely appropriate that Marston's satirist searches in vain for a *man*: masculinity, which should provide the foundation to any semiotic system because of its absolute ontology, is itself revealed to be nothing more than a copy without original, a reality-effect cobbled together out of the play of surfaces.

The opposition between representation and simulation is directly relevant to *The Devil is an Ass*, not least through our introduction to the problem of urban vice in Satan's induction. The ability of London to create its own vices demonstrates a shift from representation to simulation: vice no longer reflects the moral absolutes of Hell, but it is generated from the semiotic interplay of the urban environment. Satan is nostalgic for a time when vice was representational, when it might be personated by a stable allegorical figure like Iniquity; now, vice is "other things...stranger, and newer" (1.1.102), a proliferating web of signification that even the prime architect of vice cannot make legible and stable. Like the urban satirists, Satan responds to this situation with a kind of perplexed helplessness: "They have their Vice there most like to Virtues; / You cannot know 'em apart by any difference" (121–22). Vice itself has turned vicious, and as a result an entire social symbology seems to have lost its moorings. Rather than existing within a moral framework that can make sense of its depravities, the London depicted in this play frustrates comprehension.

As in *film noir*, we are presented with a palpable sense of wrongness that cannot be alleviated because there is no way to get to its source: within a semiotics of simulation, it is impossible to strip away a false surface and show what lies beneath it. As a result, our attention must focus on that surface: on the *medium* through which the city is perceived. From one perspective, this medium is theatricality, the virtualizing operator that stands "in between," providing a relational and situation context through which meaning is transmitted.[23] The concerns of *The Devil is an Ass* connect in this regard with those of the antitheatrical discourse, which persistently imagines a theater that will not stay where it belongs, in the bounded space of the playhouse, but instead infiltrates all spaces of the city. "What voice is heard in our streets?" asks the author of *This World's Folly*; "Not but the squeaking out of those...obscene and light jigs...sucked from the poisonous dugs of sin-swelled theatres."[24] "Players by sticking of their bills in London, defile the streets with their infectious filthiness," writes the author of *A Mirror of Monsters*, imagining a city written over with theatrical signifiers.[25]

But *The Devil is an Ass* goes beyond the ostensible concerns of the antitheatrical writers by explicitly suturing theatricality to capital.[26] The play persistently emphasizes the commercial basis of the theater, especially through the focus on clothes-broking and the use of Engine as the catalyst of the play. As various critics have recently demonstrated, the early modern theater operated within the larger dimensions of the clothing industry, and the purpose of playing cannot be extricated from these mercantile concerns.[27] It is especially appropriate that the place of commerce in the play is the tiring house behind the arras, into which Fitzdottrel repeatedly retreats with Merecraft to talk business. In complementary fashion, Merecraft's "projects" are the purest form of theatrical speculation, entirely virtual except for the "the black bag of papers" he uses to call them into being (2.1.63). Merecraft builds his scams around palpable objects—dog-skins, beer bottles, raisins, toothpicks—that exist only in his sales patter. Instead of trade monopolies, as the word "projects" would suggest, he proffers novel (and imaginary) techniques of consumer manufacture, promising to spin gold out of the dross of the world:

> Sir, money's a whore, a bawd, a drudge,
> Fit to run out on errands: let her go.
> *Via pecunia!* When she's run and gone,
> And fled and dead, then will I fetch her again
> With aqua-vitae out of an old hogshead!
> While there are lees of wine, or dregs of beer,
> I'll never want her! Coin her out of cobwebs,
> Dust, but I'll have her! (2.1.1–8)[28]

The alchemical language of material transcendence underscores how perfectly the projects fit into an urban economy of simulation, built on the fantasy conversion of the real to the notional. In this regard, London as "city of angels" might ultimately be not only a mercenary city but also a city of free-floating capital, an urban world built on the perpetual mutations and recombinations of signifiers of money and goods—a prescient nightmare of "the City" of stocks, futures, derivatives, and arbitrage.

As Satan indicates, the name that *The Devil is an Ass* provides for the urban medium—this hybrid of theater and capital—is simply "vice." Within the protocols of urban simulation, this medium does not occlude the city, as a semiotics of representation would posit, distorting its features. Rather, it *comprises* the city: as Satan's opening monologue suggests, the city is merely a machine for producing vice. To extend my use of the term still further, vice is not only the various signifiers that the play trades in—social hypocrisy, effeminate imposture, unchecked greed, moral corruption, cardinal sin—but also the mechanism of trading itself. Like the semiotic materials through which Merecraft articulates his virtual cons, the individual signifiers are less important than the generative process that stands behind them, even if our only access to that process is through these traces of its operation.

Understanding London's integral viciousness helps us to reconceive the action of the possession scene, especially through the dialogue between Fitzdottrel and Justice Paul Eitherside. As the stage direction at the start of Fitzdottrel's fit indicates, "The Justice interprets all" (5.8.29)—each gesture or expression Fitzdottrel initiates causes Eitherside to offer a clear interpretation within the established hermeneutics of diabolical possession:

> *Tailbush.* What does he now, sir?
> *Paul.* Show
> The taking of tobacco, with which the Devil
> Is so delighted.
> *Fitzdottrel.* *Hum!*
> *Paul.* And calls for hum.
> You takers of strong waters and tobacco,
> Mark this.
> *Fitzdottrel.* Yellow, yellow, yellow, yellow, & c.
> *Paul.* That's starch! The Devil's idol of that colour.
> He ratifies it with clapping of his hands.
> The proofs are pregnant. (69–77)

As these interpretive points pile up, the scene increasingly gives the strange sense that we are less witnessing the gulling of a foolish or inept judge than the autonomous operation of a signifying machine. This is not possession as representation—in which Fitzdottrel's behavior would appear symptomatic of a metaphysical reality—but possession as simulation, the circulation of a semiotic system without external referent. In this regard, it is striking that "Eitherside" is a rough Englishing of "Ambidexter," the famous Vice of the morality plays, who declares in *King Cambises*: "Now with both hands will you see me play my parte."[29] Vice speaks to vice in the possession scene, call and response dovetailing perfectly, the infernal semiotic engine running smoothly. Rather than putting theatricality on trial, the possession scene suggests that theatricality is the very process that keeps the city going. "The author of *The Devil is an Ass* seems at war with his own medium," asserts Greenblatt, a verdict that imagines a more antagonistic and resistant antitheatricality than the play really supports.[30] Instead, we might say that *The Devil is an Ass* seems in search of a way outside of the trap of its own signifying machine—not least, paradoxically, by including itself within its frame.

* * *

In the parlance of *film noir*, the intradramatic "The Devil is an Ass"—or simply "The Devil," as Fitzdottrel repeatedly names it—is a MacGuffin, an object of desire like the Maltese Falcon, less important for itself than as a means of organizing narratival actions: Fitzdottrel's desire to see "The Devil" prompts his desire for new clothes, which leads him to accept Wittipol's strange bargain for the cloak, which leads (eventually) into the central action of the play. But having the play as its own object of desire introduces a remarkable torsion to our experience of its reality. At the start of the play, Fitzdottrel "expresses a longing to see the Devil," but he also worries that the Devil does not exist:

> Ay they do now name Bretnor, as before
> They talked of Gresham, and of Doctor Forman...
> But there's not one of these that ever could
> Yet show a man the Devil in true sort.
> They have their crystals, I do know, and rings,
> And virgin parchment, and their dead men's skulls
> Their ravens' wings, their lights, and pentacles
> With characters; I ha'seen all these. But—
> Would I might see the Devil. I would give
> A hundred o' these pictures, so to see him
> Once out of picture. May I prove a cuckold,
> And that's the one main mortal thing I fear,
> If I begin not now to think the painters
> Have only made him. (1.2.1–15)

In effect, the play sets itself an impossible problem: to show the Devil "out of picture" within the frame of a theatrical representation. This Devil "in true sort" and "The Devil" as theatrical event form a strange lamination of the real and the imaginary in the play, each undercutting the other: while the existence of Satan, the "real" Devil, within the play reduces "The Devil" to mere fiction, this existence itself occurs only within the frame of "The Devil." To experience the Devil is the motivating desire of the play, but it is necessarily an impossible desire, always deferred. Put another way, it stands as a way of marking an impossible path, one that paradoxically would lead us both out of the theater and further into the theater.

The Devil, in fact, is the specific "anamorphotic distortion" that pushes the play into the realm of *noir*. To explain the operations of *noir*, Žižek turns to a painting by René Magritte, *La Lunette d'approche*:

> [The painting shows] a half-open window where, through the windowpane, we see external reality (a blue sky with some dispersed white clouds), while in the narrow opening that gives direct access to the reality beyond the pane we see nothing but a dense black mass. The frame of the windowpane is, of course, the fantasy frame that constitutes reality, whereas the narrow opening between the panes opens onto the "impossible" real, the Thing-in-itself.... This, then is the "*noir*" that defines the *noir* universe: that crack in the half-open window that shakes our sense of reality.[31]

What shakes the reality of *The Devil is an Ass* is the Devil himself—not the faintly preposterous Satan we see at the beginning of the play, who is thoroughly contaminated by the theatricality of "The Devil," but the impossible Devil: the one that cannot be shown, that is "out of picture," that exceeds the space of representation.[32] In 5.6 Satan appears again, to carry Pug out of Newgate prison back to Hell, his mission a failure. The next scene begins with the stage direction "A great noise is heard in Newgate"; the frightened keepers run on to the stage wondering at the explosion and the "steam of brimstone" and "sulphur of hell-coal" (5.7.2, 10) that remains.[33] This crack and stink of sulfur is a rent in the play, a theatrical device that points impossibly to something beyond the theatrical.[34] This is the asignifying Devil, the Devil that is not "The Devil," the hard kernel that resists metaphorization.

The encounter with the impossible-real sends the play scrambling into the space of unreality. Looking at a series of films (*noir* and otherwise) that involve pushing past a frontier into an unknowable land, Žižek remarks: "the structure is that of a Möbius strip—if we progress far enough on the side of reality, we suddenly find ourselves on its reverse, in the domain of pure fantasy."[35] The point of this "mysterious reversal of horror into bliss" is "the transmutation of the real into the symbolic: the impossible-real changes into an object of symbolic prohibition."[36] At the start of the play Fitzdottrel worries about the *possibility* of the Devil; at the end he affirms the *prohibition* of the Devil: "I do defy him.... I will tell truth / And shame the fiend" (5.8.139, 142–43). And through this prohibition the world is apparently healed, and the redemptive conclusion becomes possible. The prophylactic process is clearly shown by the complex progression of the final scenes, through which we encounter the Devil twice. Within the narrative of the play, the revelation of the "great noise" *concludes* the possession scene: at the end of 5.8 the Newgate keepers run in to report the explosion, which causes Fitzdottrel to leave counterfeiting. But from the perspective of the theater audience, the traumatic appearance of the asignifying Devil in 5.7 *inaugurates* the possession scene; indeed, the "infernal stink and steam" (5.8.132) it leaves behind must linger on stage throughout Fitzdottrel's performance, increasing its chaos and danger. Recoiling from the truth of this self-consuming performance, Fitzdottrel chooses the dream of stable identity, decorous theatricality (representation, not simulation), and—as personated by the manly Manly—genuine masculinity.

Rather than rejecting fantasy for reality, as the typical reading of the play would suppose, *The Devil is an Ass* rejects reality for fantasy; as Žižek remarks, " 'reality' stabilizes itself when some fantasy frame of a 'symbolic bliss' forecloses the view into the abyss of the real."[37] Nevertheless, the stability of the play's final position is far from certain. Commenting on Jonson's abandonment of the public stage after *The Devil is an Ass*, Happé asserts, "In this play Jonson reached a metaphysical position which, arising from a retrospect of his previous works, rounded them off with a new emphasis."[38] But the uneasy feeling lingers that this metaphysical position stands on quicksand; the hurried ending—Fitzdottrel's conversion comes less than forty lines from the end of the play—reinforces the play's palpable anxiety about what it has chosen to believe in.

For *The Devil is an Ass*, "the abyss of the real" is specifically urban: it is entirely appropriate that the "infernal stink" of the real is described as general all over London, covering the metropolis, creeping into every nook and cranny: "You cannot see St. Pulchre's steeple yet; / They smell't as far as Ware as the wind lies / By this time" (5.8.133–35). Like *film noir*, the play makes us aware of the abyssal city—not the city of surfaces observed by the urban satirists, but the condition of possibility that allows the superficial city to appear as such. It would seem appropriate to historicize the generic transformations that subtend *The Devil is an Ass*: city comedy's turn to *noir* surely relates to the increasing complexity of the city it seeks to anatomize and portray.[39] However, in making this argument it is important not to construct an imagined time when urban sign and referent naturally joined, when urban reality had a stable presence. The operation of the Žižekian *noir* suggests that this is itself a compensatory fiction. Rather than losing its coherence, early modern London loses its illusion of coherence: the city's legibility has become virtualized, no longer believable as reality. The loss of this illusion, moreover, relates closely to city comedy's pervasive theatricalization of the urban milieu. Rather than providing the city with a stable set of meanings, the proliferation of urban representation leaves only "the dark suspicion that society is entirely—only—what it appears to be: a concatenation of self-generating and self-perpetuating roles, structures, and functions without moral foundations."[40]

In the world of *The Devil is an Ass*, the theater merely battens on the city, appropriating its raw materials and disseminating processed fictions. Ultimately, however, the self-generating quality of urban simulation threatens this symbiosis. At the start of the play, the Prologue entreats the real-life Fitzdottrels who crowd the stage to move their stools back a little, commenting: "This tract / Will ne'er admit our vice, because of yours" (8–9). The space of theatrical vice, the "tract" of representation, is increasingly constrained by the expanding parameters of urban vice: with no clear lines drawn or drawable between the play and its environs, the licensed space of the stage is vulnerable to encroachment or even erasure. Although Fitzdottrel spends most of the play desperate to see "The Devil is an Ass," he has no desire to view the play itself: as his speech to his wife about the cloak suggests, all that matters is the *occasion*. Informed that business matters will preclude his attendance, he implores Merecraft, "I must not lose the play! .... If I could but see a piece.... Come but to one act, and I did not care— / But to be seen to rise, and go away, / To vex the players, and to punish their poet" (3.5.36–44).

The theoretical endpoint of this trajectory is indicated in one of Satan's attacks on the outmoded Vice Iniquity: "He ne'er will be admitted there when Vennor comes" (1.1.94). As Happé explains, Richard Vennar "issued playbills about a non-existent play called *England's Joy*...and made off with the takings."[41] Vennar is a more successful Vice than Iniquity because Vennar's theater signals an evolutionary leap in theatrical practice: no longer a staple of fantasy, the theater becomes a mere conduit, a media focal point, a nexus of advertisement. If the antitheatrical discourse shows the theater infiltrating the city, it also shows the city consuming the theater, removing its significance, incorporating it into the apparatus of urban meaning. As in the *Mirror of Monsters*, what matters is less the play than the playbills: there is no actual play, no actual venue, merely a swarm of pointers. In a world of Vennars, the theater finds itself in the same position as Hell: its privileged role as producer of theatrical vice has been rendered obsolete.

NOTES

1. Ben Jonson, *The Devil is an Ass*, ed. Peter Happé (Manchester: Manchester University Press, 1996).
2. See Happé, *Devil*, for translations of Fitzdottrel's foreign expressions. Fitzdottrel's rant is pervasively commented upon by the other characters; I have elided these interjections in order to give a sense of the overall trajectory of the speech.
3. Lawrence Manley, *Literature and Culture in Early Modern London* (Cambridge: Cambridge University Press, 1995), 472.
4. Happé, *Devil*, 4.
5. Stephen Greenblatt, "Loudun and London," *Critical Inquiry* 12.2 (Winter 1986): 326–46, 342. Avoiding such direct assessments, Manley sees the play as strategically adopting the motifs of romantic citizen comedy "for new social purposes," particularly the promotion of urbane gentility (471). The principal shortcoming of this productive line of analysis is that it makes Wittipol more of a central figure than the play allows; as I will discuss, the hapless Fitzdottrel is the only character that truly unifies the action.
6. See Kaja Silverman, *Male Subjectivity at the Margins* (New York: Routledge, 1992) and Frank Krutnik, *In a Lonely Street: Film Noir, Genre, Masculinity* (New York: Routledge, 1991). For the urban aspect of *film noir*, see Edward Dimendberg, *Film Noir and the Spaces of Modernity* (Cambridge, MA: Harvard University Press, 2004).
7. Slavoj Žižek, "The Thing that Thinks: The Kantian Background of the *Noir* Subject," in *Shades of Noir: A Reader*, ed. Joan Copjec (New York: Verso, 1993), 199, 200.
8. Ibid., 214.
9. On the subject of urban legibility in city comedy, see Jean Howard, *Theater of a City: The Places of London Comedy, 1598–1642* (Philadelphia: University of Pennsylvania Press, 2006); on the topic of urban competence, see Adam Zucker, "The Social Logic of Ben Jonson's *Epicoene*," *Renaissance Drama* 33 (2004): 37–62.
10. The point here is instruction in vice, not defense from it, but the impulse is identical to the coney-catching pamphlets.
11. Happé, *Devil*, 12.
12. See ibid., 4.
13. On the duel as an "overdetermined sign of masculine identity," see Jennifer Low, *Manhood and the Duel: Masculinity in Early Modern Drama and Culture* (New York: Palgrave Macmillan, 2003), 3.
14. Plato, *The Collected Dialogues of Plato*, ed. Edith Hamilton (Princeton, NJ: Princeton University Press, 1996), 830.
15. Victoria Silver, "Totem and Taboo in the Tribe of Ben: The Duplicity of Gender and Jonson's Satires," *ELH* 62.4 (1995): 729–757, 730.
16. Ibid.

17. See Silver's essay for a considerably more extensive and subtle treatment of these issues.
18. On this point, cf. Ian Munro, *The Figure of the Crowd in Early Modern London: The City and Its Double* (New York: Palgrave Macmillan, 2005), 49.
19. Cf. Gail Kern Paster's comments on the opening exchanges of *The Alchemist*: "What seems contradictory about Jonson's rhetorical strategy is that it proceeds by a recitation of vivid details, and yet the cumulative effect of such details is undifference, the collapse of individuation back into chaotic urban environment." *The Body Embarrassed: Drama and the Disciplines of Shame in Early Modern England* (Ithaca, NY: Cornell University Press, 1993), 148.
20. John Marston, *The scourge of villanie* (London, 1598), lines 13–16.
21. Manley, *Literature and Culture*, 385.
22. Ibid.
23. On this topic, see Samuel Weber's *Theatricality as Medium* (New York: Fordham University Press, 2004), esp. chap. 1.
24. I. H., *This Worlds Folly: or, A Warning-Peece discharged upon the Wickednesse thereof* (London, 1615), sig. B1v.
25. William Rankins, *A mirrour of monsters....* (London, 1587), sig. C2.
26. David Hawkes has persuasively argued that antitheatrical writers *are* attacking capitalism (or more precisely the commodity fetish) via the example of the theater. See *Idols of the Marketplace: Idolatry and Commodity Fetishism in English Literature, 1580–1680* (New York: Palgrave Macmillan, 2001).
27. See in particular Peter Stallybrass and Ann Rosalind Jones, *Renaissance Clothing and the Materials of Memory* (Cambridge: Cambridge University Press, 2001) and Natasha Korda, "Women's Theatrical Properties," in *Staged Properties in Early Modern English Drama*, ed. Jonathan Gil Harris and Natasha Korda (Cambridge: Cambridge University Press, 2006), 202–29.
28. For more on Merecraft's projects, see Happé, *Devil*, 15–16 and 98n.
29. Quoted in Robert Weimann, *Author's Pen and Actor's Voice: Playing and Writing in Shakespeare's Theater* (Cambridge: Cambridge University Press, 2000), 24. See Weimann for a discussion of the persistent significance of the ambidextrous Vice figure to Elizabethan and Jacobean theater.
30. Greenblatt, "Loudun and London," 342.
31. Žižek, "The Thing that Thinks," 219–20.
32. Early modern England's most famous example of "anamorphotic distortion" may help to clarify this point. The skull in Hans Holbein's *The Ambassadors* is of a higher order than a typical memento mori because it exceeds the fantasy frame of the painting: it is *present* in the portrait of worldly vanity without being *pictured within* that portrait. See Marjorie Garber's analysis of Jacques Lacan's use of this

painting in Chapter 6 of *Shakespeare's Ghost Writers: Literature as Uncanny Causality* (London: Methuen, 1987). Žižek, building upon Lacan, also discusses *The Ambassadors* on a number of occasions; see especially *Looking Awry: An Introduction to Jacques Lacan through Popular Culture* (Cambridge, MA: MIT Press, 1991), esp. chap. 5.

33. It is significant, I believe, that the great noise and stink come *after* the appearance of Satan, not before, and with a cleared stage in between the two events; this increases the sense that the character Satan and the asignifying Devil are in fact two different things.
34. This is not the only play where Jonson stages such an unstageable event; see especially the explosion of the Staple in *The Staple of News* and (somewhat differently) the alleged explosion of Subtle's alchemical apparatus in *The Alchemist.*
35. Žižek, "The Thing that Thinks," 216.
36. Ibid.
37. Ibid, 218.
38. Happé, *Devil*, 4.
39. On London's increasing complexity, see (among others) Steven Mullaney, *The Place of the Stage: License, Play and Power in Renaissance England* (Chicago: University of Chicago Press, 1988); Manley, *Literature and Culture*; and Munro, *The Figure of the Crowd.*
40. Manley, *Literature and Culture*, 385.
41. Happé, *Devil*, 63.

Afterword

A Question of Morality

Lawrence Manley

> Where are these vices most frequented & vsed, but in London? Like as the disease that lyeth ranckling in the hart, ransacking euerie lym and ioynt of the body, and by that meanes makes all the members of the same subiect to his infirmitie. So the couetousnes of London, the pride of London, the wantonness of London, the ryotousnes of London, doth poison the whole realme of England, and maketh it apt to all wickednesse.
>
> —John Wharton, *Whartons Dreame* (1578)

> The knowledge and survey of vice is in this world is . . . necessary to the constituting of human vertue.
>
> —John Milton, *Areopagitica* (1544)[1]

John Wharton's 1578 attack on the wickedness of London is written in the sweeping spirit of the Psalmist, who had seen

> violence and strife in the city.
> Day and night they go about it upon the walls thereof: mischief also and sorrow are in the midst of it.
> Wickedness is in the midst thereof: deceit and guile depart not from her streets.
>
> (Psalm 55: 9–11)

Scripture held that the first city was founded by the first murderer Cain, who went out from the presence of God and into the land of Nod (the name means "wandering"), where he sought refuge in a place of his own making, a human creation in potential opposition to God's.[2] From this episode came the two cities of Augustine ("Cain was the first-born, and he belonged to the city of men; after him was born Abel, who belonged to the city of God," 15.1) and the deeply rooted associations through which earthly cities were linked to corruption and vice. God had bent himself to humanity so far as to give sojourning Israel "great and goodly cities, which thou buildest not" (Deut. 6:11), but according to the Bible, which contrasts to pagan traditions of centering the city at the *mundus* or physical intersection of the human with the divine, the builders of cities (witness Babel and Nineveh) were given to sinfulness and crime.

Moral condemnation of early modern London as a city of vice was driven not only by the Scripturalist bias of the reformation but also by the city's apparently corrosive effects on traditional English society and its moral values. The perception that "our country lives was more godly than the life of the city"[3] was fuelled by the transformative effects of London's expansion into a teeming early modern metropolis. The city's commerce, the presence of the court in Westminster, the legal proceedings of the chief courts of the realm drew Englishman from throughout the provinces. As the main conduit for the exchange of landed wealth, London became home to the aristocratic marriage market; its social season and developing luxury and leisure industries were attractive to urbanizing gentry disposed to conspicuous consumption. The city also harbored a large "youth culture" of apprentices and domestic servants, male and female, recruited from the often-distant countryside. Substantial portions of the greater London population were immigrant "strangers" and nonfree English migrants: the artisans, casual laborers, criminals, homeless, and unemployed who frequented the rapidly growing suburbs outside the city walls. The ravages of poverty and epidemic disease meant that London's expansion could only be fueled by patterns of migration: in 1590, one-eighth of the English people became Londoners at some point in their lifetimes.[4] London thus exerted its growing influence through centrifugal and solvent effects, through forces that, by undermining traditional values and structures, led to greater heterogeneity, mobility, and innovation, and hence to increasing specialization in social roles and to diversity in morals and behavior. It was in opposition to the urbanizing process that King James I sought in 1616 to restore English society to its ancient moral footing by urging gentlemen to abandon the effeminate and foreign fashion of London living. Otherwise, he declared,

> With time, *England will onely be* London, and the whole countrey be left waste: For as wee now doe imitate the French fashion, in the fashion of Clothes, and lackeys to follow every man; So we haue wee got vp the Italian fashion, in liuing miserably in our houses, and dwelling all in the Citie: but let us in Gods name leaue these idle forreine toyes, and keep the old fashion of *England*.[5]

In their examination of urban geography and illicit social mingling, of the patterns of luxury consumption, of the hazards of commerce and credit, and of the performative dimensions of self-fashioning, the chapters in this volume provide ample evidence that moral condemnation of London vice was partly a response to the destabilizing effects of the metropolis on the social order. At the same time, however, the chapters also suggest that in its possibilities for exchange and combination London fostered novel modes of association and deportment that, by transvaluing values, transformed the moral potential of urban living. This is in keeping with Georg Simmel's observation that great cities exercise their most important influence when they transcend their visible expanse and the "quantitative aspect of life is transformed directly into qualitative traits of character."[6]

In their focus on masculinities and the homosocial dimensions of urban morals, several of the chapters in this volume (those by Bloom, Ellinghausen, Zucker, Johnston, and Bly especially) remind us of the ways in which such transformations in character are mediated by the "secondary," voluntary modes of association that in large cities displace the "primary" associations of the family and the local community.[7] At issue for London's large population of young males—consisting of apprentices, servants, students at the inns of court, fashionable gentlemen, demobbed soldiers, casual students, and university graduates in search of place and patronage—was the potential for conflict between imperatives deriving from authority and those deriving from regard for the respect and confirmation of peers.[8] The church, civic authority, the writ of law, the rules of apprenticeship and servitude, and the sheer discipline of labor and force placed many curbs upon any freedom from the "primary" authority of the family or small community. Nevertheless, the voluntary associations formed in social spaces such as those examined here—the alehouse, the barber shop, the theater, the middle aisle of St. Paul's—or in associations such as gangs, criminal enterprises, clubs, conventicles, or gathered congregations[9]—were the basis for subcultures that provided for assimilation to London living. They offered what Pierre Bourdieu has called "inter-legitimation" by peers, and they helped to constitute what, before the advent of cultural geography, the urban sociologist Robert Park called the "moral regions" of a city, the places of rendezvous and resort rather than abode where populations segregate "not merely in accordance with . . . interests, but in accordance with tastes or . . . temperaments."[10]

An obverse to such voluntary modes of association, and a corollary to their moral "segregation," is the element of differentiation or dissociation that is one of the most elemental forms of socialization and one of the means by which urban populations diversify and specialize. Such dissociation—the affinity for the regard of some that is a disaffinity or scorn for others—may involve the affectation of "the most tendentious pecularities . . . the specifically metropolitan extravagances of mannerism, caprice, and capriciousness."[11] In their treatment of the outrageous "flaunting" of fashionable excess, the ludic functions of prandial indulgence and gambling, or the distancing effects of aggressive jest and wit, the chapters above examine several of the ways in which alternative moralities were fashioned through deliberate deviation from traditional norms. As the game of "vapours" in Jonson's *Bartholomew Fair* suggests, additional examples of "effecting distances" might be found in the many varieties of capricious male violence in early modern London, from apprentice riots and the practice of "roaring" to the well-documented cases of liverymen clashing at the theaters or in the streets and to the extravagant drunken carouses of the Restoration period. In such escapades, as in other forms of libertine behavior, the flaunting of traditional morals and the violation of class norms through illicit interclass rendezvous were not simply ways of repudiating a traditional past; they also expressed the enlarged and liberating possibilities of a newly expansive phase in the life of London.

To be sure, there is something deeply suspect in this idea of moral innovation. Some of the contributions to this volume (such as Adam Zucker's chapter on gambling), take note of the elements of "misrecognition," obsessionality, and economic exploitation associated with vice, thereby pointing to the ways in which apparent moral deviance was but participation by another means in the dominant structures of society. Moreover, the religious authorities who claimed youths not otherwise "prone vnto euill" were "carried cleane away" by "this violent streame and blustering tempest of ill company" were not ignorant of the ideological component in moral rebellion; they shared, perhaps, something like Eric Erikson's insight that "it is the ideological outlook of a society," rather than adult moral autonomy, that is most apt to speak "to the adolescent who is eager to be affirmed by his peers."[12] Moreover, civic authorities charged with the protection of peace, life, and property were certainly familiar with the predatory aspects of vice, its indifference to the victimization of others, and its roots in the kinds narcissistic, antisocial impulses that lead perpetrators to regard themselves as exceptions to the rules that apply to the rest of society.[13]

Whatever its potential for intellectual provocation, the transvaluation of value from the outlaw perspective—as in the rogue pastoral tradition by which criminals might eloquently claim "all conditions of men seeke to liue by their wittes, and he is counted wisest, that hath the deepest insight into the getting of gaines" (the modern equivalent is the rhetorical question of Brecht's Macheath, "What's breaking into a bank compared with founding a bank?")—could also be discounted as mere self-justification by "the worser sort," who, "espying…infirmities in the godlie, run vpon them with open mouth and take vpon them to condemne them vtterly, and to iudge their hearts, saying; they be hypocrites, dissemblers, and there is none worse then they."[14] Shakespeare, as we shall see below, recognized the impasse of such moral "othering" in the mutually undermining banter of the tavern gallants of *Measure for Measure*, who are, morally speaking, not much different from the pirate who went to sea with the Ten Commandments but razed out the one against stealing. As one gentleman protests to the other, "Thou are always figuring diseases in me; but thou art full of error, I am sound" (1.2.53–54). The reversible symmetry in such antitheses is a predictable consequence of moral skepticism,[15] and it could lead to the kinds of *noir*-ish or "abyssal" moral consciousness discussed in Ian Munro's chapter on Jonson's *The Devil is an Ass.*

Nevertheless, in the emerging literature of early modern London a case was made for the novel kinds of moral authority to be derived from the secular experience of urban life and its vices. The young Sir Francis Bacon, observing from the sidelines at the Inns of Court a clergy preoccupied with ecclesiastical minutiae of the Marprelate controversy, objected that contemporary divines were failing to prepare a generation for the complexities of moral choice in an increasingly worldly setting: "The word (the bread of life) they toss up and down, they break it not. They draw not their directions down *ad casus conscientiae*; that a man may be warranted whether they be lawful or not."[16] Thomas Nashe, too, echoing Matthew 7:9 ("What man is there of you, whom if his son ask bread, will he give him a stone?") complained of preachers who offered their congregations "Bread made of stones" because they were "not halfe so well acquainted as them that live about the Court and Citty" with the threats of abundance and unbelief.[17] Noting that preachers "fitte vs with a cheape religion...being couetous your selues," Nashe claimed they had forgotten that Christ was "a mean-titled man" who "kept company with Publicans and sinners, the very out cast of the people" (*Works*, 2:18, 107). The "heauy-gated lumberers" who had stumbled into the ministry were, moreover, "growne to such an austeritie, as they would haue vs straight of children to become old-men. They will allowe no time for a gray bearde to grow in" (*Works* 1:122). On the grounds that "men are men, and with those thinges must be mooued, that men wont be be moued," Nashe parlayed his own novel status and experience, as a placeless, degraded urbanite and print celebrity, into a previously unrecognized form of moral authority, promising his readers to probe morality "more searchingly than common soule-Surgions accustome" and "to build virtue a church on that foundation that the devil built his chapel" (*Works*, 2:80, 1: 305). Adopting tactics from the popular stage Vice, a hybrid figure whose theatrical authority derived from his status as a demonic, roguish villain, Nashe and his popular contemporaries converted homiletics into bedevilling irony and based their "representational authority" on their adaptation of writing to "the material world and lived experience" of readers.[18]

The preponderance of evidence assembled in *Masculinity and the Metropolis of Vice* is drawn from literary rather than historical sources, and especially from the theater. Moreover, several of the chapters underline early modern tendencies to implicate the theater in the moral geography of London vice. These links between vice and theater are partly owing to the ludic, recreational nature of theater and to the low decorum of popular comic genres, that is, to their concern with the forms of deviance Aristotle said were "laughable" errors and disgraces and that Sir Philip Sidney called "the common errors of our life."[19] The view that comedy was "nothing but scurrility," combined with the Platonically inspired fear that "vice is learned with beholding," helped to fuel the antitheatrical campaign against the London stage.[20] But just as important to the association of the stage with vice was the extent to which the contemporary theater, as an aspect of the urbanizing process, was transforming the low decorum of comedy into a discursive challenge to the more traditional practices of public preaching and public justice in early modern London. In this traditional alliance of ministracy with magistracy, word with sword, it was for "the preacher to reprove" and "the magistrate to punish" the deviations from moral norms that threatened the social order.[21] But as Natasha Korda suggests in her chapter, the theater's own ways of representing and punishing vice (and thus of defining virtue) were a means by which the players could query the official keepers of morals and "bolster their own claim to virtuous, civic masculinity." The systemic outrage of the claims of theater to traditional moralists is underlined in the antitheatrical complaint that "God only gave authority of public instruction and correction but to two sorts of men: to his ecclesiastical ministers and temporal magistrates. He never instituted a third authority of players, or ordained that they should serve in his ministry, and therefore are they to be rejected with their use and quality."[22]

In her analysis, Korda takes note of two effects in the theatrical representation of urban vice and its punishment—in *A Chaste Maid in Cheapside*'s exploration of illicit trading in flesh, she sees the theater's capacity to expose the moral failings of the "official" worlds constructed by commerce and civic regulation, and in *Bartholomew Fair*'s exposure of the failings of Justice Adam Overdo ("remember you are but Adam, flesh and blood! You have your frailty," 5.2.92–93) she sees additionally the possibility of a reformation in self-knowledge through the experience of vice and human frailty. Both effects can be found as well in Shakespeare's *Measure for Measure*, another play focused on a "city of vice" that is clearly a version of contemporary London.[23] But in Shakespeare's case, it is not the skeptical power of theater to disarm traditional constructions of virtue and vice but rather its capacity to represent moral transformation through the experience of vice and moral failing that is the theater's most striking innovation.

The undermining of external moral authority in the manner of *A Chaste Maid* is the more immediate, and also the easier, of the play's effects to grasp. It is readily apparent in the many complaints of Pompey and his associates against the hypocrisies of the law and its power—for example, in the observation that while "All houses in the suburbs of Vienna must be pluck'd down...those in the city...shall stand for seed. They had gone down too but that a wise burgher put in for them" (1.2.95–100) or in the quip "'Twas never merry world since of two usuries the merriest [i.e. fornication] was put down, and the worser [i.e., usury] allow'd by order of law" (3.2.5–7). Though pungent enough, such ironic reversals in the usual pattern of moral "othering" are shown for what they are (the reverend Arthur Dent might have referred to them as "the worser sort" merely "espying . . . infirmities in the godlie") and then swiftly undercut. When Pompey vows to turn from "unlawful bawd" to "lawful hangman" and the hangman Abhorson protests that Pompey will "discredit our mystery," the more reliable provost promptly disallows the difference ("You weight equally; a feather will turn the scale," 4.2.15–30). In the same sceptical and even-handed way, one of the quarreling gentlemen in the play's second scene concedes "there went but a pair of shears between" the gallants' narcissistically inflated moral differences (1.2.27). What the play suggests, however, is not just that putative differences between virtue and vice, licit and illicit, can be unstable or easily reversed. It suggests also that a narrow insistence on moral differences can become a means of preventing self-knowledge and of disowning the complicated obligations to others on which any viable morality must depend. Thus excessive moral rigor (and reliance on the state and its law) and an "othering" of vice goes with the ignorance of the self-denying Angelo, a man so precise that (in contravention of Matthew 7:9) he "scarce confesses / That his blood flows; or that his appetite / Is more to bread than stone" (1.3.51–53).

The deepest moral innovation of the play, however, lies in the extent to which it links transformative self-knowledge to the experience of vice and personal frailty. The pattern is first set in the comment of Escalus when Angelo orders the Provost to execute Claudio:

> Well, heaven forgive him! And forgive us all!
> Some rise by sin, and some by virtue fall;
> Some run from brakes of ice and answer none,
> And some condemned for a fault alone. (2.1.37–40)[24]

At first glance the referent of "him" must be Claudio, the man who is condemned for a single fault while others run safely from the consequences of lives that are as morally crazen as breaking ice. Further thought, however, suggests the referent might be Angelo, a much-flawed man who, having risen to power through hypocrisy and sinfulness, is himself much in need of forgiveness. Finally, however, in the radically opposite idea that some may fall morally as the result of their supposed virtue, while others may rise morally through the very experience of sinfulness ("some rise by sin" is in one way just good protestant doctrine), the play reverses the positions of Angelo and Claudio, thereby engaging a different sort of moral project, the acquisition of self-knowledge and ethical development through the experience of moral failing and humbled recognition of the world's moral complications.[25]

One key to this project is the Aristotelian distinction between *akrasia*, that is, the incontinence or other habitual vice we indulge while knowing instinctually it is wrong to do so (there is plenty of this in *Measure for Measure*), and *kakia*, the evil act that results from ignorance and incomplete self-knowledge, as we make bad choices thinking they are good (this is the more interesting kind of failing that makes "problems" of all the play's major characters).[26] A second key to the project is the passage in the gospel of Matthew which not only supplies the play's title ("with what measure ye mete, it shall be measured to you again") but goes on to ask "Why seest thou the mote that is in thy brother's eye and perceivest not the beam that is in thine own eye?" (7: 2–3). Hypocrisy (7:5) is the principle upshot of this passage, but Rabelais, for one, linked the passage also to the Delphic/Socratic injunction to "know thyself," and so, I believe, does Shakespeare.[27]

That, in any case, would appear to be the point of Mariana's flawed plea for the upright Isabella to join her on her knees in behalf of the seemingly irredeemable Angelo:

> Isabel!
> Sweet Isabel, do yet but kneel by me.
> Hold up your hands, say nothing, I'll speak all.
> They say, best men are moulded out of faults;
> And for the most part, become much more the better
> For being a little bad; so may my husband.
> O, Isabel! will you not lend a knee? (5.1.436–42)

The apparent lameness of Mariana's plea—even the best men are faulty and so (*therefore?*) even the extremely crazen or faulty Angelo may reform and be redeemable—contains a deeper insight: that the best sort of men are precisely those who are molded out of their own faults and "become much more the better / For being a little bad."

This can hardly be called a heterodox perception, fashioned as it is from such exemplary biblical and classical sources. But in its account of the role of personal experience, including the experience of vice, in the fashioning of virtue, and in its manner of representing the moral development of its characters through their encounters with and within a city of vice, *Measure for Measure* does, by offering its audience bread rather than stones, participate in the parallel innovations of early modern theater and early modern urban living. In both of these spheres, as the editors observe, manhood "was negotiated, made visible, and even engendered through the performance of misconduct." That is certainly a fine description of what *Measure for Measure* does. As powerfully as Milton's *Areopagitica*, *Measure for Measure* rejects "a fugitive and cloister'd vertue, unexercis'd & unbreath'd"; and just as powerfully as Milton's tract, it too insists that "that which purifies us is triall, and triall is by what is contrary."

Yet Milton speaks of contemplating and knowing evil while *rejecting* it and of considering "vice with all her baits and seeming pleasures" while abstaining and preferring "that which is truly better." This ability to experience vice *vicariously* "was the reason why," Milton explained, "our sage and serious poet *Spencer*... describing true temperance under the person of *Guion*, brings him in with his palmer through the cave of Mammon, and the bowr of earthly blisse, that he might see and know, and yet abstain."[28] It was in ignorance or forgetfulness of the Aristotelian idea of vicariousness that early modern antitheatricalists and other enemies of popular literature insisted that the traffic with misconduct on the page or stage was morally aberrant and "attracted the mind to imitate such vices as are portrayed out."[29] In fact, it was because of what the London stage inherited from the norms of comedy and because of the place the stage had taken in the assessment of contemporary urban mores, that it could offer a vicarious experience of the role of vice in the shaping of the early modern city and the lives of its denizens. In the ways they handle evidence and argument, the chapters in this volume are attentive not just to the dynamics of the stage but to the mediated and performative aspects of moral conduct and moral discourse in the period. They remind us—as *Measure for Measure* and early modern theatre remind us—that the material development of early modern London was not just infrastructural or economic but behavioral and discursive.

NOTES

1. *Whartons Dreame*, sigs. A3–A3v; *Areopagitica*, in *The Complete Prose Works of John Milton*, gen. ed. Don M. Wolfe, 8 vols. (New Haven, CT: Yale University Press, 1953–82), 2: 516.
2. See Jacques Ellul, *The Meaning of the City* (Grand Rapids: William B. Eerdmans, 1970), chap. 1.
3. *Civil and Uncivil life*, sig. B2v.
4. Roger Finlay, *Population and Metropolis: The Demography of London 1580–1650* (Cambridge: Cambridge University Press, 1981), 9.

5. Speech in Star Chamber, June 20, 1616, in *Political Writings*, ed. Johann P. Sommerville (Cambridge: Cambridge University Press, 1994), 226.
6. Simmel "The Metropolis and Mental Life," in *Classic Essays on the Culture of Cities*, ed. Richard Sennett (Englewood Cliffs, NJ: Prentice-Hall, 1969), 47–50.
7. Robert Park, "The City: Suggestions for the Investigation of Human Behavior," in *Classic Essays on the Culture of Cities*, ed. Sennet, 115
8. On the distinction between these imperatives, see Alexander Welsh, *What Is Honour? A Question of Moral Imperatives* (New Haven, CT: Yale University Press, 2008), chap. 1.
9. Michael Walzer, for example, observes that for "men newly come to the city, uneasy there, not yet urbane, not yet sharing the sophistication of the town-dweller or the courtier...the congregational discipline taught them an urban style, provided new standards of order and a new routine, set them apart from the motley population of the expanding city and eventually produced a new self-confidence," *The Revolution of the Saints* (Cambridge, MA: Harvard University Press, 1965), 243.
10. Pierre Bourdieu, *Distinction: A Social Critique of the Judgment of Taste*, trans. Richard Nice (Cambridge, MA: Harvard University Press, 1984), 53; Park, "The City," 128.
11. Simmel, "The Metropolis and Mental Life," 57.
12. Arthur Dent, *The plaine mans path-way to heauen* (1607), 313; Eric Erikson, *Childhood and Society* (New York: Basic Books,1963), 261–63.
13. See Freud, "Some Character-Types Met with in Psycho-Analytic Work: (I) The Exceptions," in *The Standard Edition of the Complete Psychological Works of Sigmund Freud*, trans. James Strachey (24 vols. London: Hogarth Press, 1953–74), 4: 312–15.
14. *The Defence of Conny catching* (1592), in *The Life and Complete Works in Prose and Verse of Robert Greene*, ed. Alexander Grosart, 15 vols. (London, 1881–86), 11: 51; *The Threepenny Opera*, trans. Ralph Manheim and John Willet (New York: Arcade publishing, 1994), 76; Dent, *The plaine mans path-way to heauen*, 21.
15. For a modern discounting of the "innocent" skepticism in the claim "the punishment created the crime," see G. K. Chesterton, *The Man Who Was Thursday* (New York: Modern Library, 2001), 45.
16. "An Advertisement Touching the Controversies of the Church of England," in *The Letters and Life of Francis Bacon*, ed. James Spedding (7 vols. London: Longman, 1861–72), 1: 92.
17. Thomas Nashe, *Christs Teares over Ierusalem*, in *the Works of Thomas Nashe*, ed. Ronald B. McKerrow, 5 vols., rev. ed. (Oxford: Basil Blackwell, 1958–66), 2: 122–25.

18. Alexandra Halasz, *The Marketplace of Print: Pamphlets and the Public Sphere in Early Modern England* (Cambridge: Cambridge University Press, 1997), 110.
19. Aristotle, *Poetics*, 1449a32v ff.; Sir Philip Sidney, *The Defence of Poesy*, in *The Oxford Authors: Sir Philip Sidney*, ed. Katherine Duncan-Jones (Oxford: Oxford University Press, 1989), 230.
20. Sidney, *The Defence of Poesy*, 244; Stephen Gosson, *Plays Confuted in Five Actions* (1582), in *Shakespeare's Theater: A Sourcebook*, ed. Tanya Pollard (Oxford: Blackwell, 2004), 108. For the Platonic notion of identification through mimesis, see *Republic*, 606B-D.
21. Nicholas Heming, *The Lawful Use of Riches* (1578), cited in Thomas Wilson, *A Discourse on Usury*, ed. R. H. Tawney (London: G. Bell and Sons, 1925), 112–13.
22. I. G. (John Greene), *A Refutation of the Apology for Actors* (1615), in Pollard, *Shakespeare's Theater*, 255.
23. See, e.g., Leah Marcus, *Puzzling Shakespeare: Local Reading and Its Discontents* (Berkeley: University of California Press, 1988), chap. 4.
24 .I quote from *The Riverside Shakespeare*, 2nd ed., ed. G. Blakemore Evans (Boston: Houghton Mifflin, 1997), 584–618.
25. For this reading of "Some rise by sin, and some by virtue fall," a line italicized in the Folio, see Lawrence J. Ross, *On "Measure for Measure": An Essay in Criticism of Shakespeare's Drama* (Newark: University of Delaware Press, 1997), 51.
26. See Aristotle, *Ethics*, 1145a15–1145b30.
27. "Il ne sçait le premier trait de philosophie, qui est: *Congnois toy*; et, se glorifiant veoir un festu en l'œil d'aultruy, ne void une grosse souche laquelle luy poche les deux œilz," *Le tiers livre*, ch xxv, in *Œuvres Complètes*, 2 vols. (Paris: Garnier, 1962), 2: 508. The same applies in *Measure for Measure* to several of the major characters, including the Duke, a man who has "contended especially to know himself" (2.3.233) but who is abruptly brought to public acknowledge of himself and his responsibilities to others at the moment when Lucio pulls off his cowl.
28. *Areopagitica*, in *The Complete Prose Works of John Milton*, 2: 514–16.
29. Henry Crosse, *Vertues common-vvealth* (1603), in Pollard, *Shakespeare's Theater*, 189.

Contributors

Amanda Bailey is assistant professor of English at the University of Connecticut. She has published essays on early modern male youth culture and the theater and more recently on early modern ideas of property and possession. She is the author of *Flaunting: Style and the Subversive Male Body in Renaissance England* (Toronto, 2007). Her current book project is on debt and dramatic economies in early modern England.

Gina Bloom is associate professor of English at the University of California, Davis, where she teaches courses in early modern literature, especially drama. She is the author of *Voice in Motion: Staging Gender, Shaping Sound in Early Modern England* (University of Pennsylvania Press, Material Texts Series, 2007) and is currently working on a book about masculinity and games in the early modern English theater.

Mary Bly is associate professor of English literature at Fordham University. She is the author of *Queer Virgins and Virgin Queans on the Early Modern Stage* (Oxford, 2000) and is currently completing *The Geography of Puns*, a project addressing the geographical, linguistic economies of early modern London with particular attention to the liberties.

Holly Dugan is assistant professor of English at The George Washington University. She is currently working on a book-length project that examines the ephemeral history of perfume and the role of smell in early modern culture. Her article, "Scent of a Woman: Performing the Politics of Smell in Early Modern England," was recently published in the Spring 2008 *Journal of Medieval and Early Modern Studies.*

Laurie Ellinghausen is associate professor of English at the University of Missouri, Kansas City. She is the author of *Labor and Writing in Early Modern England, 1567–1667* (Ashgate, 2008). Her current projects include a book that investigates intersections between "renegade" religion, national identity, and exile in early modern drama;

she is also developing a continuing education course dedicated to the pedagogy of Shakespeare in high schools and colleges in the Kansas City metropolitan area.

Roze Hentschell is associate professor of English at Colorado State University, where she teaches courses in British literature and culture of the early modern period. She is the author of *The Culture of Cloth in Early Modern England: Textual Constructions of a National Identity* (Ashgate, 2008). She is at work on a new book on the cultural space of St. Paul's Cathedral precinct and, with Kathryn Lavezzo, is editing a collection of essays in memory of Richard Helgerson.

Mark Albert Johnston is assistant professor of English at the University of Windsor, Canada, where he teaches courses on early British literature, early modern culture, and Shakespearean drama. He has published articles in *ELR*, *ELH*, and *SEL*, and is particularly interested in early modern constructions of race, gender, and sexuality. He is currently completing a monograph study of beards and barbers in late Tudor and early Stuart England.

Natasha Korda is associate professor of English at Wesleyan University. She is author of *Shakespeare's Domestic Economies: Gender and Property in Early Modern England* (University of Pennsylvania Press, 2002) and coeditor of *Staged Properties in Early Modern English Drama* (Cambridge University Press, 2002). She is currently completing a book entitled "Labors Lost: Women's Work and the Early Modern English Stage" and coediting a collection of essays on "Working Subjects in Early Modern English Drama."

Lawrence Manley is the William R. Kenan, Jr. Professor of English at Yale University. He is the author of *Convention, 1500–1750* (1980) and *Literature and Culture in Early Modern London* (1995) and the editor of *London in the Age of Shakespeare* (1986). He is currently editing *The Cambridge Companion to London in English Literature* and completing (with Sally-Beth MacLean) *Lord Strange's Men and Their Plays.*

Ian Munro is associate professor of Drama at the University of California, Irvine. He is the author of *The Figure of the Crowd in Early Modern London: The City and Its Double* (Palgrave Macmillan, 2005) and the editor of *A Woman's Answer Is Never to Seek: Early Modern Jestbooks, 1526–1635* (Ashgate, 2007), part of the "Early Modern Englishwoman" facsimile series. He is currently working on a project about early modern wit and jesting.

Adam Zucker is assistant professor of English at the University of Massachusetts, Amherst. He is the coeditor (with Alan B. Farmer) of *Localizing Caroline Drama: Politics and Economics of the Early Modern English Stage, 1625–1642* (Palgrave Macmillan, 2006). His recent articles on city comedy in *Renaissance Drama* and the *Journal for Early Modern Cultural Studies* are part of a book project on wit, material place, and comic form in early modern England.

Index